Keras 2.x Projects

9 projects demonstrating faster experimentation of neural network and deep learning applications using Keras

Giuseppe Ciaburro

BIRMINGHAM - MUMBAI

Keras 2.x Projects

Commissioning Editor: Pravin Dhandre
Acquisition Editor: Devika Battike
Content Development Editor: Nathanya Dias
Technical Editor: Joseph Sunil
Copy Editor: Safis Editing
Project Coordinator: Kirti Pisat
Proofreader: Safis Editing
Indexer: Mariammal Chettiyar
Graphics: Jisha Chirayil
Production Coordinator: Shraddha Falebhai

First published: December 2018

Production reference: 1311218

Published by Packt Publishing Ltd.
Livery Place
35 Livery Street
Birmingham
B3 2PB, UK.

ISBN 978-1-78953-664-5

www.packtpub.com

`mapt.io`

Mapt is an online digital library that gives you full access to over 5,000 books and videos, as well as industry leading tools to help you plan your personal development and advance your career. For more information, please visit our website.

Why subscribe?

- Spend less time learning and more time coding with practical eBooks and Videos from over 4,000 industry professionals

- Improve your learning with Skill Plans built especially for you

- Get a free eBook or video every month

- Mapt is fully searchable

- Copy and paste, print, and bookmark content

Packt.com

Did you know that Packt offers eBook versions of every book published, with PDF and ePub files available? You can upgrade to the eBook version at `www.packt.com` and as a print book customer, you are entitled to a discount on the eBook copy. Get in touch with us at `customercare@packtpub.com` for more details.

At `www.packt.com`, you can also read a collection of free technical articles, sign up for a range of free newsletters, and receive exclusive discounts and offers on Packt books and eBooks.

Contributors

About the author

Giuseppe Ciaburro holds a PhD in environmental technical physics and two master's degrees. His research was focused on machine learning applications in the study of the urban sound environments. He works at Built Environment Control Laboratory—Università degli Studi della Campania Luigi Vanvitelli (Italy). He has over 15 years of professional experience in programming (Python, R, and MATLAB), first in the field of combustion and then in acoustics and noise control. He has several publications to his credit.

About the reviewer

Sudharsan Ravichandiran is a data scientist, researcher, artificial intelligence enthusiast, and YouTuber (search for Sudharsan reinforcement learning). He completed his bachelors in information technology at Anna University. His area of research focuses on practical implementations of deep learning and reinforcement learning, which includes natural language processing and computer vision. He is an open source contributor and loves answering questions on Stack Overflow. He also authored a best seller, *Hands-On Reinforcement Learning with Python*, published by Packt Publishing.

Packt is searching for authors like you

If you're interested in becoming an author for Packt, please visit `authors.packtpub.com` and apply today. We have worked with thousands of developers and tech professionals, just like you, to help them share their insight with the global tech community. You can make a general application, apply for a specific hot topic that we are recruiting an author for, or submit your own idea.

Table of Contents

Preface

Keras 2.x Projects explains how to leverage the power of Keras to build and train state-of-the-art deep learning models through a series of practical projects that look at a range of real-world application areas.

To begin with, you will quickly set up a deep learning environment by installing the Keras library. Through each of the projects, you will explore and learn the advanced concepts of deep learning and will learn how to compute and run your deep learning models using the advanced offerings of Keras. You will train fully-connected multilayer networks, convolutional neural networks, recurrent neural networks, autoencoders and generative adversarial networks using real-world training datasets. The projects you will undertake are all based on real-world scenarios of all complexity levels, covering topics such as language recognition, stock volatility, energy consumption prediction, faster object classification for self-driving vehicles, and more.

By the end of this book, you will be well versed with deep learning and its implementation with Keras. You will have all the knowledge you need to train your own deep learning models to solve different kinds of problems.

Who this book is for

If you are a data scientist, machine learning engineer, deep learning practitioner or an AI engineer who wants to build speedy intelligent applications with minimal lines of codes, then this book is the best fit for you.

What this book covers

Chapter 1, *Getting Started with Keras*, covers an overview of the Keras environment. We will learn how to install and configure Keras, how to work with the Keras library, and we will discover the basic concepts of the Keras architecture. We will also see how Keras uses TensorFlow as its tensor manipulation library, as well as how we can switch the Keras backend from TensorFlow (which is the default option) to Theano and CNTK, which are other available frameworks. Finally, we will understand the different types of Keras models, looking at model classes used with sequential layers and model classes used with functional API layers.

Chapter 2, *Modeling Real Estate Using Regression Analysis*, looks at the different types of regression techniques. We will apply regression methods to your data and understand how the regression algorithm works. We will then understand the basic concepts that multiple linear regression methods use to fit equations to data using the Keras layers. We will also learn how to evaluate the model's performance and how to tune a model to improve the model's performance.

Chapter 3, *Heart Disease Classification with Neural Networks*, covers the basic concept of the classification problem. We will look at a practical case of heart disease classification using Keras. The basic concepts of classification methods and how to implement them in the Keras environment will be covered. How to import and organize data for neural network classification analysis, and how to implement a Keras classification model using a real-life example, will be explored.

Chapter 4, *Concrete Quality Prediction Using Deep Neural Networks*, covers the basic concepts of **multilayer neural networks** (**MNNs**) and how to implement them in the Keras environment. Many variations of MNNs will be introduced, such as CNNs, RNNs, **deep belief networks** (**DBNs**), and **restricted Boltzmann machines** (**RBMs**). We will look at an example of a multilayered artificial network. We will learn about how to implement a model that allows us to calculate the compressive strength of concrete according to the ingredients used in the mixture. Finally, we will see how to remove outliers to improve the performance of the model.

Chapter 5, *Fashion Article Recognition Using Convolutional Neural Networks*, covers the connection pattern between neurons in CNNs, which is inspired by the structure of the visual cortex in the brain. We will see how the individual neurons present in this part of the brain (visual cortex) respond to certain stimuli in a narrow region of observation called the receptive field. The receptive fields of different neurons are partially overlapped so that together they cover the entire field of view. The response of a single neuron to stimuli taking place in its receptive field can be mathematically approximated by a convolution operation. In this chapter, a CNN will be trained to solve a pattern recognition problem.

Chapter 6, *Movie Review Sentiment Analysis Using Recurrent Neural Networks*, covers the RNN, which is a neural model wherein a bidirectional flow of information is present. In other words, while the propagation of signals in feedforward networks takes place only in a continuous manner in a direction from inputs to outputs, RNNs are different. In them, this propagation can also occur from a neural layer following a previous one, or between neurons belonging to the same layer, and even between a neuron and itself. In this chapter, an RNN is used to solve a language recognition problem.

Chapter 7, *Stock Volatility Forecasting Using Long-Short Term Memory*, covers the basic concepts of forecasting techniques. Forecast horizon and several forecast methods will be analyzed. Time series data will also be dealt with. A time series constitutes a sequence of observations of a phenomenon. In a time series, we can identify several components—trend, seasonality, cycle, and residual. We will learn how to remove seasonality from a time series with a practical example. We will address the most-used models to represent time series—AR, MA, ARMA, and ARIMA. For each one, the basic concepts will be analyzed and then a mathematical formulation of the model will be provided. Finally, a Keras LSTM model for time series analysis will be proposed. Using a practical example, we will see how to deal with a time series regression problem with an RNN model of the LSTM type.

Chapter 8, *Reconstruction of Handwritten Digital Images Using Autoencoders*, looks at autoencoders. The autoencoder is a neural network whose purpose is to code its input into small dimensions, where the result obtained helps to reconstruct the input itself. Autoencoders are made up of the union of two subnets: an encoder and a decoder. The encoder and the decoder will be differentiable with respect to the distance function, so the parameters of the encoding/decoding functions can be optimized to minimize the loss of reconstruction, using the stochastic gradient. In this chapter, an autoencoder is used to reconstruct handwritten digit images.

Chapter 9, *Robot Control System Using Deep Reinforcement Learning*, introduces the basic concepts of reinforcement learning and how to use these techniques to control a mechanical system. To start with, an overview of robot control will be addressed. Then, the OpenAI Gym library will be introduced, which helps us to implement algorithms based on reinforcement learning. It includes a growing collection of benchmark issues that are shared on a common interface, and a website where people can share their results and compare algorithm performance. We will explore the different environments available and how to install the library. Finally, the CartPole system will be used to implement Q-learning and Deep Q-learning algorithms. The CartPole system is a classic problem of reinforcement learning. The system consists of a pole (which acts like an inverted pendulum) attached to a cart via a joint. The system is controlled by applying a force of +1 or -1 to the cart. The force applied to the cart can be controlled, and the objective is to swing the pole upward and stabilize it.

Chapter 10, *Reuters Newswire Topics Classifier in Keras*, covers **natural language processing** (**NLP**), which is the process of automatically processing information that is written or spoken in a natural language using an electronic calculator. This process is made particularly difficult and complex due to the intrinsic ambiguity of human language. In this chapter, Keras layers are used to build a model to classify Reuter's newswire topics. Data is available from a dataset that contains 11,228 newswires from Reuters with 46 labeled topics. This dataset is from Keras, and each wire is encoded as a sequence of word indexes.

Chapter 11, *What is Next?*, will summarize what will have been covered in this book and what the next steps are that you can take. You will learn how to apply the skills you have gained to other projects, including real-life challenges in building and deploying Keras deep learning models and other common technologies that data scientists often use. By the end of this chapter, you will have a better understanding of the real-life challenges in building and deploying machine learning models, and the additional resources and technologies that you can use to sharpen your machine learning skills.

To get the most out of this book

Sound knowledge of machine learning and a basic familiarity with the Keras library would be useful.

Download the example code files

You can download the example code files for this book from your account at www.packt.com. If you purchased this book elsewhere, you can visit www.packt.com/support and register to have the files emailed directly to you.

You can download the code files by following these steps:

1. Log in or register at www.packt.com.
2. Select the **SUPPORT** tab.
3. Click on **Code Downloads & Errata**.
4. Enter the name of the book in the **Search** box and follow the onscreen instructions.

Once the file is downloaded, please make sure that you unzip or extract the folder using the latest version of:

- WinRAR/7-Zip for Windows
- Zipeg/iZip/UnRarX for Mac
- 7-Zip/PeaZip for Linux

The code bundle for the book is also hosted on GitHub at https://github.com/PacktPublishing/Keras-2.x-Projects. In case there's an update to the code, it will be updated on the existing GitHub repository.

We also have other code bundles from our rich catalog of books and videos available at https://github.com/PacktPublishing/. Check them out!

Download the color images

We also provide a PDF file that has color images of the screenshots/diagrams used in this book. You can download it here:
http://www.packtpub.com/sites/default/files/downloads/9781789536645_ColorImages.pdf.

Conventions used

There are a number of text conventions used throughout this book.

CodeInText: Indicates code words in text, database table names, folder names, filenames, file extensions, pathnames, dummy URLs, user input, and Twitter handles. Here is an example: "We will add a Flatten() layer:"

A block of code is set as follows:

```
import autokeras as ak
clf = ak.ImageClassifier()
clf.fit(x_train, y_train)
results = clf.predict(x_test)
```

When we wish to draw your attention to a particular part of a code block, the relevant lines or items are set in bold:

```
[default]
exten => s,1,Dial(Zap/1|30)
exten => s,2,Voicemail(u100)
exten => s,102,Voicemail(b100)
exten => i,1,Voicemail(s0)
```

Any command-line input or output is written as follows:

```
$ pip install autokeras
```

Warnings or important notes appear like this.

Tips and tricks appear like this.

Get in touch

Feedback from our readers is always welcome.

General feedback: If you have questions about any aspect of this book, mention the book title in the subject of your message and email us at customercare@packtpub.com.

Errata: Although we have taken every care to ensure the accuracy of our content, mistakes do happen. If you have found a mistake in this book, we would be grateful if you would report this to us. Please visit www.packt.com/submit-errata, selecting your book, clicking on the Errata Submission Form link, and entering the details.

Piracy: If you come across any illegal copies of our works in any form on the Internet, we would be grateful if you would provide us with the location address or website name. Please contact us at copyright@packt.com with a link to the material.

If you are interested in becoming an author: If there is a topic that you have expertise in and you are interested in either writing or contributing to a book, please visit authors.packtpub.com.

Reviews

Please leave a review. Once you have read and used this book, why not leave a review on the site that you purchased it from? Potential readers can then see and use your unbiased opinion to make purchase decisions, we at Packt can understand what you think about our products, and our authors can see your feedback on their book. Thank you!

For more information about Packt, please visit packt.com.

Getting Started with Keras
1

Keras is an open source neural network library written in Python. This book will help you to experiment with deep neural networks as simply as possible. Its principal author and maintainer is François Chollet, a Google engineer. In 2017, Google's TensorFlow team decided to support Keras in TensorFlow's main library. Keras contains several implementations of commonly used neural network blocks, such as levels, objectives, activation functions, optimizers, and a set of tools to facilitate work with image and text data. In this chapter, an overview of the Keras environment will be addressed.

The following topics are covered:

- Introduction to Keras
- Keras backend options
- Installation
- Model fitting in Keras

At the end of the chapter, the reader will learn how to work with the `keras` library, and how to install and configure Keras. We will also discover the basic concepts of the Keras architecture. We will learn how Keras uses TensorFlow as its tensor manipulation library. We will also understand the different type of Keras models, sequential and functional APIs, and learn how to implement Keras layers.

Introduction to Keras

Keras is a Python library that provides a simple and clean way to create a range of deep learning models. Keras code was released under the MIT license. Keras has been structured based on austerity and simplicity, and it provides a programming model without ornaments that maximizes readability. It allows expressing neural networks in a very modular way, considering a model like a sequence or a single graph. This is a good approximation, because the components of a deep learning model are discrete elements that can be arbitrarily combined. The new components are easily aggregated and modifiable within the framework designed for engineers, to quickly test and explore new ideas. Last but not least, using the Python programming language provides constructs that allow clear programming on both a small and large scale. In the following screenshot, we can see the Keras official home page (`https://keras.io/`):

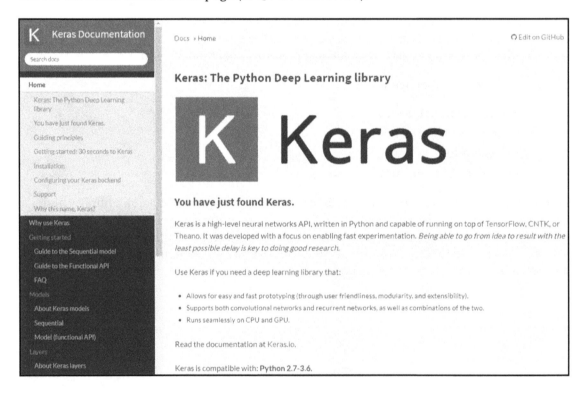

Ease of use is the strongpoint of Keras. During the design phase, the user has been the focus of attention of the developers, producing a product that reduces the user's work via simple and consistent APIs. In this way, the number of actions necessary to solve common use cases is reduced. In addition, the results are returned in a clear manner, making the identification of possible errors very simple.

In Keras, a model is represented by a sequence of autonomous and completely configurable modules that can be connected with the lowest possible number of restrictions. Everything in Keras is a module—neural layers, cost functions, optimizers, initialization schemes, activation functions, and regularization schemes. These independent modules can be combined to create new, more complex models.

All modules available in Keras are simple to add, and so are new classes and functions in a programming language. In addition, the modules are already available, and are accompanied by numerous examples that explain their practical use. But Keras is not limited to the availability of the built-in modules. The user will be able to easily create new modules, making Keras an easily extensible environment.

The `keras` library bases its technology on the levels that are used to manage input and output. An application in Keras can be implemented through the following four simple steps:

1. Prepare input and output data.
2. Create the first level to manage the input data.
3. Set up intermediate levels to perform the analysis.
4. Create the output level to manage the targets.

Keras works as a specific high-level API for neural networks. It can act as a user interface and can extend the functionality of other deep learning framework backends on which it runs. Thanks to this feature, Keras has become a wrapper for migration between frameworks. Not only can algorithms and models of neural networks for deep learning be exchanged, but also networks and preliminary weights.

Wrapper libraries consist of a thin layer of code that translates a library's existing interface into a compatible interface.

On the other hand, since Keras is autonomous, it can be used without having to interact with the backend framework on which it is running. Keras has its own chart data structures for defining computational charts; it is not based on the data structures of the underlying backend framework. This way, you will not have to learn how to program the backend framework.

Keras is easy to learn and use. Using Keras is like working with Lego blocks, you just have to put in sequence a series of compatible modules. It was created so that people can quickly perform the experimental phase of the model using a highly modular and extensible framework. Keras focuses on defining levels for the neural network. You do not have to deal with tensors, but it's easy to write with less code.

Keras backend options

Keras is a model-level library that provides high-level blocks for the development of deep learning models. Keras developers have focused their efforts on creating high-level models by neglecting low-level operations such as tensor products, convolutions, and so on. These operations have been entrusted to specialized and well-optimized tensor manipulation libraries that already exist, thus acting as a backend engine for Keras. Several backend engines can be connected perfectly to Keras. Actually, Keras has three backend implementations available—TensorFlow, Theano, and **Microsoft Cognitive Toolkit (CNTK)**.

TensorFlow

TensorFlow is an open source software library for numerical calculation based on graph modeling (data flow graphs). A **graph** is defined as an abstract pipeline of mathematical operations operating on tensors, and are also known as multidimensional arrays. Each graph consists of nodes and arcs, wherein the nodes are operations on the data, and the arcs represent the tensors that pass through the various operations.

 You can find the updated version of the library and all the documentation supplied at the following link: (http://www.tensorflow.org).

TensorFlow is the most commonly used library in the field of machine learning and neural networks. It has numerous APIs, including the lowest level, that is, TensorFlow Core, allows complete control over programming. These APIs are those typically used in the field of machine learning, since they make it possible to check in detail all the elements of the model being implemented. The highest level APIs are available and built from TensorFlow Core. In some cases, they can make some operations such as repetitive and predefined tasks faster and simpler, but generally preclude the possibility of going into detail, and in the implementation of a neural network it is often necessary to have a more precise control over operations. However, they can still be useful for the development of standard machine learning models.

TensorFlow provides interfaces for different languages, including Python and C or C ++, with full support, and Go or Java in Beta. It also supports parallel computing on GPUs or CPUs, and distributed computation allows execution even on mobile devices.

A TensorFlow program is typically structured in the following two distinct phases:

- **Construction**: In this phase, the various operations of the graph that will be performed on the input tensors are defined.
- **Execution**: In this phase, the operations defined in the previous phase are evaluated so as to retrieve the numerical output. The execution of operations is managed through the `session` object of TensorFlow.

The fundamental unit in TensorFlow is the **tensor**. A tensor consists of a set of primitive type values modeled as a multidimensional array. In TensorFlow, almost all the functions contained in the API take tensors as inputs and always output tensors. Each tensor contained in the graph has a unique name that can be specified by the user, or otherwise automatically assigned.

For more information on tensors and any other resources related to TensorFlow, you can refer to the official site of the framework, as shown in the following screenshot:

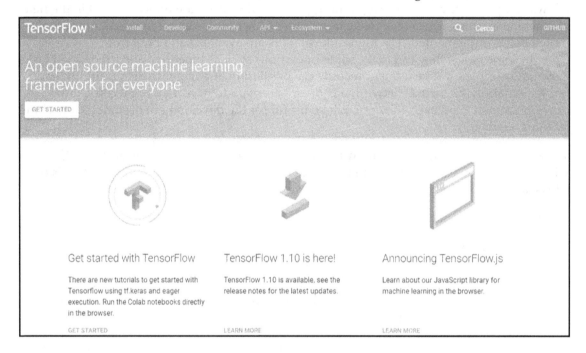

The default behavior in TensorFlow is to allocate all the components (tensors and operations) in the GPU memory (if it has been installed with computational support on a GPU). However, you can manually specify where to allocate each tensor and operation. It is recommended to minimize switches between the CPU and GPU as these slow down execution.

TensorFlow also allows you to define scopes for variables through which a namespace mechanism is managed; they facilitate the definition of complex models. Scopes are also very important for sharing variables between multiple graphs.

TensorFlow provides the following two options for reading input data:

- **Manual**: Observations are manually read and organized in batches, and then passed to the model. It is a simple mechanism to use, but it can become very slow because the data must be continually copied from the Python environment to the TensorFlow environment.

- **Integrated**: All operations to read data and organize them in batches of observations are implemented within the graph. It is a less intuitive mechanism to use, but presents a large increase in performance, since all data always remains in the TensorFlow environment.

All basic operations for neural networks are implemented in TensorFlow as graph nodes. The framework automatically manages everything needed to implement the forward and backward pass, including the automatic calculation of derivatives.

Among the main operations available for the construction of neural networks models, we find the following:

- Convolutions
- Sum of the bias
- Fully connected levels
- Activation functions
- Pooling
- Prediction functions

Finally, there is a suite of tools for graphic display that is fully integrated into TensorFlow called **TensorBoard**. It allows visualizing the computational graph of the model and many other statistics useful for the analysis of the training process.

Theano

Theano is an open source library of numerical computation for the Python programming language developed by a group of machine learning experts at the University of Montreal. In Theano, calculations are expressed using a syntax that is similar to NumPy's, and is compiled to perform efficiently on both CPU and GPU architectures.

 You can find the updated version of the library and all the documentation supplied at the following link: http://deeplearning.net/software/theano.

It is named after a Greek mathematician, Theano of Crotone. Theano is a compiler for mathematical expressions written in Python. It allows defining, optimizing, and evaluating mathematical expressions, in particular those with multidimensional arrays. Using Theano, it is possible to achieve comparable speeds with C or C ++ applications for problems with large amounts of data. Theano combines aspects of a computer algebra system with aspects of an optimizing compiler. These characteristics are useful when complex mathematical expressions are evaluated repeatedly, and the evaluation speed is crucial. In the following screenshot, we can see the official home page of Theano:

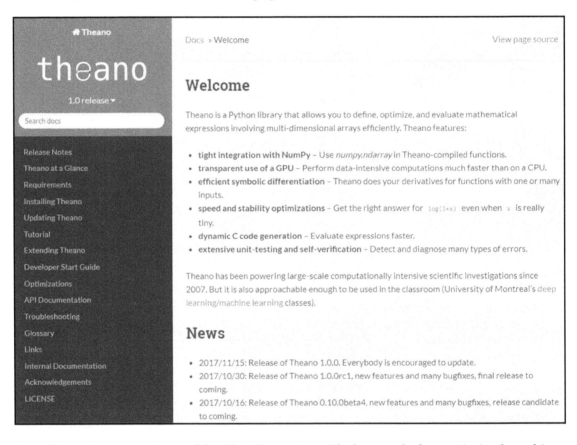

It combines the convenience of the NumPy syntax with the speed of an optimized machine language. The user composes mathematical expressions in a high-level description that mimics the syntax and semantics of NumPy, even though it is statically typed. These expressions allow Theano to provide symbolic differentiation. Before performing the calculation, Theano optimizes the choice of expressions, translates them into C ++ (or CUDA for GPU), and automatically compiles them into dynamically loaded Python modules. The machine learning algorithms implemented with Theano are particularly fast.

CNTK

The CNTK is an open source toolkit for commercial-grade applications that is distributed in deep learning. CNTK implements neural networks as a series of computational steps via a directed graph. CNTK is a command-line program that can do simple and deep neural network analyses. CNTK was originally developed as an internal Microsoft tool.

 You can find the updated version of the library and all the documentation supplied at the following link: `https://github.com/Microsoft/CNTK`.

Using CNTK, the most common machine learning models are easily achievable and can be combined. CNTK is available as a library in Python, C#, or C++ environments, or it can be used as a standalone machine learning tool through its own model description language. In addition, CNTK model evaluation functionality can be used from Java programs. CNTK supports 64-bit Linux or 64-bit Windows operating systems. To install CNTK, you can either choose precompiled binary packages, or compile the toolkit from the source provided in GitHub. In the following screenshot, we can see the official home page of CNTK:

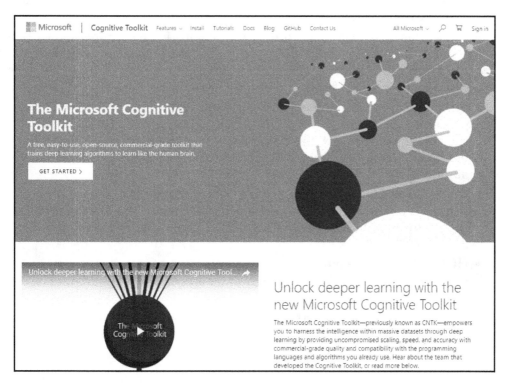

In the **Tutorials** section, there is a collection of code samples, recipes, and tutorials on the various ways you can use the toolkit with scenarios for images, text, and speech data.

Installation

Previously, we have already said that Keras is written in Python, so in order for it to work, it is necessary to have a previously installed version of Python (Keras is compatible with **Python 2.7-3.6**). Platforms that support Python development environments can support Keras as well. Furthermore, before installing Keras, it is necessary to provide for the installation of the backend engine, and some optional dependencies useful for the implementation of machine learning models.

Optional dependencies

Some useful optional dependencies are listed in the following list:

- **NumPy**: This is an open source library of the Python programming language, which adds support for multidimensional and large vectors, and even matrices with high-level mathematical functions to work with.
- **SciPy**: This is an open source library of mathematical algorithms and tools. It contains modules for optimization, linear algebra, integration, special functions, **fast fourier transform** (**FFT**), signal and image processing, **ordinary differential equation** (**ODT**) solvers, and other common tools in science and engineering.
- **Scikit-learn**: This is an open source machine learning library for the Python programming language. It contains classification, regression, clustering algorithms, support vector machines, logistic regression, bayesian classifier, k-means, and DBSCAN, and is designed to work with the NumPy and SciPy libraries.
- **cuDNN**: This is a GPU accelerated library of primitives for deep neural networks. cuDNN provides highly tuned implementations for standard routines, such as forward and backward convolution, pooling, normalization, and activation layers.
- **HDF5**: This is a data model, library, and file format for storing and managing data. It supports an unlimited variety of datatypes, and is designed to be flexible and efficient.
- **H5py**: This is a Python interface to the HDF5 binary data format.

- **Graphviz**: This is an open source program used to draw graphs described in the DOT language. It provides libraries for applications using the tools provided. Graphviz is free software licensed under the **Common Public License** (**CPL**).
- **Pydot**: This is a Python interface for Graphviz and the DOT language.

We can now proceed with the installation of every single library or install all the dependencies with a single line of code. Alternatively, you can install the Anaconda Python module, which will automatically install these libraries and a lot of other libraries that are needed for scientific computing.

Installing the backend engine

After installing the dependencies, it is necessary to select the backend engine and proceed with its installation. Keras developers recommend the TensorFlow backend. This is the one set by default.

Links to installation instructions for all the available backends are listed in the following list:

- TensorFlow installation instructions: `https://www.tensorflow.org/install/`
- Theano installation instructions: `http://deeplearning.net/software/theano/install.html#install`
- CNTK installation instructions: `https://docs.microsoft.com/en-us/cognitive-toolkit/setup-cntk-on-your-machine`

In all cases, we can use the `pip` command to install the correct packages.

Keras installation and configuration

At this point, the environment is ready for Keras installation. If all the dependencies and the backend engine have been correctly installed, we can proceed. Actually, the work that remains to be done is very simple and immediate.

There are two ways to install Keras as follows:

The first step involves the use of the **Python Package Index** (**PyPI**).

> This is a repository of software for the Python programming language. PyPI helps you find and install software developed and shared by the Python community. This is the recommended option.

After installing the PyPI package, simply type the following command:

```
$ sudo pip install keras
```

If you are using a `virtualenv`, you may want to avoid using `sudo`:

```
$ pip install keras
```

Alternatively, we can install Keras from the GitHub source. To do this, we first need to clone Keras using `git`:

```
$ git clone https://github.com/keras-team/keras.git
```

Then, add `cd` to the `keras` folder and run the `install` command:

```
cd keras
sudo python setup.py install
```

We have the Keras environment available to implement our deep learning models. Let us look at some more information about the configuration. As we have already mentioned, Keras uses TensorFlow as the default backend. If we want to use the other two options, Theano and CNTK, we must modify the Keras configuration file. This is a file with the `.json` extension, and is named `keras.json..`

The file's position depends on the operating system that is in use in our PC:

```
$ HOME/.keras/keras.json
```

We can use the following command for Unix-like OSes:

```
%USERPROFILE%/.Keras/keras.json
```

And, for Windows OS, the contents of the configuration file are of the following type:

```
{
    "image_data_format": "channels_last",
    "epsilon": 1e-07,
    "floatx": "float32",
    "backend": "tensorflow"
}
```

The parameters have the following meaning:

- `image_data_format`: String, either `channels_last` or `channels_first`. It specifies which data format convention Keras will follow.
- `epsilon`: Float, a numeric fuzzing constant used to avoid dividing by zero in some operations.
- `floatx`: String, `float16`, `float32`, or `float64`. Default float precision.
- `backend`: String, `tensorflow`, `theano`, or `cntk`.

Switching from one backend to another is very fast. Simply change the field backend to `theano`, `tensorflow`, or `cntk`, and Keras will use the new configuration the next time you run any Keras code.

Model fitting in Keras

We have just installed and configured our Keras environment, and we can now focus on the implementation of our model based on deep neural networks. When developing a deep learning application, we follow a general pipeline characterized by the following steps:

1. **Collecting the data**: Everything starts from the data, no doubt about it, but one might wonder where so much data comes from. In practice, it is collected through lengthy procedures that may, for example, derive from measurement campaigns or face-to-face interviews. In all cases, the data is collected in a database so that it can then be analyzed to derive knowledge.

If we do not have specific requirements, to save time and effort we can use publicly available data. In this regard, a large collection of data is available in the UCI Machine Learning Repository at the following link: `https://archive.ics.uci.edu/ml/index.php`.

2. **Preparing the data**: We have collected the data; now we have to prepare it for the next step. Once we have this data, we must make sure it is in a format usable by the algorithm we want to use. To do this, you may need to do some formatting. Recall that some algorithms need data in an integer format, whereas others require data in the form of strings. Finally, others need to be in a special format. We will get to this later, but the specific formatting is usually simple compared to data collection.

The following diagram shows the deep learning process workflow:

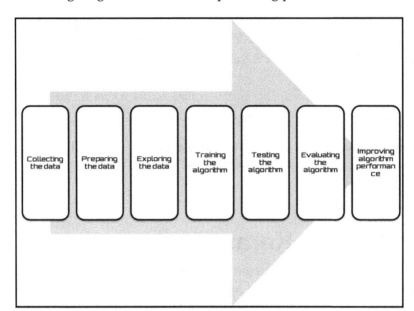

3. **Exploring the data**: At this point, we can look at data to verify that it is actually working and we do not have a bunch of empty values. In this step, through the use of plots, we can recognize patterns or whether there are some data points that are vastly different from the rest of the set. Plotting data in one, two, or three dimensions can also help.

4. **Training the algorithm**: Now, let's get serious. In this step, the deep learning begins to work with the definition of the model and the next training round. The model starts to extract knowledge from large amounts of data that we had available. For unsupervised learning, there's no training step because you don't have a target value.

5. **Testing the algorithm**: In this step, we use the information learned in the previous step to see if the model actually works. The evaluation of an algorithm verifies how well the model approximates the real system. In the case of supervised learning, we have some known values that we can use to evaluate the algorithm. In unsupervised learning, we may need to use some other metrics to evaluate success. In both cases, if we are not satisfied, we can return to the previous steps, change some things, and retry the test.

6. **Evaluating the algorithm**: We have reached the point where we can apply what has been done so far. We can assess the approximation ability of the model by applying it to real data. The model, preventively trained and tested, is then valued in this phase.

7. **Improving algorithm performance**: Finally, we can focus on the finishing steps. We've verified that the model works, we have evaluated the performance, and now we are ready to analyze the whole process to identify any possible room for improvement.

In Keras, there are two ways to define a model—sequential, and functional API. The sequential model lets you create layer-by-layer models for most problems. Limits are dictated by the inability to create models that share levels or that have multiple inputs or outputs. Alternatively, the functional API allows you to create models with greater flexibility. We can easily define models in which the levels are connected in different ways and not just from the previous level to the next. In fact, we can link a layer to any other level, thus creating complex networks.

The Keras sequential model architecture

Keras is structured according to the object-oriented programming methodology. Therefore, the creation of a model is very simple: select the basic architecture and then add the layers necessary to create the desired model. As just mentioned, the sequential model lets you create a layer-by-layer model as a linear stack of layers. However, it is not possible to create models that share levels or that have multiple inputs or outputs.

A sequential model is created by passing a list of layer instances to the constructor. To create a model, we should follow these steps:

1. Import the sequential class from `keras.models`

2. Stack layers using the `.add()` method

3. Configure the learning process using the `compile()` method

4. Import the data

5. Train the model on the train dataset using the `.fit()` method

The first step is solved by importing the classes that we will use later for the construction of the model. An example of an import is shown in the following command:

```
from keras.models import Sequential
from keras.layers import Dense, Activation
```

Three layer classes have been imported: `Sequential`, `Dense`, and `Activation`. Then, we instantiate an object from the `Keras.model.Sequential` class:

```
model = Sequential()
```

All information about your network, such as weights, layers, and operations will be stored in this object.

After instantiating our object, we will move on to adding layers using the `add()` method:

```
model.add(Dense(32, activation='relu', input_dim=100))
model.add(Dense(1, activation='sigmoid'))
```

We have added two `Dense` layers, which is the basic feedforward fully connected layer.

All operations of a layer can be passed as arguments to the `Dense` object, as follows:

- Number of hidden units
- Activation function
- Bias
- Weight/bias initialization
- Weight/bias regularization
- Activation regularization

You can create any level in the network using the following command:

```
model.add (layer_name)
```

This method will preserve the order of the levels you add. There are lots of layers implemented in Keras. When you add a layer to your model, a gradient operation will be created in the background and it will take care of computing the backward gradient automatically. Before training a model, you need to configure the learning process, which is done via the `compile()` method; we can see it in the following code block:

```
model.compile(optimizer='rmsprop',
              loss='binary_crossentropy',
              metrics=['accuracy'])
```

The three arguments that are passed are as follows:

- An optimizer
- A loss function
- A list of metrics

At this point, we have set the model architecture and before proceeding to the training we have to import the data.

In this case, we generate simple dummy data by performing a random sampling using `numpy`:

```
import numpy as np
data = np.random.random((1000, 100))
labels = np.random.randint(2, size=(1000, 1))
```

To train a model, the `fit ()` method is used, as seen in the following code block:

```
model.fit(data, labels, epochs=10, batch_size=32)
```

In this way, we have trained the model, iterating on the data in groups of 32 samples. With these few lines of code, we have already built our first network in Keras. This is a simple example of binary classification that uses a single entry model with two classes.

In Keras, to summarize a model, it is possible to use the `summary()` function. The summary is returned in text format and includes the following information:

- The layers and their order in the model
- The output shape of each layer
- The number of parameters (weights) in each layer
- The total number of parameters (weights) in the model

To print a summary of the model, we simply type the following command:

```
model.summary()
```

In the following screenshot, the results are shown:

```
Layer (type) Output Shape Param #
=================================================================
dense_1 (Dense) (None, 32) 3232

dense_2 (Dense) (None, 1) 33
=================================================================
Total params: 3,265
Trainable params: 3,265
Non-trainable params: 0
```

Here, we can clearly see the output shape and number of weights in each layer.

Keras functional API model architecture

The functional API is much better when you want to do something that diverges from the basic idea of having an input, a succession of levels, and an output, for example, models with multiple inputs, multiple outputs, or a more complex internal structure, such as using the output of a given layer as an input to multiple layers or, on the contrary, combining the output of different layers to use them together as an input of another level.

In fact, as already said, the functional API allows you to create models with greater flexibility. We can easily define models in which the levels are connected in different ways and not just from the previous level to the next. In fact, we can link a layer to any other level, thus creating complex networks.

To understand the difference between the two models that Keras offers, we will use a simple example. This is a densely connected network of the type already seen in *The Keras sequential model architecture* section. In a densely connected network, every input is connected to every output by a weight, which is generally followed by a non-linear activation function. Again, we recommend it for its simplicity. The first step is solved by importing the classes that we will use later for the construction of the model. We will run the example using the following steps:

We will begin by importing the required libraries using the following code block:

```
from keras.layers import Input, Dense
from keras.models import Model
```

Three layer classes have been imported: Input, Dense, and Model.

Then, we have to instantiate a Keras `Tensor`. In fact, in this case we must define an autonomous input level that specifies the shape of the input data (tensor). The input layer accepts a shape argument, which is a tuple indicating the dimensionality of the input data:

```
InputTensor = Input(shape=(100,))
```

This returns a tensor.

> A Keras tensor is a tensor object from the underlying backend that we can add to certain attributes that allow us to construct a Keras model only by knowing the inputs and outputs of the model.

Now, we can define the layers using the following code block:

```
H1 = Dense(10, activation='relu')(InputTensor)
```

The first dense layer is created, which connects the input layer output (`InputTensor`) as the input to the dense layer, `(x)`. It is this way of connecting layers (layers by layer) that gives the functional API its flexibility. A layer instance is callable on a tensor, and returns a tensor.

Let's move on to the next layer:

```
H2 = Dense(20, activation='relu')(H1)
```

So, a second dense layer is created, that connects the `Dense` layer output, `(x)`, as the input to the other dense layer, `(H2)`.

Let's move on to the final layer creation:

```
Output = Dense(1, activation='softmax')(H2)
```

Finally, a third dense layer is created that connects the `Dense` layer output, `(H2)`, as the input to the other dense layer, `(Output)`.

Now, we can create a model that includes the `Input` layer and three `Dense` layers:

```
model = Model(inputs=InputTensor, outputs= Output)
```

The model created has 100 inputs, two hidden layers with 10 and 20 neurons, and an output layer with one output.

To print a summary of the model, simply type the following command:

```
model.summary()
```

In the following screenshot, we can see the results:

```
Layer (type) Output Shape Param #
=================================================================
input_1 (InputLayer) (None, 100) 0
_____
dense_1 (Dense) (None, 10) 1010
_____
dense_2 (Dense) (None, 20) 220
_____
dense_3 (Dense) (None, 1) 21
=================================================================
Total params: 1,251
Trainable params: 1,251
Non-trainable params: 0
```

All these terms will become clearer in the following chapters.

Summary

In this chapter, an overview of the Keras environment has been explored. We have learned how to install and configure Keras and how to work with the `keras` library, and have discovered the basic concepts of the Keras architecture. We have also seen how Keras uses TensorFlow as its tensor manipulation library, how we can switch the Keras backend from TensorFlow, which is the default option, to Theano and CNTK, and other available frameworks. Finally, we have understood the different types of Keras model, and we discussed model classes used with sequential layers and those used with functional API layers.

In the next chapter, you will learn the different types of regression techniques and how to apply regression methods to your data, and will understand how the regression algorithm works. We will understand the basic concepts that multiple linear regression methods use to fit equations to data using Keras layers. We will also learn how to evaluate the model's performance, and learn how to tune a model to improve its performance.

2
Modeling Real Estate Using Regression Analysis

The real estate market is a type of market where the sales and purchases between sellers and buyers refer to the exchange of real estate of any kind, such as housing, land, commercial premises, and so on. Real estate prices depend on a series of factors that make the asset more palatable for potential buyers. Regression analysis is the statistical process of studying the relationship between a set of independent variables (explanatory variables) and the dependent variable (response variable). Through this technique, it is possible to understand how the value of the response variable changes when the explanatory variable is varied. In this chapter, the real estate market will be modeled through a regression analysis.

In this chapter, we will cover the following topics:

- Defining a regression problem
- Creating a linear regression model
- Multiple linear regression concepts
- Neural networks for regression using Keras

By the end of this chapter, we will have learned about the different types of regression techniques. We will apply regression methods to your data and understand how the regression algorithm works. We will then understand the basic concepts that multiple linear regression methods use to fit equations to data using the Keras layers. We will also learn how to evaluate the model's performance and how to tune a model to improve the model's performance.

Defining a regression problem

Regression analysis is the starting point in data science. This is because regression models represent the most well-understood models in numerical simulation. Once we experience the workings of regression models, we will be able to understand all other machine learning algorithms. Regression models are easily interpretable as they are based on solid mathematical bases (such as matrix algebra, for example). In the following sections, we will see that linear regression allows us to derive a mathematical formula that's representative of the corresponding model. Perhaps this is why such techniques are extremely easy to understand.

Regression analysis is a statistical process that's implemented to study the relationship between a set of independent variables (explanatory variables) and the dependent variable (response variable). Through this technique, it will be possible to understand how the value of the response variable changes when the explanatory variable is varied.

Consider some data that is collected about a group of students, on the number of study hours per day, attendance at school, and the scores that they have obtained on the final exam. Through regression techniques, we can quantify the average increase in the final exam score when we add one more hour of study. Lower attendance in school (decreasing the student's experience) lowers the scores in the final exam.

A regression analysis can have two objectives:

- **Explanatory analysis**: To understand and weigh the effects of the independent variable on the dependent variable, according to a particular theoretical model

- **Predictive analysis**: To locate a linear combination of the independent variable to predict the value assumed by the dependent variable optimally

However, regression, given its cross-disciplinary characteristics, has numerous and varied areas of applications, right from psychology to agrarianism, and from economics to medicine and business management, just to name a few.

The purpose of regression as a statistical tool is of two types, namely to synthesize and generalize, as we can see in the following diagram:

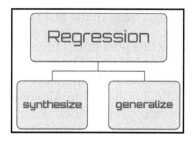

Synthesize: The first purpose (**synthesize**) means predisposing collected data into a form (tables, graphs, or numerical summaries), which allows you to understand better, the phenomena on which the detection was performed. The synthesis is met by the need to simplify, which in turn results from the limited ability of the human mind to handle articulated, complex, or multidimensional information. In this way, we can use techniques that allow for a global study of a large number of quantitative and qualitative information to highlight features, ties, differences, or associations between detected variables.

Generalize: The second purpose (**generalize**) is to extend the result of an analysis performed on the data of a limited group of statistical units (sample) to the entire population group (population). The contribution of regression is not limited to the data analysis phase. It's true that the added value is expressed in the formulation of research hypotheses, argumentation of theses, adoption of appropriate solutions and methodologies, choices of methods of detection, formulation of the sample, and the procedure of extending the results to the reference universes.

Keeping these phases under control means producing reliable and economically useful results, and mastering descriptive statistics and data analysis as well as inferential ones. In this regard, we recall that the descriptive statistics are concerned with describing the experimental data with a few significant numbers or graphs. Therefore, they photograph a given situation and summarize its salient characteristics. Inferential statistics use statistical data that is also appropriately summarized by the descriptive statistics to make probabilistic forecasts on future or otherwise uncertain situations.

People, families, businesses, public administrations, mayors, ministers, and researchers constantly make decisions. For most of them, the outcome is uncertain, in the sense that it is not known exactly what will result, although the expectation is that they will achieve the (positive) effects they are hoping for. Decisions would be better and the effects would be expected closer to those desired if they were made on the basis of relevant data in a decision-making context.

Let's look at some applications of regression in the real world in the following section:

- A student who graduates this year must choose the faculty and university degree in which he or she will enroll. Perhaps he or she has already gained a vocation for his or her future profession, or studies, and may have confirmed his or her predisposition for a particular discipline. Maybe a well-established family tradition advises him or her to follow their parent's profession. In these cases, the uncertainty of choice will be greatly reduced. However, if the student does not have genuine vocations or is not geared particularly to specific choices, he or she may want to know something about the professional outcomes of the graduates. In this regard, some statistical studies on graduate data from the previous years may help him or her make a decision.

- A distribution company such as a supermarket chain wants to open a new sales outlet in a big city and must choose the best location. It will use and analyze numerous statistical data on the density of the population in different neighborhoods, the presence of young families, the presence of children under the age of six (if it is interested in selling to this category of consumers), and the presence of schools, offices, other supermarkets, and retail outlets.

- Another company wants to invest its profits. It must make a portfolio choice and it has to decide whether to invest in government bonds, national shares, foreign securities, funds, or real estate. To make this choice, it will first conduct an analysis of the returns and risks of different investment alternatives based on statistical data.

- National governments are often called upon to make choices and decisions. To do this, they have statistical production equipment. They have population data and forecasts about population evolution over the coming years, which will calibrate their interventions. A strong decline in birth rates will, for example, recommend school consolidation policies; the emergence of children from the non-community component will signal the need for reviewing multiethnic programs and, more generally, school integration policies. On the other hand, statistical data on the presence of national products in foreign markets will suggest the need to export support actions or interventions to promote innovation and business competitiveness.

In the examples we have seen so far, the usefulness of statistical techniques, and particularly of regression in the most diverse working situations, is clear. It is therefore clear how much more information and data companies are required to have to ensure the rationality of decisions and economic behaviors by those who direct them.

Basic regression concepts

Regression is an inductive learning task that has been widely studied, and is widely used in practical applications. Unlike classification processes where you are trying to predict discrete class labels, regression models predict numeric values.

From a set of data, we can find a model that describes observations by the use of regression algorithms. For example, we can identify a correspondence between the input variables and output variables of a given system. One way to do this is to postulate the existence of some kind of mechanism for the parametric generation of data. This, however, does not contain the exact values of the parameters. This process typically makes reference to statistical techniques.

The extraction of general laws from a set of observed data is called **induction**, as opposed to deduction, in which we start from general laws and try to predict the value of a set of variables. Induction is the fundamental mechanism underlying the scientific method in which we want to derive general laws (typically described in mathematical terms), starting from the observation of phenomena.

The observation of the phenomena requires the measurement of a set of variables, and the subsequent acquisition of measured data. Then, the resulting model can be used to make predictions on additional data. The overall process is so that we start from a set of observations, and we aim to make predictions on new situations, which is called inference.

The generalization ability of the regression model is crucial for all other machine learning algorithms as well. Regression algorithms must not only detect the relationships between the target function and attribute values in the training set, but they also generalize them so that they may be used to predict new data.

It should be emphasized that the learning process must be able to capture the underlying regimes from the training set and not the specific details. Once the learning process is completed through training, the effectiveness of the model is tested further on a dataset named `testset`.

Different types of regression

The power of regression techniques is due to the quality of their algorithms, which have been improved and updated over the years. These are divided into several main types, depending on the nature of the dependent and independent variables used or the shape of the regression line.

The reason for such a wide range of regression techniques is the variety of cases to be analyzed. Each case is based on data with specific characteristics, and each analysis is characterized by specific objectives. These specifications require the use of different types of regression techniques to obtain the best results.

How do we distinguish between different types of regression techniques? Previously, we said that a first distinction can be made based on the form of the regression line. Based on this feature, regression analysis is divided into linear regression and nonlinear regression, as shown in the following diagram:

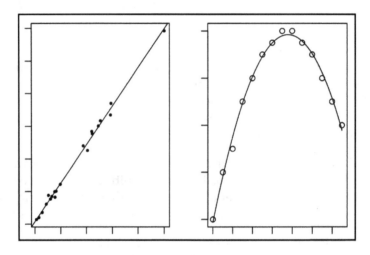

Linear regression on the left and nonlinear quadratic regression on the right

It's clear that the shape of the regression line is dependent on the distribution of data. There are cases where a straight line is the regression line that best approximates the data, while in other cases you need to fall into a curve to get the best approximation. That said, it is easy to understand that a visual analysis of the distribution of data we are going to analyze is a good practice to be done in advance. By summarizing the shape of distribution, we can distinguish the type of regression between the following:

- Linear regression
- Nonlinear regression

The difference between the two models lies in the type of relationships existing between the variables: linear and nonlinear. Let's analyze the nature of the variables involved. In this regard, a question arises spontaneously: *Can the number of explanatory variables affect the choice of regression technique?* The answer to this question is surely positive. For example, in the case of linear regression, if there is only one input variable, then we will do simple linear regression. Alternatively, if the input variables are two or more, we will need to perform multiple linear regression.

By summarizing a simple linear regression, it shows the relationship between a dependent variable Y and an independent variable X. A multiple regression model shows the relationship between a dependent variable Y and multiple independent variables X. In the following diagram, we can see the types of regression imposed from the **Number of the explanatory variables**:

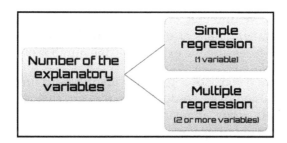

Another question that arises is, what if we have multiple response variables rather than explanatory variables? In that case, we move from univariate models to multivariate models. As suggested by the name itself, multivariate regression is a technique with the help of which a single regression model can be estimated with more than one response variable. When there is more than one explanatory variable in a multivariate regression model, the model is a multivariate multiple regression.

Finally, let's see what happens when we analyze the type of variables. Usually, regression analysis is used when you want to predict a continuous response variable from a number of explanatory variables, which are also continuous. But this is not a limitation of regression, in the sense that such an analysis is also applicable when categorical variables are at stake.

In the case of a dichotomous explanatory variable (which takes a value of zero or one), the solution is immediate. There are already two numbers (zero and one) associated with this variable, so the regression is immediately applicable. Categorical explanatory variables with more than two values can also be used in regression analyses; however, before they can be used, they need to be converted into variables that have only two levels (such as zero and one). This is called dummy coding or indicator variables. Logistic regression should be used if the response variable is dichotomous.

Creating a linear regression model

A simple linear regression is easy to understand, but represents the basis of regression techniques. Once these concepts are understood, it will be easier for us to address the other types of regression. To begin with, let's take an example of applying linear regression that's been taken from the real world.

Consider some data that has been collected on a group of bikers, which consists of the following aspects:

- Number of years of use
- Number of kilometers traveled in one year
- Number of falls

Through these techniques, we find that, on average, when the number of kilometers traveled increases, the number of falls also increases. By increasing the number of years of motorcycle usage and by increasing the experience, the number of falls tends to decrease.

The linear regression method consists of precisely identifying a line that is capable of representing point distribution in a two-dimensional plane, that is, if the points corresponding to the observations are near the line, then the chosen model will be able to describe the link between the variables effectively.

In theory, there are an infinite number of lines that may approximate the observations, while in practice, there is only one mathematical model that optimizes the representation of the data. In the case of a linear mathematical relationship, the observations of the variable y can be obtained by a linear function of the observations of the variable x. For each observation, we will have the following:

$$y = \alpha * x + \beta$$

In the preceding formula, x is the explanatory variable and y is the response variable. The parameters α and β, which represent the slope of the line and the intercept with the y-axis, respectively, must be estimated based on the observations collected for the two variables included in the model.

Slope α is of particular interest, that is, the variation of the mean response for every single increment of the explanatory variable. What about a change in this coefficient? If the slope is positive, the regression line increases from left to right, and if the slope is negative, the line decreases from left to right. When the slope is zero, the explanatory variable has no effect on the value of the response. But it is not just the sign of α that establishes the weight of the relationship between the variables. More generally, its value is also important. In the case of a positive slope, the mean response is higher when the explanatory variable is higher, while in the case of a negative slope, the mean response is lower when the explanatory variable is higher.

If we have a set of observations in the form $(x_1, y_1), (x_2, y_2), ... (x_n, y_n)$, for each of these pairs, we can write an equation. In this way, we get a system of linear equations. We can represent this equation in matrix form, as shown in the following diagram:

$$\begin{bmatrix} y_1 \\ y_2 \\ ... \\ y_n \end{bmatrix} = \begin{bmatrix} x_1 & 1 \\ x_2 & 1 \\ ... & ... \\ x_n & 1 \end{bmatrix} \times \begin{bmatrix} \alpha \\ \beta \end{bmatrix}$$

We will name the terms contained in this formula as follows:

$$Y = \begin{bmatrix} y_1 \\ y_2 \\ ... \\ y_n \end{bmatrix} ; X = \begin{bmatrix} x_1 & 1 \\ x_2 & 1 \\ ... & ... \\ x_n & 1 \end{bmatrix} ; A = \begin{bmatrix} \alpha \\ \beta \end{bmatrix}$$

This can be expressed using a condensed formulation:

$$Y = X \times A$$

This represents a system of linear equations, and to locate the solution, we will resolve the following equation:

$$A = (X^T * X)^{-1} * X^T * Y$$

In the previous equation, there are three mathematical operations involving matrices: transpose, inverse, and matrix multiplication.

But how does least squares regression work? In the least squares method, the coefficients are estimated by determining numerical values that minimize the sum of the squared deviations between the observed responses and the fitted responses.

As we said, given n points (x_1, y_1), (x_2, y_2), ... (x_n, y_n) in the observed population, a least squares regression line is defined as follows:

$$y = \alpha * x + \beta$$

This is the equation line for which the following quantity is minimal:

$$E = \sum_{i=1}^{n}(\alpha x_i + \beta - y_i)^2$$

This quantity represents the sum of the squares of the distances of each experimental datum (x_i, y_i) from the corresponding point on the straight line, as shown in the following graph:

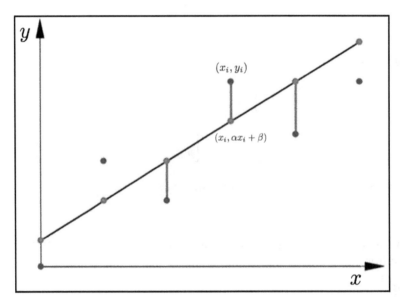

To understand this concept, it is easier to draw the distances between these points, formally called residuals, for a couple of pieces of data. Once the coefficients are obtained, calculating the residuals is really simple – the observed minus the estimated values, that is:

$$r_i = y_i - (\alpha x_i + \beta)$$

A residual is a measure of how well a regression line fits an individual data point. Therefore, the model is said to fit the data well if the residuals appear to behave randomly. However, the model is clearly said to fit the data poorly if the residuals happen to display a systematic pattern.

Multiple linear regression concepts

So far, we have resolved simple linear regression problems that study the relation between a dependent variable, y, and an independent variable, x, based on the following regression equation:

$$y = \alpha * x + \beta$$

In this equation, the explanatory variable is represented by x and the response variable is represented by y. To solve this problem, the least squares method was used. In this method, we can find the best fit by minimizing the sum of squares of the vertical distances from each data point on the line. As mentioned previously, we don't find that a variable depends solely on another very often. Usually, we find that the response variable depends on at least two predictors. In practice, we will have to create models with a response variable that depend on more than one predictor. These models are known as multiple linear regression models. It is a straightforward generalization of single predictor models. According to multiple linear regression models, the dependent variable is related to two or more independent variables.

The general model for n variables is of the following form:

$$y = \beta_0 + \beta_1 * x_1 + \beta_2 * x_2 + ... + \beta_n * x_n$$

Here, $x_1, x_2, .. x_n$ are the n predictors and y is the only response variable. The coefficients β_i measure the change in the y value, associated with a change in x_i, keeping all the other variables constant. The simple linear regression model is used to find a straight line that best fits the data. On the other hand, multiple linear regression models, for example, with two independent variables, are used to find a plane that best fits the data; more generally, it is a multidimensional plane. The goal is to find the surface that best fits our predictors in terms of minimizing the overall squared distance between itself and the response variable.

To estimate β similarly to what we did in the simple linear regression case, we want to minimize the following term over all possible values of intercepts and slopes:

$$\sum_i = [y_i - (\beta_0 + \beta_1 * x_1 + \beta_2 * x_2 + ... + \beta_n * x_n)]^2$$

Just as we did in the case of simple linear regression, we can represent the previous equation in matrix form, as follows:

$$
\begin{bmatrix} y_1 \\ y_2 \\ \dots \\ y_n \end{bmatrix} = \begin{bmatrix} 1 & x_{1,1} & x_{1,2} & \dots & x_{1,n} \\ 1 & x_{2,1} & x_{2,2} & \dots & x_{2,n} \\ \dots & & & & \\ 1 & x_{n,1} & x_{n,2} & \dots & x_{n,n} \end{bmatrix} \times \begin{bmatrix} \beta_0 \\ \beta_1 \\ \beta_2 \\ \dots \\ \beta_n \end{bmatrix}
$$

We can name the terms contained in this formula as follows:

$$
Y = \begin{bmatrix} y_1 \\ y_2 \\ \dots \\ y_n \end{bmatrix} ; X = \begin{bmatrix} 1 & x_{1,1} & x_{1,2} & \dots & x_{1,n} \\ 1 & x_{2,1} & x_{2,2} & \dots & x_{2,n} \\ \dots & & & & \\ 1 & x_{n,1} & x_{n,2} & \dots & x_{n,n} \end{bmatrix} ; \beta = \begin{bmatrix} \beta_0 \\ \beta_1 \\ \beta_2 \\ \dots \\ \beta_n \end{bmatrix}
$$

This can be reexpressed using a condensed formulation:

$$
Y = X * \beta
$$

Finally, to determine the intercept and slope through the least squares method, we have to solve the previous equation with respect to β, as follows (we must estimate the coefficients with the normal equation):

$$
\beta = (X^T * X)^{-1} * X^T * Y
$$

Basically, it represents the same equation that we looked at previously. We can then calculate the intercept and slope of the regression line.

Neural networks for regression using Keras

The real estate market is a market where the sales and purchase between sellers and buyers refer to the exchange of real estate of any kind, such as housing, land, commercial premises, and so on. Real estate prices depend on a series of factors that make the asset more palatable for potential buyers.

These factors include the socioeconomic conditions, environmental conditions, and educational facilities of the area in which the property is located. Analyzing how these factors affect the cost of real estate can be a valuable tool for technicians in the sector in order to predict the market trends, depending on the changes that are occurring.

To do this, we will run a neural network regression for the Boston dataset; the median values of owner-occupied homes are predicted for the test data. The dataset describes 13 numerical properties of houses in Boston suburbs, and is concerned with modeling the price of houses in those suburbs in thousands of dollars. As such, this is a regression predictive modeling problem. Input attributes include features such as the crime rate, the proportion of nonretail business acres, chemical concentrations, and more.

 To get the data for this section, we will draw on the large collection of data available in the UCI Machine Learning Repository at `http://archive.ics.uci.edu/ml`.

The following list shows all the variables, followed by a brief description:

- **Number of instances**: 506
- **Number of attributes**: 14 continuous attributes (including the class attribute `medv`), and one binary-valued attribute

Each of the detailed attributes areas are as follows:

- `crim`: Per capita crime rate by town
- `zn`: Proportion of residential land zoned for lots over 25,000 square feet
- `indus`: Proportion of nonretail business acres per town
- `chas`: Charles River dummy variable (= 1 if tract bounds river; 0 otherwise)
- `nox`: Nitric oxides concentration (parts per ten million)
- `rm`: Average number of rooms per dwelling
- `age`: Proportion of owner-occupied units built prior to 1940
- `dis`: Weighted distances to five Boston employment centers
- `rad`: Index of accessibility to radial highways
- `tax`: Full-value property tax rate per $10,000
- `ptratio`: Pupil-teacher ratio by town
- `black`: 1000(Bk - 0.63)^2, where Bk is the proportion of blacks by town
- `lstat`: Percent of the lower status of the population
- `medv`: Median value of owner-occupied homes in $1,000

Of these, `medv` is the response variable, while the other 13 variables are possible predictors. The goal of this analysis is to fit a regression model that best explains the variation in `medv`. Is there a relationship between the first 13 columns and the `medv` response variable? Can we predict the `medv` value based on the 13 input columns? As we stated previously, the objective of this example is to predict the median value of owner-occupied homes. The answers to these questions will allow us to predict the median value of the houses according to a series of factors.

The data is available in a `.data` file named `housing.data` from the UCI dataset. To start, let's look at how we can import the data into Python. To do this, we will use the `read_csv` module of the `pandas` library. The `read_cs` method loads the data in a pandas DataFrame.

The first thing to do is import the library that we will use, as follows:

```
import pandas as pd
```

From now on, to refer to any function contained in the `pandas` library, we just use the string `pd`. We have changed the `pandas` library name, and the **as** clause can be added to do that.

The `pandas` library is an open source, BSD-licensed library providing high-performance, easy-to-use data structures and data analysis tools for the Python programming language. In particular, it offers data structures and operations for manipulating numericals.

The available data does not contain the header, so it is necessary to retrieve the names of the variables that are contained in another file, and always make it available in the UCI archive.

Now, let's put them in a list:

```
BHNames= ['crim','zn','indus','chas','nox','rm',
         'age','dis','rad','tax','ptratio','black','lstat','medv']
```

Let's look at how we can import the data contained in the dataset in Python:

```
url='https://archive.ics.uci.edu/ml/machine-learning-databases/housing/hous
ing.data'
data = pd.read_csv(url, delim_whitespace=True, names=BHNames)
```

As we said, to import a dataset, we use the `read_csv` module of the `pandas` library. In this function, instead of the filename, we can also enter a complete URL of a file contained on a website repository. To do this, first, we have set the complete URL in the `url` variable, and then this variable has been passed to the function. Furthermore, two other parameters have been passed to the function, namely `delim_whitespace` and `names`. The first specifies whether or not whitespace will be used as `sep`. The second specifies a list of column names to use.

Exploratory analysis

Before starting with data analysis through multiple linear regression, we conduct an exploratory analysis to understand how the data is distributed and extract preliminary knowledge:

To display the first 20 rows of the DataFrame that have been imported, we can use the `head()` function, as follows:

```
print(data.head(20))
```

The following results are returned:

	crim	zn	indus	chas	nox	rm	age	dis	rad	tax	ptratio	black	lstat	medv
0	0.00632	18.0	2.31	0	0.538	6.575	65.2	4.0900	1	296.0	15.3	396.90	4.98	24.0
1	0.02731	0.0	7.07	0	0.469	6.421	78.9	4.9671	2	242.0	17.8	396.90	9.14	21.6
2	0.02729	0.0	7.07	0	0.469	7.185	61.1	4.9671	2	242.0	17.8	392.83	4.03	34.7
3	0.03237	0.0	2.18	0	0.458	6.998	45.8	6.0622	3	222.0	18.7	394.63	2.94	33.4
4	0.06905	0.0	2.18	0	0.458	7.147	54.2	6.0622	3	222.0	18.7	396.90	5.33	36.2
5	0.02985	0.0	2.18	0	0.458	6.430	58.7	6.0622	3	222.0	18.7	394.12	5.21	28.7
6	0.08829	12.5	7.87	0	0.524	6.012	66.6	5.5605	5	311.0	15.2	395.60	12.43	22.9
7	0.14455	12.5	7.87	0	0.524	6.172	96.1	5.9505	5	311.0	15.2	396.90	19.15	27.1
8	0.21124	12.5	7.87	0	0.524	5.631	100.0	6.0821	5	311.0	15.2	386.63	29.93	16.5
9	0.17004	12.5	7.87	0	0.524	6.004	85.9	6.5921	5	311.0	15.2	386.71	17.10	18.9
10	0.22489	12.5	7.87	0	0.524	6.377	94.3	6.3467	5	311.0	15.2	392.52	20.45	15.0
11	0.11747	12.5	7.87	0	0.524	6.009	82.9	6.2267	5	311.0	15.2	396.90	13.27	18.9
12	0.09378	12.5	7.87	0	0.524	5.889	39.0	5.4509	5	311.0	15.2	390.50	15.71	21.7
13	0.62976	0.0	8.14	0	0.538	5.949	61.8	4.7075	4	307.0	21.0	396.90	8.26	20.4
14	0.63796	0.0	8.14	0	0.538	6.096	84.5	4.4619	4	307.0	21.0	380.02	10.26	18.2
15	0.62739	0.0	8.14	0	0.538	5.834	56.5	4.4986	4	307.0	21.0	395.62	8.47	19.9
16	1.05393	0.0	8.14	0	0.538	5.935	29.3	4.4986	4	307.0	21.0	386.85	6.58	23.1
17	0.78420	0.0	8.14	0	0.538	5.990	81.7	4.2579	4	307.0	21.0	386.75	14.67	17.5
18	0.80271	0.0	8.14	0	0.538	5.456	36.6	3.7965	4	307.0	21.0	288.99	11.69	20.2
19	0.72580	0.0	8.14	0	0.538	5.727	69.5	3.7965	4	307.0	21.0	390.95	11.28	18.2

The `head()` function, with no arguments, gets the first five rows of data from the DataFrame.

Now, the dataset is available in our Python environment. To extract further information, we can invoke the `info()` function, as follows:

```
print(data.info())
```

The `print()` method prints a concise summary of a DataFrame, including the index `dtypes` and column `dtypes`, non-null values, and memory usage.

The following results are returned:

```
<class 'pandas.core.frame.DataFrame'>
RangeIndex: 506 entries, 0 to 505
Data columns (total 14 columns):
crim        506 non-null  float64
zn          506 non-null  float64
indus       506 non-null  float64
chas        506 non-null  int64
nox         506 non-null  float64
rm          506 non-null  float64
age         506 non-null  float64
dis         506 non-null  float64
rad         506 non-null  int64
tax         506 non-null  float64
ptratio     506 non-null  float64
black       506 non-null  float64
lstat       506 non-null  float64
medv        506 non-null  float64
dtypes: float64(12), int64(2)
memory usage: 55.4 KB
None
```

A series of additional information is returned for all the variables contained in the dataset. To get a preview of the data contained in it, we can calculate a series of basic statistics.

To do so, we will use the `describe()` function in the following way:

```
summary = data.describe()
summary = summary.transpose()
print(summary)
```

We have simply transposed the results to make printing on the screen easier.

The following results are returned:

	count	mean	std	min	25%	50%	75%	max
crim	506.0	3.613524	8.601545	0.00632	0.082045	0.25651	3.677082	88.9762
zn	506.0	11.363636	23.322453	0.00000	0.000000	0.00000	12.500000	100.0000
indus	506.0	11.136779	6.860353	0.46000	5.190000	9.69000	18.100000	27.7400
chas	506.0	0.069170	0.253994	0.00000	0.000000	0.00000	0.000000	1.0000
nox	506.0	0.554695	0.115878	0.38500	0.449000	0.53800	0.624000	0.8710
rm	506.0	6.284634	0.702617	3.56100	5.885500	6.20850	6.623500	8.7800
age	506.0	68.574901	28.148861	2.90000	45.025000	77.50000	94.075000	100.0000
dis	506.0	3.795043	2.105710	1.12960	2.100175	3.20745	5.188425	12.1265
rad	506.0	9.549407	8.707259	1.00000	4.000000	5.00000	24.000000	24.0000
tax	506.0	408.237154	168.537116	187.00000	279.000000	330.00000	666.000000	711.0000
ptratio	506.0	18.455534	2.164946	12.60000	17.400000	19.05000	20.200000	22.0000
black	506.0	356.674032	91.294864	0.32000	375.377500	391.44000	396.225000	396.9000
lstat	506.0	12.653063	7.141062	1.73000	6.950000	11.36000	16.955000	37.9700
medv	506.0	22.532806	9.197104	5.00000	17.025000	21.20000	25.000000	50.0000

The describe() function generates descriptive statistics that summarize the central tendency, dispersion, and shape of a dataset's distribution, excluding **not a number (NaN)** values. It analyzes both numeric and object series, as well as the DataFrame column sets of mixed data types. The output will vary depending on what is provided.

In the preceding screenshot, we can see that the variables have different ranges. When the predictors have different ranges, the impact on response variables by the features having a greater numeric range could be more than the one having a lesser numeric range, and this could in turn impact the prediction's accuracy. Our goal is to improve predictive accuracy and not allow a particular feature to impact the prediction due to a large numeric value range. Thus, we may need to scale values under different features so that they fall under a common range. Through this statistical procedure, it is possible to compare identical variables belonging to different distributions and also different variables or variables expressed in different units.

Remember, it is a good practice to rescale the data before training a regression algorithm. With rescaling, data units are eliminated, allowing you to compare data from different locations easily.

In this case, we will use the min-max method (usually called feature scaling) to get all the scaled data in the range [0, 1]. The formula to achieve this is as follows:

$$x_{scaled} = \frac{x - x_{min}}{x_{max} - x_{min}}$$

To perform feature scaling, we can use the preprocessing package available in the `sklearn` library. The `sklearn` library is a free software machine learning library for the Python programming language. It features various classification, regression, and clustering algorithms, including **support vector machines** (**SVMs**), random forests, gradient boosting, k-means, and DBSCAN, and is designed to interoperate with the Python numerical and scientific libraries NumPy and SciPy.

Remember, to import a library that is not present in the initial distribution of Python, you must use the `pip install` command, followed by the name of the library. This command should be used only once and not every time you run the code.

The `sklearn.preprocessing` package provides several common utility functions and transformer classes to modify the features available in a representation that best suits our needs. We will begin using the following steps:

As always, we start by importing the package:

```
from sklearn.preprocessing import MinMaxScaler
```

To scale features between a given minimum and maximum value, in our case, between zero and one, so that the maximum absolute value of each feature is scaled to unit size, the `MinMaxScaler` function can be used.

Let's start by defining the `scaler` object:

```
scaler = MinMaxScaler()
```

Now, just to have a confirmation of what we are going to do, we print the parameters that we will use for the next resizing:

```
print(scaler.fit(data))
```

The `fit` method computes the minimum and maximum that is to be used for later scaling. The result is as follows:

```
MinMaxScaler(copy=True, feature_range=(0, 1))
```

Now, we can scale the features:

```
DataScaled = scaler.fit_transform(data)
```

The `fit_transform` method fits to the data and then transforms it.

A NumPy array shape is returned. It is advisable to report the results in the starting format (`pandas` **DataFrame**), at least for comparison purposes.

Let's do this using the following code block:

```
DataScaled = pd.DataFrame(DataScaled, columns=BHNames)
```

To verify that the transformation was carried out, we will print the basic statistics that we had already calculated previously:

```
summary = DataScaled.describe()
summary = summary.transpose()
print(summary)
```

The following results are returned:

	count	mean	std	min	25%	50%	75%	max
crim	506.0	0.040544	0.096679	0.0	0.000851	0.002812	0.041258	1.0
zn	506.0	0.113636	0.233225	0.0	0.000000	0.000000	0.125000	1.0
indus	506.0	0.391378	0.251479	0.0	0.173387	0.338343	0.646628	1.0
chas	506.0	0.069170	0.253994	0.0	0.000000	0.000000	0.000000	1.0
nox	506.0	0.349167	0.238431	0.0	0.131687	0.314815	0.491770	1.0
rm	506.0	0.521869	0.134627	0.0	0.445392	0.507281	0.586798	1.0
age	506.0	0.676364	0.289896	0.0	0.433831	0.768280	0.938980	1.0
dis	506.0	0.242381	0.191482	0.0	0.088259	0.188949	0.369088	1.0
rad	506.0	0.371713	0.378576	0.0	0.130435	0.173913	1.000000	1.0
tax	506.0	0.422208	0.321636	0.0	0.175573	0.272901	0.914122	1.0
ptratio	506.0	0.622929	0.230313	0.0	0.510638	0.686170	0.808511	1.0
black	506.0	0.898568	0.230205	0.0	0.945730	0.986232	0.998298	1.0
lstat	506.0	0.301409	0.197049	0.0	0.144040	0.265728	0.420116	1.0
medv	506.0	0.389618	0.204380	0.0	0.267222	0.360000	0.444444	1.0

With reference to the preceding screenshot, every variable is included in a range between 0 and 1. Now, all features have values between 0 and 1. We will now move on to a visual analysis. For example, what we can do is plot the boxplot of the variables.

A boxplot, which is also referred to as a whiskers chart, is a graphical representation that's used to describe the distribution of a sample by simple dispersion and position indexes. A boxplot can be represented – either horizontally or vertically – by means of a rectangular partition divided by two segments. The rectangle (box) is delimited by the first quartile (25th percentile) and the third quartile (75th percentile), and divided by the median (50th percentile), as shown in the following diagram:

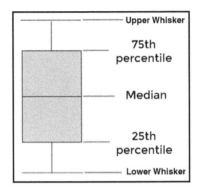

Segments outside the box (whiskers) represent the lower and the upper whiskers. By default, the whiskers will extend up to 1.5 times the interquartile range from the top or bottom of the box to the furthest datum within that distance. In this way, the four equally populated ranges delineated by quartiles are graphically represented. To plot a boxplot in Python, we can use the matplotlib library.

The matplotlib library is a Python 2-D plotting library that produces publication-quality figures in a variety of hard copy formats and interactive environments across platforms. The matplotlib library tries to make easy things and hard things possible. You can generate plots, histograms, power spectra, bar charts, error charts, scatter plots, and so on with just a few lines of code. The matplotlib.pyplot function consists of a collection of command-style functions that make matplotlib work, such as MATLAB. Each pyplot function makes a change to a figure, such as creating a figure, creating a plotting area in a figure, plotting some lines in a plotting area, decorating the plot with labels, and so on.

As always, let's start by importing the library into Python:

```
import matplotlib.pyplot as plt
```

The available data is in `pandas` DataFrame format. For this reason, we can use the `pandas.DataFrame.boxplot` function. This function makes a box plot from the `DataFrame` columns, which are optionally grouped by some other columns:

```
boxplot = data.boxplot(column=BHNames)
plt.show()
```

Finally, to print on video, the `plt.show()` function will be used.

This function displays all figures and blocks until the figures have been closed. In the following diagram, the boxplots of all the variables contained in the `DataScaled` DataFrame are shown:

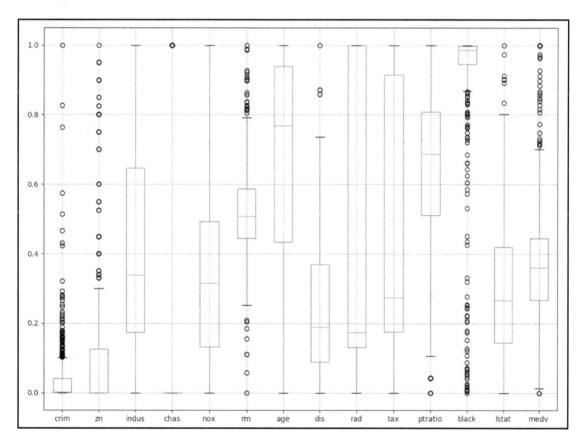

From the analysis of the previous diagram, we can note that several variables have outliers, with the `crim` variable being the one that has the largest number.

Outlier values are numerically different from the rest of the collected data. Statistics derived from samples containing outliers can be misleading.

In the following chapters, we'll look at how we can handle this problem. Furthermore, from the analysis of the previous diagram, we can see that the predictors are many; often, this can create problems rather than give us a hand. We can then find which of the available predictors are most correlated with the response variable. A standardized measurement of the relationship between two variables is instead represented by correlation, which can be calculated, starting from covariance. In Python, correlation coefficients are calculated by the `pandas.DataFrame.corr()` function; it computes pairwise correlation of columns, excluding NA/null values. Three methods are available, namely:

- `pearson` (standard correlation coefficient)
- `kendall` (Kendall Tau correlation coefficient)
- `spearman` (Spearman rank correlation)

Remember, the correlation coefficient of two random variables is a measure of their linear dependence.

In the following code block, we calculate the correlation coefficients for the `DataScaled` DataFrame:

```
CorData = DataScaled.corr(method='pearson')
```

To display all DataFrame columns on video, we can use `option_context` with one or more options:

```
with pd.option_context('display.max_rows', None,
            'display.max_columns', CorData.shape[1]):
    print(CorData)
```

In the following screenshot, we can see the results:

```
              crim        zn     indus      chas       nox        rm       age  \
crim      1.000000 -0.200469  0.406583 -0.055892  0.420972 -0.219247  0.352734
zn       -0.200469  1.000000 -0.533828 -0.042697 -0.516604  0.311991 -0.569537
indus     0.406583 -0.533828  1.000000  0.062938  0.763651 -0.391676  0.644779
chas     -0.055892 -0.042697  0.062938  1.000000  0.091203  0.091251  0.086518
nox       0.420972 -0.516604  0.763651  0.091203  1.000000 -0.302188  0.731470
rm       -0.219247  0.311991 -0.391676  0.091251 -0.302188  1.000000 -0.240265
age       0.352734 -0.569537  0.644779  0.086518  0.731470 -0.240265  1.000000
dis      -0.379670  0.664408 -0.708027 -0.099176 -0.769230  0.205246 -0.747881
rad       0.625505 -0.311948  0.595129 -0.007368  0.611441 -0.209847  0.456022
tax       0.582764 -0.314563  0.720760 -0.035587  0.668023 -0.292048  0.506456
ptratio   0.289946 -0.391679  0.383248 -0.121515  0.188933 -0.355501  0.261515
black    -0.385064  0.175520 -0.356977  0.048788 -0.380051  0.128069 -0.273534
lstat     0.455621 -0.412995  0.603800 -0.053929  0.590879 -0.613808  0.602339
medv     -0.388305  0.360445 -0.483725  0.175260 -0.427321  0.695360 -0.376955

               dis       rad       tax   ptratio     black     lstat      medv
crim     -0.379670  0.625505  0.582764  0.289946 -0.385064  0.455621 -0.388305
zn        0.664408 -0.311948 -0.314563 -0.391679  0.175520 -0.412995  0.360445
indus    -0.708027  0.595129  0.720760  0.383248 -0.356977  0.603800 -0.483725
chas     -0.099176 -0.007368 -0.035587 -0.121515  0.048788 -0.053929  0.175260
nox      -0.769230  0.611441  0.668023  0.188933 -0.380051  0.590879 -0.427321
rm        0.205246 -0.209847 -0.292048 -0.355501  0.128069 -0.613808  0.695360
age      -0.747881  0.456022  0.506456  0.261515 -0.273534  0.602339 -0.376955
dis       1.000000 -0.494588 -0.534432 -0.232471  0.291512 -0.496996  0.249929
rad      -0.494588  1.000000  0.910228  0.464741 -0.444413  0.488676 -0.381626
tax      -0.534432  0.910228  1.000000  0.460853 -0.441808  0.543993 -0.468536
ptratio  -0.232471  0.464741  0.460853  1.000000 -0.177383  0.374044 -0.507787
black     0.291512 -0.444413 -0.441808 -0.177383  1.000000 -0.366087  0.333461
lstat    -0.496996  0.488676  0.543993  0.374044 -0.366087  1.000000 -0.737663
medv      0.249929 -0.381626 -0.468536 -0.507787  0.333461 -0.737663  1.000000
```

Due to the large number of variables, the obtained matrix is not easily interpretable. To overcome this inconvenience, we can plot a correlogram. A correlogram is a graph of a correlation matrix. It is very useful to highlight the most correlated variables in a data table. In this plot, correlation coefficients are colored according to their value. A correlation matrix can also be reordered according to the degree of association between variables. We can plot a correlogram in Python using the `matplotlib.pyplot.matshow()` function. This function displays a DataFrame as a matrix in a new figure window. The origin is set at the upper left-hand corner, and rows (first dimension of the array) are displayed horizontally. The aspect ratio of the figure window is that of the array, unless this would make an excessively short or narrow figure. Tick labels for the x-axis are placed on top. Let's view these steps in the following code block:

```
plt.matshow(CorData)
plt.xticks(range(len(CorData.columns)), CorData.columns)
plt.yticks(range(len(CorData.columns)), CorData.columns)
plt.colorbar()
plt.show()
```

From the preceding code block, we come to know that `plt.xticks` and `plt.yticks` set the current tick locations and labels of the x-axis and y-axis. `plt.colorbar()` adds a colorbar to a plot. Finally, `plt.show()` shows the plot on video. The correlogram is shown in the following diagram:

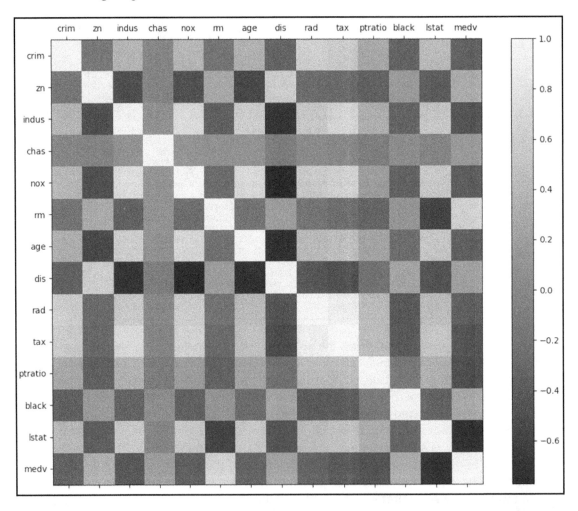

As we are interested in the existing relationship between the response variable (`medv`) and predictors, we will only analyze the last line of the correlation matrix. In it, we can see the predictors that are most closely related, namely `rm`, `lstat`, and `ptratio`. Indeed, these variables have colors that approach the extremes of the color label (the different color is due to the positive or negative correlation, as shown in the color label in the right-hand part of the plot).

Data splitting

Training the parameters of a prediction function and testing it on the same data is an incorrect procedure from a methodological point of view. A model is used simply to predict the sample labels. If used during the training phase, it would have a perfect score, but would not be able to predict anything useful on the data that hasn't previously been explored. This situation is called overfitting. To avoid this, it is a common practice to run an automatic learning experiment (data splitting) to provide some of the data that's available as a training set and a test set.

Data splitting is an operation that allows us to divide the available data into two sets, generally for cross-validation purposes. A dataset is used to train a predictive model, and the other to test the model's performance. Training and testing the model forms the basis for further usage of the model for prediction in predictive analytics. For example, if given a dataset that has 100 rows of data, which includes the predictor and response variables, we will split the dataset into a convenient ratio (say 70:30) and allocate 70 rows for training and 30 rows for testing. The rows will be selected randomly to reduce bias. Once the training data is available, the data is fed to the neural network to get the massive universal function in place. The training data determines the weights, biases, and activation functions to be used so that we can get to output from input.

Once sufficient convergence is achieved, the model is stored in memory and the next step is testing the model. We pass the 30 rows of data to check if the actual output matches the predicted output from the model. The evaluation is used to get various metrics that can validate the model. If the accuracy is too wary, the model has to be rebuilt with changes in the training data and other parameters passed to the neural network builder.

To split the data, the `scikit-learn` library has been used. More specifically, the `sklearn.model_selection.train_test_split()` function has been used. This function quickly computes a random split into training and test sets.

Let's start by importing the function:

```
from sklearn.model_selection import train_test_split
```

At this point, to make work easier for us, we will divide the starting DataFrame into two: predictors (X) and target (Y).

To do this, the `pandas.DataFrame.drop()` function will be used:

```
X = DataScaled.drop('medv', axis = 1)
print(X.describe())
Y = DataScaled['medv']
print(Y.describe())
```

The `pandas.DataFrame.drop()` function drops specified labels from rows or columns. We will remove rows or columns by specifying label names and the corresponding axis, or by specifying the index or column names directly. When using a multi-index, labels on different levels can be removed by specifying the level. To extract X, we have removed the target column (`medv`) from the starting `DataScaled` DataFrame.

The following results are returned:

```
X shape = (506, 13)
Y shape = (506,)
```

So, X has 13 columns (predictors) and Y has only one column (target). Now, we have to split the two DataFrames:

```
X_train, X_test, Y_train, Y_test = train_test_split(X, Y, test_size = 0.30,
random_state = 5)
print('X train shape = ',X_train.shape)
print('X test shape = ', X_test.shape)
print('Y train shape = ', Y_train.shape)
print('Y test shape = ',Y_test.shape)
```

In the `train_test_split()` function, four parameters are passed, namely X, Y, `test_size`, and `random_state`. X and Y are predictors and target DataFrames. The `test_size` parameter can take the following types: float, integer or none, and optional (default=0.25). If float is between 0.0 and 1.0, it represents the proportion of the dataset to include in the test split. If the parameter is `int`, it represents the absolute number of test samples. If the parameter is `None`, the value is set to complement the train size. By default, the value is set to 0.25. In our case, we set `test_size = 0.30`, which means that 30% of the data is divided up as test data. Finally, the `random_state` parameter is used to set the seed used by the random number generator. In this way, the repetitive splitting of the operation is guaranteed.

The following results are returned:

```
X train shape = (354, 13)
X test shape = (152, 13)
Y train shape = (354,)
Y test shape = (152,)
```

So, the starting DataFrame is split into two datasets that have 354 rows (X_train) and 152 rows (X_test). A similar subdivision was made for Y.

Neural network Keras model

To perform a neural network regression analysis, we will use the Keras Sequential model. As we mentioned in `Chapter 1`, *Getting Started with Keras*, to create a Keras Sequential model, we must follow these steps:

1. Import the `Sequential` class from `keras.models`.

2. Stack the layers using `.add()` method.

3. Configure the learning process using `.compile()` method.

4. Train the model on the train dataset using `.fit()` method.

We have omitted the import data step because our data is already available in the Python environment. We will use the following steps to perform the analysis:

First, we have to load the libraries needed to run the analysis:

```
from keras.models import Sequential
from keras.layers import Dense
from keras import metrics
```

Three layer classes have been imported, namely `Sequential`, `Dense`, and `metrics`:

- **Sequential class**: This is used to define a linear stack of network layers that make up a model. In the following code block, we will use the `Sequential` constructor to create the model, which will then be enriched with layers using the `add ()` method.
- **Dense class**: This is used to instantiate a `Dense` layer, which is the basic feedforward fully connected layer. Finally, the `metrics` class is imported.
- **Metric class**: This is a function that is used to evaluate the performance of your model. Metric functions are to be supplied in the metrics parameter when a model is compiled.

Now, let's move on to building the model:

```
model = Sequential()
model.add(Dense(20, input_dim=13, activation='relu'))
model.add(Dense(10, activation='relu'))
model.add(Dense(1, activation='linear'))
```

From the preceding code block, for the first row, we have set the type of the model to `Sequential()`. Then, we have added the layers. We have already said that we will use a completely connected network structure with three levels. Fully connected levels are defined using the `Dense` class.

The first is the most important because it is the level that defines the input, and it must have the right number of inputs. This can be specified with the `input_dim` argument and set to 13 for the 13 predictors. We passed three parameters: `20`, `input_dim = 13`, and `activation = 'relu'`. `20` (units) is a positive integer representing the dimensionality of the output space, and denotes the number of neurons in the level. The `input_dim = 13` attribute is the number of the input variables. Finally, the `activation = 'relu'` action is used to set the activation function. The second layer has `10` neurons and a `relu` activation function. Finally, the output layer has a single neuron (output) and a `linear` activation function.

Before training a model, you need to configure the learning process, which is done via the `compile()` method:

```
model.compile(optimizer='adam',loss='mean_squared_error',
                                metrics=['accuracy'])
```

In the preceding code block, three arguments are passed:

- The `adam` optimizer: This is an algorithm for the first-order, gradient-based optimization of stochastic objective functions, based on adaptive estimates of lower order moments.
- The `mean_squared_error` loss function: The **mean squared error** (MSE) measures the average of the squares of the errors, that is, the average squared difference between the estimated values and what is estimated. MSE is a measure of the quality of an estimator. It is always nonnegative and values that are closer to zero are better.
- The `accuracy` metric: The accuracy metric is a function that is used to evaluate the performance of your model during training and testing.

To train the model, the `fit()` method is used, as follows:

```
model.fit(X_train, Y_train, epochs=1000, verbose=1)
```

In the preceding code block, four arguments are passed:

- `X_train`: Array of predictors training data.
- `Y_train`: Array of target (label) data.
- `epochs=1000`: Number of epochs to train the model. An epoch is an iteration over the entire x and y data provided.
- `verbose`: `verbose=1`: This is an integer: 0, 1, or 2. For verbosity mode, 0 = silent, 1 = progress bar, and 2 = one line per epoch.

When the `fit()` function is performed, the `loss` and the `accuracy` at the end of each training epoch are displayed, as shown in the following output:

```
Epoch 990/1000
354/354 [===] - 0s 56us/step - loss: 0.0021 - acc: 0.0282
Epoch 991/1000
354/354 [===] - 0s 28us/step - loss: 0.0021 - acc: 0.0282
Epoch 992/1000
354/354 [===] - 0s 27us/step - loss: 0.0020 - acc: 0.0282
Epoch 993/1000
354/354 [===] - 0s 35us/step - loss: 0.0021 - acc: 0.0282
Epoch 994/1000
354/354 [===] - 0s 32us/step - loss: 0.0021 - acc: 0.0282
Epoch 995/1000
354/354 [===] - 0s 23us/step - loss: 0.0020 - acc: 0.0282
Epoch 996/1000
354/354 [===] - 0s 56us/step - loss: 0.0020 - acc: 0.0282
Epoch 997/1000
354/354 [===] - 0s 28us/step - loss: 0.0023 - acc: 0.0282
Epoch 998/1000
354/354 [===] - 0s 28us/step - loss: 0.0020 - acc: 0.0282
Epoch 999/1000
354/354 [===] - 0s 34us/step - loss: 0.0022 - acc: 0.0282
Epoch 1000/1000
354/354 [===] - 0s 38us/step - loss: 0.0020 - acc: 0.0282
```

To print a summary of the model, we will type the following command:

```
model.summary()
```

In the following code block, we can see the results:

```
Layer (type) Output Shape Param #
================================================================
dense_1 (Dense) (None, 20) 280

dense_2 (Dense) (None, 10) 210

dense_3 (Dense) (None, 1) 11
================================================================
Total params: 501
Trainable params: 501
Non-trainable params: 0
```

Here, we can clearly see the output shape and the number of weights in each layer. To test the model's capacity for predicting the median value of owner-occupied homes as a function of the thirteen variables assumed, we can display the predicted values against the current ones.

To do this, we must first perform the prediction on all the observations contained in the test dataset. We can use the `predict()` function for this.

This is a generic function for predictions from the results of various Keras models:

```
Y_predKM = model.predict(X_test)
```

For the time being, we don't need to add anything else. This data will be useful to us later to make a comparison with another model.

To evaluate the performance of the model we have just adapted, we must use the `evaluate()` function:

```
score = model.evaluate(X_test, Y_test, verbose=0)
print('Keras Model')
print(score[0])
```

This function returns the loss value and metrics values for the model in test mode. Computation is done in batches. The following result is returned:

```
Keras Model
0.0038815933421901066
```

At first glance, it seems to be a good result, but to have confirmation of this, it is necessary to compare these results with those deriving from the application of another model. As we are doing a regression analysis, this model seems to be the most suitable one.

Multiple linear regression model

Multiple linear regression is a straightforward generalization of single predictor models. In a multiple linear regression model, the dependent variable is related to two or more independent variables. To perform a multiple linear regression analysis, the `scikit-learn` library will be used. From the `sklearn.linear_model` field, the `LinearRegression` class performs an ordinary least squares linear regression:

As usual, we will load the library through the following command:

```
from sklearn.linear_model import LinearRegression
```

Now, we can use the `LinearRegression()` function, as follows:

```
LModel = LinearRegression()
```

To fit the linear model, the `fit()` function will be used:

```
LModel.fit(X_train, Y_train)
```

In this case, in the training phase, we used the data extracted for this phase. At this point, we can use the model to make predictions.

To do this, the `predict()` function is also available in the `scikit-learn` library:

```
Y_predLM = LModel.predict(X_test)
```

Usually, a scatterplot is used to determine whether or not there is a relationship between data. However, a scatterplot can also be used to analyze the performance of a linear model. By reporting the actual and predicted values on the two axes, it is possible to check how this data is arranged. To help with the analysis, it is possible to trace the bisector of the quadrant, that is, the line of equation $Y = X$. Theoretically, all observations should rest on this line, but we can be satisfied that the data is closer to this line. About half of the data points must be below the line and the other half must be above the line. The points that move away significantly from this line represent possible outliers.

To plot the two scatterplots, we will use the `matplotlib` library:

```
plt.figure(1)
plt.subplot(121)
plt.scatter(Y_test, Y_predKM)
plt.xlabel("Actual values")
plt.ylabel("Predicted values")
plt.title("Keras Neural Network Model")

plt.subplot(122)
```

```
plt.scatter(Y_test, Y_predLM)
plt.xlabel("Actual values")
plt.ylabel("Predicted values")
plt.title("SKLearn Linear Regression Model")
plt.show()
```

In the following diagram, we can see two scatterplots:

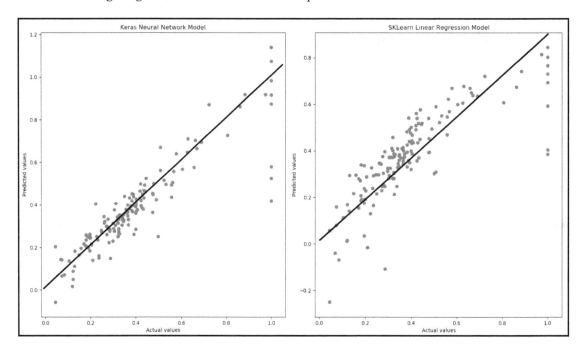

Analyzing the preceding graphs, it is clear that the Keras model (on the left) returns better results. The points are better suited to the line (they are divided equally in equal parts above and below the line), and isolated points are fewer. To confirm this first intuition, we must also calculate the MSE for the linear regression model. To do this, the `sklearn.metrics.mean_squared_error()` function will be used. This function computes MSE regression loss.

First, we have to import the function:

```
from sklearn.metrics import mean_squared_error
```

Then, we can compute the MSE, as follows:

```
mse = mean_squared_error(Y_test, Y_predLM)
print('Linear Regression Model')
print(mse)
```

The following result is returned:

```
Linear Regression Model
0.014089115439987464
```

Comparing this value (`0.014089115439987464`) with the one returned by the Keras model (`0.0038815933421901066`), we can state that the Keras model is more performant and recording a decidedly lower error (one order of magnitude).

Summary

In this chapter, you've learned about the different types of regression techniques. Regression analysis is a statistical process that's done to study the relationship between a set of independent variables (explanatory variables) and a dependent variable (response variable). Regression algorithms show you how the value of the response variable changes when the explanatory variable is varied. The concepts underlying regression were explored. Furthermore, we gained an understanding of the differences between simple and multiple regression. Later, we saw how a simple and multiple linear regression problem is represented algebraically. Thus, we have analyzed how a regression problem is solved through the least squares algorithm.

The second part of this chapter was dedicated to the practical resolution of a multiple regression problem using the `keras` library. Modeling a real estate market is a typical regression problem that different operators in the sector face daily. We started with an exploratory analysis to understand the data at our disposal, performing visual analysis by tracing a barplot to identify possible trends. After that, we built a fully densely connected neural network to model this problem. Finally, to evaluate the performance of the model, the problem was addressed by constructing a multiple linear regression model: two models were then compared. The Keras model produced much better results.

In the next chapter, we will be introduced to the basic concepts of the classification problem. We will explore different types of classification techniques, understand the basic concepts of classification methods, and how to implement them in the Keras environment. We will also learn how to import and organize data for neural network classification analysis, learn how to implement a Keras classification model using a real-life example, and how to evaluate the model's performance. Finally, we will learn how to tune a model to improve its performance.

3
Heart Disease Classification with Neural Networks

Classification algorithms help us to automatically learn how to make accurate predictions based on our observations. Starting from a set of predefined class labels, the classifier gives each piece of data a class label in accordance with the training model. Classification is somewhat similar to regression, which we studied in Chapter 2, *Modeling Real Estate Using Regression Analysis*. As well as regression, classification uses known labels of a training dataset to predict the response of the new test dataset. The main difference between regression and classification is that regression is used to predict continuous values, whereas classification works with categorical data.

For example, regression can be used to predict the future price of housing based on prices over the last 10 years. However, we should use the classification method to predict whether the price of housing will grow or decrease in the near future. In the first case, we use continuous data for the prediction and choose a continuous data response (the exact price of housing, as we did in Chapter 2, *Modeling Real Estate Using Regression Analysis*). In the second case, starting with continuous values (housing prices over the last 10 years), we begin by classifying the various phases where a growth or diminution of price has been recorded, and then we use that classification to predict a relative trend in the near future. In this chapter, you'll learn how to classify heart disease using Keras classification algorithms.

We will cover the following topics in this chapter:

- Basics of classification problems
- Different types of classification
- Pattern recognition using a Keras neural network
- Exploratory analysis
- Data visualization
- Keras binary classifier

By the end of this chapter, we will have learned about the basic concepts of the classification problem. We will explore different types of classification techniques. Then, we will understand the basic concepts of classification methods, learn to implement them in the Keras environment, and also learn how to import and organize data for a neural network classification analysis. Finally, we will learn how to implement a Keras classification model using a real-life example.

Basics of classification problems

Classifiers identify the class of a new objective, based on knowledge that's been extracted from a series of samples (dataset). Starting from a dataset, a classifier extracts a model, which is then used to classify the new instances. Examples of classifiers are as follows:

- **The texts classifier**: This classifier is able to say whether a piece of text is relevant to a pre-established topic, based only on the terms that appear
- **The image classifier**: This is a classifier that, given some points of a simple drawing, is able to reconstruct the underlying pattern
- **The medical classifier**: This is a classifier that, from a sufficient amount of clinical data, is able to find out whether a patient is suffering from a certain disease, or what the severity of the disease is

Therefore, the classifier is a system with some characteristics that allow you to identify the class of the sample examined. In different classification methods, groups are called classes. The goal of a classifier is to establish the classification criterion to maximize performance. The performance of a classifier is measured by evaluating the capacity for generalization. Generalization means attributing the correct class to each new experimental observation. The way in which these classes are identified discriminates between the different methods that are available.

Different types of classification

The power of the classification methods is due to the quality of its algorithms, which have been improved and updated over the years. These are divided into several main types, depending on the nature of the signal used for learning or the type of feedback adopted by the system.

They are as follows:

- **Supervised learning**: The algorithm generates a function that links input values to a desired output through the observation of a set of examples, in which each piece of data that's input has its relative output data. This is used to construct predictive models.
- **Unsupervised learning**: The algorithm tries to derive knowledge from a general input, without the help of a set of preclassified examples, which are used to build descriptive models. Typical examples of the application of these algorithms are search engines.

The following diagram shows examples of supervised learning (on the left) and unsupervised learning (on the right):

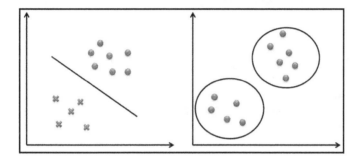

In summary, the classification is called **supervised** if the classes are known prior and the training set patterns are labeled, and **unsupervised** when classes are unknown and must be derived from the data itself.

It is possible to make a further distinction—parametric and non-parametric methods, which can be described as follows:

- **Parametric**: This makes assumptions about class distributions and derives related parameters from a training set. This is based on the statistical probability distribution of each class. An example would be **linear discriminant analysis (LDA)**.
- **Non-parametric**: This only takes into account the distances among objects in space, regardless of their distribution, which is then used to estimate the probability density function. An example would be **k-nearest neighbors (KNN)**.

In parametric methods, we look for a good data model. In non-parametric methods, a good discriminating surface is searched. In the following diagram, several classification methods are displayed, grouped by their types:

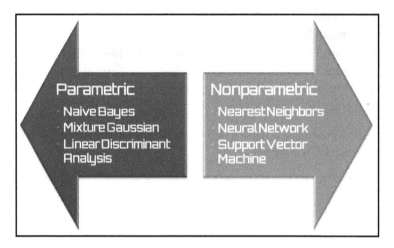

Finally, a classification or recognition system has the task of providing a user with an assessment of the observed physical reality. This evaluation uses a subdivision of reality (consisting of objects called samples or patterns) in sets, having homogeneous characteristics, and the said classes.

Classification algorithms

We have seen that there are different approaches available for a classification problem. Furthermore, for each of these approaches, different solutions are available. To answer how it's possible to make a choice on the most appropriate algorithm for your use case, we will dive deep into the most used algorithms.

Naive Bayes algorithm

A Bayesian classifier is a classifier based on the application of Bayes' theorem. This classifier requires the knowledge of apriori and conditional probabilities related to the problem, quantities that, in general, are not known but are typically estimable. If reliable estimates of the probabilities involved in the theorem can be obtained, the Bayesian classifier is generally reliable and potentially compact.

In texts classification, with the term Bayesian classifier, we conventionally refer to the Naive Bayes classifier, that is, a simplified Bayesian classifier with an underlying probability model that makes the assumption of independence of the features, or assumes that the presence or absence of a particular feature in a textual document is not related to the presence or absence of other features.

Gaussian mixture models

Mixture models are types of density models that are made up of a certain number of density functions, usually Gaussian. These functions are combined to provide multimode density. Mixed models allow you to represent probability distributions in the presence of subpopulations. For example, it can be used to model the colors of an object and exploit this information to perform color-based tracking or segmentation.

For the training of such models, the **expectation maximization** (**EM**) algorithm is used. This algorithm allows for learning with incomplete datasets or with datasets that have been generated by mixtures of probability distributions, that is, if neither of the parameters of the distribution functions is known, nor where each piece of data to a date distribution function belongs.

It is assumed that the patterns were generated from a mix of distributions: each class generated data according to a specific distribution, but at the end of the generation the patterns appear as products from a single multi-modal distribution. The goal of the algorithm is to trace-starting from the training set patterns-to the parameters of the individual distributions that generated them. To this end, the form of the distributions is assumed and it is assumed, for simplicity, that they are all of the same type. The most frequent case is that of mixing multinormal (Gaussian) distributions, whose definition parameters are to be estimated.

Discriminant analysis

Discriminant analysis is a form of statistical analysis that dates back to Fisher in 1936. It is a method for describing a one-dimensional function, that is, the difference between two or more groups, and allocating each observation to the group of origin. This is a classification problem where the groups are known a priori and one or more new observations are classified into one of the known groups based on the measured characteristics. Each observation must have a score on one or more quantitative predictor measures, and a score on a group measure. Discriminant analysis is useful in determining whether a set of variables is effective in predicting category membership.

K-nearest neighbors

KNN is an algorithm that's used in pattern recognition for object classification based on the characteristics of the nearest objects. An object is classified according to the majority of the votes of its neighboring k cluster. The k integer is a positive integer that is typically not very large. If the value of k is 1, then the object is assigned to its neighbor's class. In a binary context in which there are only two classes, it is appropriate to choose k with an odd value to avoid being in a situation of parity. It is the simplest algorithm among those used in machine learning.

Therefore, KNN identifies the class of belonging to a tested sample based on its distance from stored and classified objects. In most cases, the Euclidean distance is used. On a bidimensional plane, the Euclidean distance represents the minimum distance between two points, which is essentially the straight line connecting two points on a graph. This distance is calculated as the square root of the sum of the squared difference between the elements of two vectors. An object is assigned to the class based on the majority vote of its neighbors, and then the most common among its KNN is chosen.

Support vector machine

The **support vector machine** (**SVM**) algorithms were born in the '90s, thanks to the research of Vladimir Vapnik and his collaborators. They are used to classify instances starting from a training set of experimental data, whose characteristic parameters are known. The goal is, therefore, to build a system that learns from already-correctly classified data. This can then be used to build a classification function that's able to catalog data, even from outside this set. The main characteristic of the SVMs, which led them to immediate success, is given by the fact that based on simple ideas, they allow for high performance in practical applications, and they are rather simple to analyze mathematically but allow you to analyze complex models. The algorithm that allows them to be trained can be traced back to the problem of quadratic programming with linear constraints. These models are used in very different contexts, among which the most common are pattern recognition, text cataloging, and image identification.

Bayesian decision theory

Bayesian decision theory is an approach to statistical inference in which the probabilities are not interpreted as frequencies, proportions, or similar concepts, but rather as levels of confidence in the occurrence of a given event. The name is derived from Bayes' theorem, which is the foundation of this approach. To understand the concepts behind this theory, it is necessary to introduce some definitions. Consider the following example.

In a bag, there are seven white balls and three black balls. Except for their color, the balls are identical. They are made of the same material, they are the same size, they are perfectly spherical, and so on. I'll put my hand in the bag without looking inside, pulling out a random ball. What is the probability that the ball that I pulled out is black? The possibilities are as follows:

- The balls, in all, are *7 + 3 = 10*. By pulling out a ball, I have ten possible cases. I have no reason to think that some balls are more privileged than others, that is, they are more likely to be pulled out. Therefore, the ten possible cases are equally probable.
- Of these ten possible cases, there are only three cases in which the ball pulled out is black. These are the cases that are favorable to the expected event.

The black ball being pulled out has three out of ten possible occurrences. We will define its probability as the ratio between the favorable and the possible cases. Therefore, we get the following:

Probability (black ball) = 3/10 = 0.3 = 30%

As we have shown in the previous example, the probability of an event can be expressed as follows:

- As a fraction, for example, *3/10*
- As a decimal number, for example, *3/10 = 3:10 = 0.30*
- As a percentage, for example, *0.30 = 30%*

Resolving this problem gives us the opportunity to give a chance definition of an event: the probability (a priori) that, a given **event (E)** occurs, is the ratio between the **number (s)** of favorable cases of the event itself and the total **number (n)** of the possible cases, provided all considered cases are equally probable. This can be better represented using the following formula:

$$P = P(E) = \frac{number\ of\ favorable\ cases}{total\ number\ of\ possible\ cases} = \frac{s}{n}$$

Let's take a look at two simple examples:

- By throwing a coin, what is the probability that it shows a head? The possible cases are two—heads and tails *{H, T}*, so the favorable cases are *1{H}*. Therefore, *P(head) = ½ =0.5 = 50%*.
- By throwing a dice, what is the probability that a 5 is thrown? The possible cases are 6, *{1, 2, 3, 4, 5, 6}*, and the favorable cases are *1{5}*. Therefore, *P(5) =1/6 =0.166 =16.6%*.

To define probability, we use the concept of equally likely events. It is therefore necessary to clarify what is meant by equally likely events. To this end, the concept of the principle of insufficient reason (or principle of indifference) can be introduced, which states the following:

> *"Given a group of events, if there are no valid reasons to think that some event occurs more or less easily than others, then all group events must be considered equally likely."*

To calculate the number of possible and favorable cases, in many cases, combinatorial calculations are required. Previously, we defined probability as the ratio between the number of favorable cases and the number of possible cases. But what values can it take? The probability of an event $P(E)$ is always a number between 0 and 1:

$$0 \leq P(E) \leq 1$$

The extreme values are defined as follows:

- An event that has a probability of 0 is called an impossible event. Suppose we have six red balls in a bag—what is the probability of picking a black ball? The possible cases are 6; the favorable cases are 0 because there are no black balls in the bag. Thus, $P(E) = 0/6 = 0$.
- An event that has a probability of 1 is called a certain event. Suppose we have six red balls in a bag—what is the probability of picking a red ball? The possible cases are 6; the favorable cases are 6 because there are only red balls in the bag. Thus, $P(E) = 6/6 = 1$.

The classical definition of probability, based on a discrete and finite number of events, is hardly extendable to the case of continuous variables. The ideal condition of perfect uniformity, where all possible outcomes (the space of events) are previously known and all are equally probable, is a weak element of that definition. The latter condition is also imposed before defining the notion of probability, resulting in circularity in the definition.

An important advance compared to the classic concept in which probability is established a priori, before looking at the data, is contained in the most frequent definition of probability; this is instead obtained later, after examining the data. According to this concept, the probability of an event is the limit to which the relative frequency of the event tends when the number of trials tends to infinity. This definition can also be applied without prior knowledge of the space of events and without assuming the condition of equally likely events. However, it is assumed that the experiment is repeatable several times, ideally infinitely, under the same conditions.

We can then say that, in a series of repeated tests under the same conditions, each of the possible events is manifested with a relative frequency that is close to its probability. This can be defined as follows:

$$relative\ frequency \approx probability$$

In the Bayesian approach, probability is a measure of the degree of credibility of one proposition. This definition applies to any event. Bayesian probability is an inverse probability; we switch from observed frequencies to probability. In the Bayesian approach, the probability of a given event is determined before making the experiment, based on personal considerations. The a priori probability is therefore tied to the degree of credibility of the event, set in a subjective way. With Bayes' theorem, on the basis of the frequencies observed, we can adjust the probability a priori to reach the probability a posteriori. Then, by using this approach, an estimate of the degree of credibility of a given hypothesis before observation of data is used to associate a numerical value with the degree of credibility of that hypothesis after data observation.

So far, we've talked about the likelihood of an event, but what happens when the possible events are more than one? Two random events, A and B, are independent if the probability of the occurrence of event A is not dependent on whether event B has occurred, and vice versa. For example, let's say we have two 52 decks of French playing cards. When extracting a card from each deck, the following two events are independent:

- **E1**: The card extracted from the first deck is an ace
- **E2**: The card extracted from the second deck is a clubs card

The two events are independent, and each can happen with the same probability, independently of the other's occurrence.

Conversely, a random event, A, is dependent on another event, B, if the probability of event A depends on whether event B has occurred or not. Suppose we have a deck of 52 cards. By extracting two cards in succession without putting the first card back in the deck, the following two events are dependent:

- **E1**: The first extracted card is an ace
- **E2**: The second extracted card is an ace

To be precise, the probability of E2 depends on whether or not E1 occurs. Hence, we can see the following:

- The probability of E1 is 4/52
- The probability of E2 if the first card was an ace is 3/51
- The probability of E2 if the first card was not an ace is 4/51

Now let's deal with other cases of mutual interaction between events. Accidental events that cannot occur simultaneously on a given trial are considered mutually exclusive or disjointed. By extracting a card from a deck of 52, the following two events are mutually exclusive:

- **E1**: The ace of hearts comes out
- **E2**: One face card comes out

Indeed, the two events just mentioned cannot occur simultaneously, meaning that an ace cannot be a figure. Two events are, however, exhaustive or joint if at least one of them must occur at a given trial. By extracting a card from a deck of 52, the following two events are exhaustive:

- **E1**: One face card comes out
- **E2**: One number card comes out

These events are exhaustive because their union includes all possible events. Now let's deal with the case of joint probability, both independent and dependent. Given two eventsA and B, if the two events are independent (the occurrence of one does not affect the probability of the other), the joint probability of the event is equal to the product of the probabilities of A and B:

$$P(A \cap B) = P(A) \times P(B)$$

Let's look at an example. We have two decks of 52 cards. By extracting a card from each deck, let's consider the two independent events:

- A: The card extracted from the first deck is an ace
- B: The card extracted from the second deck is a clubs card

What is the probability that both of them occur?

- The probability that A will occur is *4/52*
- The probability that B will occur is *13/52*
- The probability that both will occur will therefore be *4/52 * 13/52 = 52 /(52 * 52) = 1/52*

If the two events are dependent (that is, the occurrence of one affects the probability of the other), then the same rule may apply, provided *P(B|A)* is the probability of event *A* given that event *B* has occurred. This condition introduces conditional probability, which we are going to dive into now:

$$P(A \cap B) = P(A) \times P(B|A)$$

A bag contains two white balls and three red balls. Two balls are pulled out from the bag in two successive extractions without reintroducing the first ball that was pulled out of the bag.

Calculate the probability that the two balls extracted are both white:

- The probability that the first ball is white is 2/5
- The probability that the second ball is white, provided that the first ball is white is 1/4

The probability of having two white balls is as follows:

P(two whites) = 2/5 * 1/4 = 2/20 = 1/10

As promised, it is now time to introduce the concept of conditional probability. The probability that event *A* occurs, calculated on the condition that event *B* occurred, is called conditional probability, and is indicated by the symbol *P(A | B)*. It is calculated using the following formula:

$$P(B|A) = \frac{P(A \cap B)}{P(A)}$$

Conditional probability usually applies when *A* depends on *B*, that is, events are dependent on each other. In the case where A and B are independent, the formula becomes as follows:

$$P(A|B) = P(A)$$

In fact, now, the occurrence of B does not affect the probability *P(A)*.

Let's look at an example. What is the probability that by extracting two cards from a deck of 52, the second one is a diamond? Note the information that the first was a diamond, too:

P(diamonds ∩ diamonds) = 13/52 * 12/51

Therefore, the conditional probability is given by the following:

P(diamonds | diamonds) = (13/52 * 12/51) / 13/52 = 12/51

As a further example, you can calculate the probability that you get the number one by throwing a dice, given that the result is an odd number. The conditional probability we want to calculate is that of the event *B|A*; that is, getting one knowing that there will be an odd number, where A is the getting an odd number event and B is the getting the number one event.

The intersection event A ∩ B corresponds to the event getting the number one and an odd number (which is equivalent to getting the number one event, since one is odd).

Therefore, the probability of getting an odd number is equal to the following:

P(A) = 3/6 = 1/2

The probability of getting the number 1 is as follows:

P(A ∩ B) = 1/6

Therefore, it is possible to calculate the conditional probability of event B with respect to event A using the following formula:

$$P(B|A) = \frac{P(A \cap B)}{P(A)} = \frac{\frac{1}{6}}{\frac{1}{2}} = \frac{1}{3} \approx 0.333$$

Let's recall, in this regard, that playing dice is always a loss-making activity, even for a statistician.

Bayes' theorem

In the previous section, *Bayesian decision theory*, we learned how to calculate many types of probabilities. Now it is time to benefit from these acquired skills. We will do this by defining Bayes' theorem as follows:

Let A and B be two dependent events. Previously, we said that the joint probability between the two events is calculated using the following formula:

$$P(A \cap B) = P(A) \times P(B|A)$$

Or, similarly, using the following formula:

$$P(A \cap B) = P(B) \times P(A|B)$$

By analyzing the two proposed formulas, it is clear that they have the first equal member. This implies that even the second members are equal, so we can write the equation as follows:

$$P(A) \times P(B|A) = P(B) \times P(A|B)$$

By solving these equations for conditional probability, we get the following:

$$P(B|A) = \frac{P(B) \times P(A|B)}{P(A)}$$

Or, in a similar way, we can calculate the following:

$$P(A|B) = \frac{P(A) \times P(B|A)}{P(B)}$$

The proposed formulas represent the mathematical statement of Bayes' theorem. The use of one or the other depends on what we are looking for.

Let's look at an example. Suppose you are given two coins. The first coin is fair (heads and tails) and the second coin is biased (heads on both sides). You randomly choose a coin and toss it, getting heads as a result. What is the likelihood of it being the second coin (the wrong coin)?

Let's start by distinguishing the various events that come into play. Let's identify these events:

- **A**: The first coin was chosen
- **B**: The second coin was chosen
- **C**: After the toss comes a head

To avoid making mistakes, let's look at what we need to calculate. The question made by the problem is simple. It asks us to calculate the likelihood of choosing the second coin, knowing that after the launch we got heads. In symbolic terms, we have to calculate $P(B|C)$.

According to Bayes' theorem, we can write the following:

$$P(B|C) = \frac{P(B) \times P(C|B)}{P(C)}$$

Now, compute the three probabilities that appear in the previous equation. Remember that $P(B|C)$ is called posterior probability, and that is what we want to calculate. $P(B)$ is called prior probability, linked to the second event (B), and is equal to 1/2, since we have two possible choices (two coins are available):

$$P(B) = \frac{1}{2}$$

$P(C|B)$ is called likelihood and is equal to 1, as it gives the chances of heads, knowing that you have chosen the second coin (which has two heads and so is a certain event). Therefore, we get the following:

$$P(C|B) = 1$$

Finally, *P(C)* is called marginal likelihood and is equal to 3/4, as the coins have four faces (possible cases), of which three have heads (favorable cases):

$$P(C) = \frac{3}{4}$$

At this point, we can enter the calculated probabilities in the Bayes' formula to get the result:

$$P(B|C) = \frac{P(B) \times P(C|B)}{P(C)} = \frac{\frac{1}{2} \times 1}{\frac{3}{4}} = \frac{2}{3}$$

The concepts underlying the Bayesian theory are sufficiently clear. Now we can focus on a practical case of classification.

Pattern recognition using a Keras neural network

Heart diseases are often underestimated, but, in reality, they are the leading cause of death in the world. Among them, **coronary artery disease** (**CAD**) accounts for about a third of all deaths worldwide in people over 35 years of age. CAD is the result of arteriosclerosis, which consists in the narrowing of the blood vessels and the hardening of its walls. In some cases, CAD can completely block the influx of oxygen-rich blood to the heart muscle, causing a heart attack.

CAD is caused by an accumulation of waxy grease deposits on the inner walls of the arteries. These deposits consist of cholesterol, calcium, and other substances that travel in the blood; the product of their accumulation is called atherosclerotic plaque. This plaque can clog the coronary arteries and make them rigid and irregular, causing the so-called hardening of the arteries or atherosclerosis. These obstructions can be single or multiple and present various levels of gravity and different locations. Gradually, the deposits restrict the lumen of the coronary arteries, thus reducing the supply of blood and oxygen to the heart muscle. This reduction in blood flow can cause chest pain (angina), difficulty in breathing (dyspnoea), and other symptoms, while complete obstruction can induce a heart attack.

Coronary angiography is used to diagnose CAD. Angiography is the diagnostic representation of the blood or lymphatic vessels of the human body through a technique that involves the infusion of a water soluble contrast agent within the vessels and the generation of medical images through various biomedical imaging techniques.

In this example, we will try to predict a condition of heart disease through a classification algorithm based on neural networks. To do this, we will use the *Heart Disease Data Set*, which is available in the UCI Machine Learning Repository.

The UCI Machine Learning Repository is available at the following link: http://mlr.cs.umass.edu/ml/datasets.html.

These databases contain several pieces of data information on heart disease instances. These are provided by the following four clinical institutions: **Cleveland Clinic Foundation (CCF)**, **Hungarian Institute of Cardiology (HIC)**, **Long Beach Medical Center (LBMC)**, and **University Hospital in Switzerland (SUH)**.

More specifically, we will refer to the data that was made available by the CCF (edited by Robert Detrano, MD, PhD). This database contains 76 attributes, but all published experiments refer to using a subset of 14 of them. The goal is to predict the presence of heart disease in the patient. The target is an integer value from 0 (no presence) to 4. Experiments with the Cleveland database have concentrated on simply attempting to distinguish presence (values 1, 2, 3, 4) from absence (value 0).

The following list shows all the variables, followed by a brief description:

- **Number of instances**: 302
- **Number of attributes**: 14 continuous attributes (including the class attribute HeartDisease)

Each of the attributes are detailed as follows:

- age: Age in years
- sex: Sex (1 = male; 0 = female)
- cp: Chest pain type (Value 1: typical angina; Value 2: atypical angina; Value 3: non-anginal pain, Value 4: asymptomatic)
- trestbps: Resting blood pressure (in mm Hg on admission to the hospital)
- chol: Serum cholestoral in mg/dl
- fbs: (fasting blood sugar > 120 mg/dl) (1 = true; 0 = false)
- restecg: Resting electrocardiographic results (Value 0: normal; Value 1: having ST-T wave abnormality (T wave inversions and/or ST elevation or depression of > 0.05 mV), Value 2: showing probable or definite left ventricular hypertrophy by Estes' criteria)
- thalach: Maximum heart rate achieved

- `exang`: Exercise induced angina (1 = yes; 0 = no)
- `oldpeak`: ST depression induced by exercise relative to rest
- `slope`: The slope of the peak exercise ST segment (Value 1: upsloping; Value 2: flat; Value 3: downsloping)
- `ca`: Number of major vessels (0-3) colored by flourosopy
- `thal`: 3 = normal; 6 = fixed defect; 7 = reversable defect
- `HeartDisease`: Diagnosis of heart disease – angiographic disease status (Value 0: < 50% diameter narrowing; Value 1: > 50% diameter narrowing)—in any major vessel: attributes 59 through 68 are vessels

The data is available in a `.xlsx` file named `ClevelandData.xlsx`, which can be downloaded from the UCI dataset. To make our job easier, the target has been reworked to present only two values (0 and 1). To start, let's look at how we can import the data into Python. To do this, we will use the `read_excel` module of the `pandas` library. The `read_excel` method reads an Excel table into a pandas DataFrame. The first thing to do is import the library that we will use:

```
import pandas as pd
```

The available data does not contain the header, so it is necessary to retrieve the names of the variables that are contained in another file, which is always available in the UCI archive. Let's put them in a list:

```
HDNames=
['age','sex','cp','trestbps','chol','fbs','restecg','thalach','exang','oldp
eak','slope','ca','hal',' HeartDisease ']
```

Now let's import the data contained in the dataset in Python:

```
Data = pd.read_excel('ClevelandData.xlsx', names=HDNames)
```

Two parameters are passed: filename, and the list of column names to use.

Exploratory analysis

Before starting with data analysis through the classification algorithm, we will conduct an exploratory analysis to understand how the data is distributed and extract preliminary knowledge. To display the first twenty rows of the DataFrame that's been imported, we can use the `head()` function, as follows:

```
print(data.head(20))
```

The following results are returned:

	age	sex	cp	trestbps	chol	fbs	restecg	thalach	exang	oldpeak	slope	ca	hal	HeartDisease
0	67	1	4	160	286	0	2	108	1	1.5	2	3	3	1
1	67	1	4	120	229	0	2	129	1	2.6	2	2	7	1
2	37	1	3	130	250	0	0	187	0	3.5	3	0	3	0
3	41	0	2	130	204	0	2	172	0	1.4	1	0	3	0
4	56	1	2	120	236	0	0	178	0	0.8	1	0	3	0
5	62	0	4	140	268	0	2	160	0	3.6	3	2	3	1
6	57	0	4	120	354	0	0	163	1	0.6	1	0	3	0
7	63	1	4	130	254	0	2	147	0	1.4	2	1	7	1
8	53	1	4	140	203	1	2	155	1	3.1	3	0	7	1
9	57	1	4	140	192	0	0	148	0	0.4	2	0	6	0
10	56	0	2	140	294	0	2	153	0	1.3	2	0	3	0
11	56	1	3	130	256	1	2	142	1	0.6	2	1	6	1
12	44	1	2	120	263	0	0	173	0	0.0	1	0	7	0
13	52	1	3	172	199	1	0	162	0	0.5	1	0	7	0
14	57	1	3	150	168	0	0	174	0	1.6	1	0	3	0
15	48	1	2	110	229	0	0	168	0	1.0	3	0	7	1
16	54	1	4	140	239	0	0	160	0	1.2	1	0	3	0
17	48	0	3	130	275	0	0	139	0	0.2	1	0	3	0
18	49	1	2	130	266	0	0	171	0	0.6	1	0	3	0
19	64	1	1	110	211	0	2	144	1	1.8	2	0	3	0

The first 20 rows are displayed. This function returns the first n rows for the object, based on position. This is useful for quickly testing whether your object has the right type of data in it. Now the dataset is available in our Python environment. To extract some information, we can invoke the info() function, as follows:

```
print(Data.info())
```

This method prints a concise summary of a DataFrame, including the dtypes index and dtypes column, non-null values, and memory usage. The following results are returned:

```
<class 'pandas.core.frame.DataFrame'>
RangeIndex: 302 entries, 0 to 301
Data columns (total 14 columns):
age 302 non-null int64
sex 302 non-null int64
cp 302 non-null int64
trestbps 302 non-null int64
chol 302 non-null int64
fbs 302 non-null int64
restecg 302 non-null int64
thalach 302 non-null int64
exang 302 non-null int64
oldpeak 302 non-null float64
slope 302 non-null int64
ca 302 non-null object
```

```
hal 302 non-null object
HeartDisease 302 non-null int64
dtypes: float64(1), int64(11), object(2)
memory usage: 33.1+ KB
None
```

Useful information is reported. The number of entries is 302, and the number of data columns is 14. Essentially, with regard to the list of all features with the number of elements, the possible presence of data and the type is returned. In this way, we can already get an idea of the type of variables we are about to analyze. In fact, analyzing the results that we've obtained, we can note that three types have been identified: float64(1), int64(11), and object(2). For the first two, there are no doubts: these are integer and real numbers. This anomaly is represented by the two columns labeled as objects. To understand what happened, it is useful to check the types of data provided by the pandas library, as shown in the following table:

Pandas dtype	Python type	Usage
object	str	Text
int64	int	Integer numbers
float64	float	Floating point numbers

Now, everything is clear: the two columns have been labeled as containing text. Why did this happen? This problem is due to the presence of missing values. Keep this in mind, as we will have to deal with this problem before proceeding with the construction of the model.

To get a preview of the data contained in it, we can calculate a series of basic statistics. To do so, we will use the describe() function in the following way:

```
summary = Data.describe()
print(summary)
```

The following results are returned:

```
                age         sex          cp    trestbps         chol         fbs  \
count    302.000000  302.000000  302.000000  302.000000  302.000000  302.000000
mean      54.410596    0.678808    3.165563  131.645695  246.738411    0.145695
std        9.040163    0.467709    0.953612   17.612202   51.856829    0.353386
min       29.000000    0.000000    1.000000   94.000000  126.000000    0.000000
25%       48.000000    0.000000    3.000000  120.000000  211.000000    0.000000
50%       55.500000    1.000000    3.000000  130.000000  241.500000    0.000000
75%       61.000000    1.000000    4.000000  140.000000  275.000000    0.000000
max       77.000000    1.000000    4.000000  200.000000  564.000000    1.000000

            restecg     thalach       exang     oldpeak       slope  \
count    302.000000  302.000000  302.000000  302.000000  302.000000
mean       0.986755  149.605960    0.327815    1.035430    1.596026
std        0.994916   22.912959    0.470196    1.160723    0.611939
min        0.000000   71.000000    0.000000    0.000000    1.000000
25%        0.000000  133.250000    0.000000    0.000000    1.000000
50%        0.500000  153.000000    0.000000    0.800000    2.000000
75%        2.000000  166.000000    1.000000    1.600000    2.000000
max        2.000000  202.000000    1.000000    6.200000    3.000000

         HeartDisease
count    302.000000
mean       0.460265
std        0.499246
min        0.000000
25%        0.000000
50%        0.000000
75%        1.000000
max        1.000000
```

The `describe()` function generates descriptive statistics that summarize the central tendency, dispersion, and shape of a dataset's distribution, excluding `NaN` values. It analyzes both numeric and object series, as well as DataFrame column sets of mixed data types. The output will vary, depending on what is provided. To continue, it is therefore necessary to address the problem of missing values.

Handling missing data in Python

The problem of missing data is quite common in data mining. One of the first problems that a researcher is faced with when analyzing results is that of an incomplete dataset and the presence of errors. This generally happens because whoever collects the data has not correctly interpreted the structure, accidentally commits some errors, does not want to deliberately insert that data because of an error in the encoding tool, or is someone who instead deals with the data entry.

There is no single technique or methodology to approach the problem of how to monitor the effect of missing data; each situation is a case in itself. In general, it is always advisable to test the survey instrument with pilot surveys to study its strengths and weaknesses, so as to intervene on the latter and prevent the presence of omitted answers. In the moment in which, despite all the tricks, the problem continues to present itself, the quantity and distribution of missing data, that is, the structure of the data and the nature of the variables involved, will be the only indication on which to make decisions.

Therefore, a missing value is a value that contains no content or is non-existent. These missing values may be due to a series of occurrences:

- Errors in the creation of the dataset; the values have been entered incorrectly, leaving empty cells
- The dataset contains fields that have been created automatically, with cells that do not contain values
- The problem of an encoding tool
- The result of an impossible calculation

If a variable contains missing values, Python cannot apply certain functions to it. For this reason, it is necessary to process the missing values in advance.

When a **Database Management System** (**DBMS**) identifies empty cells, it can behave unpredictably. For example, you can enter special characters to indicate that something has gone wrong with data encoding. If we analyze the Excel file that we are using as a data source, we can see that, in correspondence to the two columns that have been presented, anomalies appear as question marks, as shown in the following screenshot:

	A	B	C	D	E	F	G	H	I	J	K	L	M	N	O	P	Q	R	S	T
264	44	1	3	120	226	0	0	169	0	0	1	0	3	0						
265	61	1	4	138	166	0	2	125	1	3,6	2	1	3	1						
266	42	1	4	136	315	0	0	125	1	1,8	2	0	6	1						
267	52	1	4	128	204	1	0	156	1	1	2	0 ?		1						
268	59	1	3	126	218	1	0	134	0	2,2	2	1	6	1						
269	40	1	4	152	223	0	0	181	0	0	1	0	7	1						
270	42	1	3	130	180	0	0	150	0	0	1	0	3	0						
271	61	1	4	140	207	0	2	138	1	1,9	1	1	7	1						
272	66	1	4	160	228	0	2	138	0	2,3	1	0	6	0						
273	46	1	4	140	311	0	0	120	1	1,8	2	2	7	1						
274	71	0	4	112	149	0	0	125	0	1,6	2	0	3	0						
275	59	1	1	134	204	0	0	162	0	0,8	1	2	3	1						
276	64	1	1	170	227	0	2	155	0	0,6	2	0	7	0						
277	66	0	3	146	278	0	2	152	0	0	2	1	3	0						
278	39	0	3	138	220	0	0	152	0	0	2	0	3	0						
279	57	1	2	154	232	0	2	164	0	0	1	1	3	1						
280	58	0	4	130	197	0	0	131	0	0,6	2	0	3	0						
281	57	1	4	110	335	0	0	143	1	3	2	1	7	1						
282	47	1	3	130	253	0	0	179	0	0	1	0	3	0						
283	55	0	4	128	205	0	1	130	1	2	2	1	7	1						
284	35	1	2	122	192	0	0	174	0	0	1	0	3	0						
285	61	1	4	148	203	0	0	161	0	0	1	1	7	1						
286	58	1	4	114	318	0	1	140	0	4,4	3	3	6	1						
287	58	0	4	170	225	1	2	146	1	2,8	2	2	6	1						
288	58	1	2	125	220	0	0	144	0	0,4	2 ?		7	0						
289	56	1	2	130	221	0	2	163	0	0	1	0	7	0						
290	56	1	2	120	240	0	0	169	0	0	3	0	3	0						
291	67	1	3	152	212	0	2	150	0	0,8	2	0	7	1						

It is precisely these values that create problems—we must treat them appropriately. Missing values of any type of variable are indicated by the **NA** code, which means not available. The **Not a Number** (**NaN**) code, on the other hand, indicates invalid numeric values, such as a numeric value divided by zero.

The first thing to do is identify these values with NaN. To do this, we can use the `pandas.replace()` function, along with the `np.nan` value, as follows:

```
import numpy as np
DataNew = Data.replace('?', np.nan)
```

The `pandas.replace()` function replaces values that have been given to replace a specific value. Values of the DataFrame are replaced with other values dynamically. The `np.nan` value is a special value that's defined in NumPy.

Let's see what has changed in the DataFrame:

```
print(DataNew.info())
```

The following results are returned:

```
<class 'pandas.core.frame.DataFrame'>
RangeIndex: 302 entries, 0 to 301
Data columns (total 14 columns):
age 302 non-null int64
sex 302 non-null int64
cp 302 non-null int64
trestbps 302 non-null int64
chol 302 non-null int64
fbs 302 non-null int64
restecg 302 non-null int64
thalach 302 non-null int64
exang 302 non-null int64
oldpeak 302 non-null float64
slope 302 non-null int64
ca 298 non-null float64
hal 300 non-null float64
HeartDisease 302 non-null int64
dtypes: float64(3), int64(11)
memory usage: 33.1 KB
None
```

Amazing! Now, all the variables are numeric. All of the variables contain 302 values, except for the variables `ca` and `hal`, which have 298 and 300 values, respectively. This is because the `describe()` function omits the NaN values. To confirm what we have just said, we will use the `describe()` function once again:

```
print(DataNew.describe())
```

The following results are returned:

```
              age         sex          cp    trestbps        chol         fbs  \
count  302.000000  302.000000  302.000000  302.000000  302.000000  302.000000
mean    54.410596    0.678808    3.165563  131.645695  246.738411    0.145695
std      9.040163    0.467709    0.953612   17.612202   51.856829    0.353386
min     29.000000    0.000000    1.000000   94.000000  126.000000    0.000000
25%     48.000000    0.000000    3.000000  120.000000  211.000000    0.000000
50%     55.500000    1.000000    3.000000  130.000000  241.500000    0.000000
75%     61.000000    1.000000    4.000000  140.000000  275.000000    0.000000
max     77.000000    1.000000    4.000000  200.000000  564.000000    1.000000

           restecg     thalach       exang     oldpeak       slope          ca  \
count   302.000000  302.000000  302.000000  302.000000  302.000000  298.000000
mean      0.986755  149.605960    0.327815    1.035430    1.596026    0.674497
std       0.994916   22.912959    0.470196    1.160723    0.611939    0.938202
min       0.000000   71.000000    0.000000    0.000000    1.000000    0.000000
25%       0.000000  133.250000    0.000000    0.000000    1.000000    0.000000
50%       0.500000  153.000000    0.000000    0.800000    2.000000    0.000000
75%       2.000000  166.000000    1.000000    1.600000    2.000000    1.000000
max       2.000000  202.000000    1.000000    6.200000    3.000000    3.000000

              hal  HeartDisease
count  300.000000    302.000000
mean     4.730000      0.460265
std      1.941563      0.499246
min      3.000000      0.000000
25%      3.000000      0.000000
50%      3.000000      0.000000
75%      7.000000      1.000000
max      7.000000      1.000000
```

We have confirmed that the two variables under control are now numeric (`float64`) and contain 298 and 300 values, respectively. We want more— proof of the presence of NaN values. To get this, we can use the `isnull()` function, as follows:

```
print(DataNew.isnull().sum())
```

The `pandas.isnull()` function detects missing values for an array-like object. This function takes a scalar or array-like object and indicates whether values are missing (NaN in numeric arrays, None or NaN in object arrays, NaT in datetimelike). The `pandas.sum()` function returns the sum of the values for the requested data. In the following code block, we can see the results:

```
age             0
sex             0
cp              0
trestbps        0
chol            0
fbs             0
restecg         0
thalach         0
exang           0
oldpeak         0
slope           0
ca              4
hal             2
HeartDisease    0
dtype: int64
```

Now, everything is clear—4 NaN for the `ca` variable and 2 NaN for the `hal` variable have been identified. Now what do we do? To fix the missing data, there are several options available:

1. Replace the values with constant values
2. Set the values with other columns' values
3. Transform the data with functions
4. Delete rows

For now, we will choose the simplest choice—we will remove the rows in which NaN values are present. It should be noted that the choice we are going to make is extremely important. A wrong choice can affect the goodness of the results. In this case, as it is a few rows on the total, we can consider the removal of these lines to be negligible. In general, it is necessary to evaluate the effect that this operation determines on the data. To remove the NaN values, we will use the `pandas.dropna()` function, as follows:

```
DataNew = DataNew.dropna()
```

Let's see how this operation changes the DataFrame:

```
print(DataNew.info())
```

The following results are returned:

```
<class 'pandas.core.frame.DataFrame'>
Int64Index: 296 entries, 0 to 300
Data columns (total 14 columns):
age 296 non-null int64
sex 296 non-null int64
cp 296 non-null int64
trestbps 296 non-null int64
chol 296 non-null int64
fbs 296 non-null int64
restecg 296 non-null int64
thalach 296 non-null int64
exang 296 non-null int64
oldpeak 296 non-null float64
slope 296 non-null int64
ca 296 non-null float64
hal 296 non-null float64
HeartDisease 296 non-null int64
dtypes: float64(3), int64(11)
memory usage: 34.7 KB
None
```

Please note that all of the variables now have the same number of instances (296). Let's see whether NaN is actually present by using the following command:

```
print(DataNew.isnull().sum())
```

The following results are returned:

```
age             0
sex             0
cp              0
trestbps        0
chol            0
fbs             0
restecg         0
thalach         0
exang           0
oldpeak         0
slope           0
ca              0
hal             0
HeartDisease 0
dtype: int64
```

NaN values are no longer present. We can therefore proceed with data analysis.

Data scaling

Analyzing the `describe()` function's results, we can see that the variables have different ranges. When the data has different ranges, the impact on the target variable by the feature having a greater numeric range could be more than the one that has a less numeric range, and this could, in turn, impact the prediction's accuracy. To remove this effect, we can scale values under different features so that they fall under a common range.

Remember, it is a good practice to rescale the data before training a deep learning algorithm. With rescaling, data units are eliminated, allowing you to easily compare data from different locations.

In this case, we will use z-score standardization. This technique consists of subtracting the mean of the column to each value in a column, and then dividing the result for the standard deviation of the column. The formula to achieve this is as follows:

$$x_{scaled} = \frac{x - mean}{sd}$$

The result of standardization is that the features will be rescaled so that they'll have the properties of a standard normal distribution, as follows:

- $\mu=0$
- $\sigma=1$

Here, μ is the mean and σ is the standard deviation from the mean.

In summary, the z score (also called the standard score) represents the number of standard deviations with which the value of an observation point or data is greater than the mean value of what is observed or measured. Values more than the mean have positive z scores, while values less than the mean have negative z scores. The z score is a quantity without dimension, which is obtained by subtracting the population mean from a single rough score and then dividing the difference for the standard deviation of the population.

Before proceeding, it is advisable to divide the data into input and target. This will be particularly useful because ad scaling will only affect the input values. Let's start from them:

```
InputNames = HDNames
InputNames.pop()
Input = pd.DataFrame(DataNew.iloc[:, 0:13],columns=InputNames)
```

First, we created a new list of names, removing the name of our target (`HeartDisease`) from the original one (`HDNames`). To do this, we used the `pop()` function. This function returns items and drops them from the frame. Then, the `iloc()` function is used to extract the first `13` columns from the `DataNew` DataFrame. Let's move to the target:

```
Target = pd.DataFrame(DataNew.iloc[:, 13],columns=['HeartDisease'])
```

To scale the input data, as we did in Chapter 2, *Modeling Real Estate Using Regression Analysis*, we will use the `sklearn.preprocessing` package once again. Specifically, we are using the `StandardScaler()` function, but as always, we start by importing the package:

```
from sklearn.preprocessing import StandardScaler
```

Let's start by defining the `scaler` variable:

```
scaler = StandardScaler()
print(scaler.fit(Input))
```

To print the parameters that we will use for the next resizing, we will use the `fit()` method, as follows:

```
print(scaler.fit(data))
```

The `fit()` method computes the `mean` and `std` to be used for later scaling. The result is as follows:

```
StandardScaler(copy=True, with_mean=True, with_std=True)
```

Now we can scale the features:

```
InputScaled = scaler.fit_transform(Input)
```

The `fit_transform()` method fits to data, and then transforms it. A `numpy` array of a specific shape is returned. It is advisable to report the results in the starting format (pandas DataFrame), at least for comparison purposes. Let's do this:

```
InputScaled = pd.DataFrame(InputScaled,columns=InputNames)
```

To verify the transformation that's been carried out, we again print the basic statistics that we calculated previously:

```
summary = InputScaled.describe()
summary = summary.transpose()
print(summary)
```

The following results are returned:

```
          count          mean       std       min        25%        50%        75%       max
age       296.0 -2.550512e-16  1.001693 -2.823438 -0.720814  0.164501  0.717823  2.488454
sex       296.0  6.001206e-18  1.001693 -1.443376 -1.443376  0.692820  0.692820  0.692820
cp        296.0  1.860374e-16  1.001693 -2.263690 -0.173043 -0.173043  0.872280  0.872280
trestbps  296.0  1.920386e-16  1.001693 -2.121540 -0.656413 -0.092903  0.470607  3.851669
chol      296.0  6.601326e-17  1.001693 -2.334999 -0.700097 -0.084604  0.554931  6.089557
fbs       296.0  2.700542e-17  1.001693 -0.406638 -0.406638 -0.406638 -0.406638  2.459191
restecg   296.0 -4.800964e-17  1.001693 -1.000046 -1.000046  0.006803  1.013652  1.013652
thalach   296.0  2.160434e-16  1.001693 -3.426010 -0.723490  0.148291  0.714949  2.284154
exang     296.0  1.342770e-16  1.001693 -0.698167 -0.698167 -0.698167  1.432322  1.432322
oldpeak   296.0  6.001206e-17  1.001693 -0.903324 -0.903324 -0.215962  0.471400  4.423733
slope     296.0 -6.901386e-17  1.001693 -0.975788 -0.975788  0.656038  0.656038  2.287865
ca        296.0  1.200241e-17  1.001693 -0.723832 -0.723832 -0.723832  0.342110  2.473994
hal       296.0 -1.800362e-16  1.001693 -0.891149 -0.891149 -0.891149  1.173666  1.173666
```

Looking at the preceding figures, we can confirm that all input variables now have the mean and the standard deviation of about zero.

Data visualization

By visualizing the data, it is possible to understand the meaning of the data by positioning it in a visual context. A numerical analysis of data can hide at first sight patterns, that is, trends and correlations that instead represent the basis of data mining. These characteristics are highlighted through graphs and diagrams that describe the nature of the data under analysis.

The first thing we can do is plot a data plot. In this way, we will be able to highlight the characteristics we have already analyzed with the statistical data returned by the describe() function. A boxplot is a graphical representation that's used to describe the distribution of a sample by simple dispersion and position indexes. As we said in Chapter 2, *Modeling Real Estate Using Regression Analysis*, to plot a boxplot in Python, we can use the matplotlib library.

As always, let's start by importing the library into Python:

```
import matplotlib.pyplot as plt
```

The available data is in pandas Dataframe format. For this reason, we can use the pandas.DataFrame.boxplot function. This function makes a boxplot from DataFrame columns, which are optionally grouped by some other columns:

```
boxplot = data.boxplot(column=BHNames)
plt.show()
```

Finally, to print the output, the `plt.show()` function will be used. This function displays all figures and block until the figures have been closed. In the following diagram, the boxplots of all the variables contained in the Input DataFrame are shown:

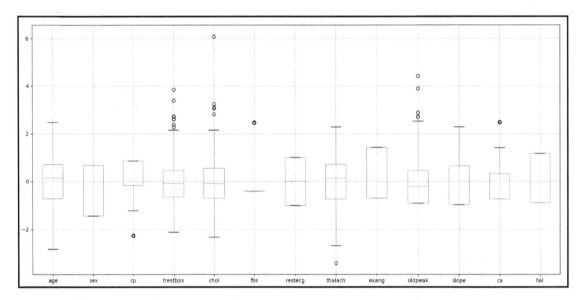

The previous diagram highlights the results of data scaling. In fact, we can see that the mean of all the variables (triangle markers) is positioned on zero. Furthermore, we can note that some variables have outliers (circles out of the whiskers). Comparing the lengths of the two whiskers (which represent the distances between the 25th percentile and the minimum and between the 75th percentile and the maximum) and the heights of the two rectangles that make up the box (representing the distances between the 25th percentile and median (50th percentile) and between the median and the 75th percentile) information on the symmetry of the distribution is obtained: this is more symmetrical, as the lengths of the whiskers are similar to each other and the heights of the two rectangles are similar to one another.

Now we will look for possible relationships among the input variables. Relationships among variables can be highlighted through a suitable graphical representation, known as a scatter plot. A scatter plot helps us study the relationship between two quantitative variables (correlation), which are detected on the same units. Let's consider a Cartesian reference, where the values of a variable appear on the horizontal axis and those of the other variable on the vertical axis. Each point in the plot is specified by a pair of numerical coordinates that represent the values of the two variables that are detected at a specific observation.

A large number of points can be observed in a single dispersion diagram. More such points are placed around a straight line, that is, the greater the correlation between the two variables. If this straight line goes from the origin out to high x-y values, then it is said that the variables have a positive correlation. If the line moves from a high value on the Y axis to a high value on the X axis, the variables have a negative correlation, as shown in the following diagram:

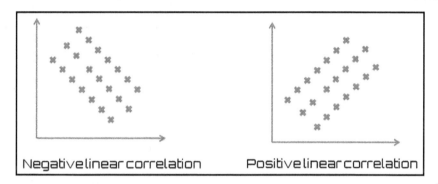

By using scatter plots, we can gain an idea of the shape and strength of the relationship among the variables. Deviations due to abnormal data, which is specific values that deviate from the general scheme or presence of different clusters, can also be highlighted.

What happens when the pairs of variables to compare are numerous? In this case, we can use a scatter plot matrix. What is the scatter plot matrix? For a set of variables, $A_1, A_2, .., A_k,$ the scatter plot matrix shows all the scatter plots of the variables in a matrix format. So, if there are n variables, the scatter plot matrix will have n rows and n columns, and the *ith* row and *jth* column of this matrix is a plot of A_i versus A_j.

To draw a scatter plot matrix, we will use the `pandas.plotting.scatter_matrix()` function, as follows:

```
pd.plotting.scatter_matrix(InputScaled, figsize=(6, 6))
plt.show()
```

The subplot in the *i*th row, *j*th column of the matrix is a scatter plot of the *i*th column of the matrix against the *j*th column of the matrix. Along the diagonal are histogram plots of each column of the matrix, as shown in the following diagram:

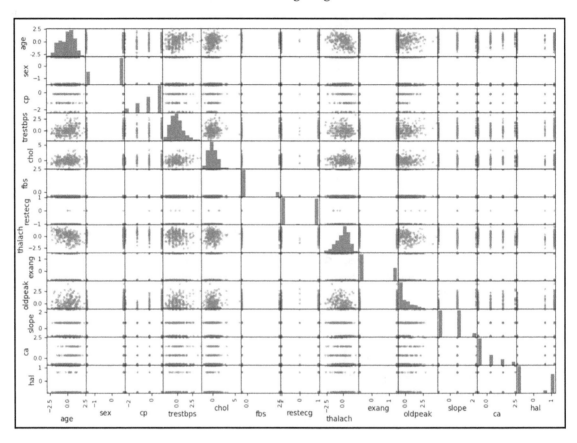

Analyzing the preceding diagram, no correlation seems to exist among the input variables, meaning that all of the variables are necessary for the correct classification of the target. To confirm this, we can perform a correlation analysis. In Python, correlation analysis is performed by the `pandas.DataFrame.corr()` function; it computes pairwise correlation of columns, excluding NA or null values, as follows:

```
CorData = InputScaled.corr(method='pearson')
with pd.option_context('display.max_rows', None,
                'display.max_columns', CorData.shape[1]):
    print(CorData)
```

The following results are returned:

```
              age       sex        cp  trestbps       chol       fbs  \
age      1.000000 -0.094802  0.118743  0.288805  0.203846  0.125821
sex     -0.094802  1.000000  0.014272 -0.068212 -0.197629  0.033539
cp       0.118743  0.014272  1.000000 -0.031599  0.070606 -0.040004
trestbps 0.288805 -0.068212 -0.031599  1.000000  0.132380  0.176636
chol     0.203846 -0.197629  0.070606  0.132380  1.000000  0.015132
fbs      0.125821  0.033539 -0.040004  0.176636  0.015132  1.000000
restecg  0.147193  0.031618  0.072291  0.147075  0.166298  0.061255
thalach -0.395204 -0.060586 -0.342089 -0.049199 -0.000058 -0.008067
exang    0.098919  0.145444  0.375759  0.068578  0.058744  0.004878
oldpeak  0.194405  0.104357  0.213564  0.189078  0.039676 -0.000472
slope    0.153807  0.028328  0.171151  0.116556 -0.007164  0.029783
ca       0.365356  0.093769  0.232361  0.099967  0.115387  0.159755
hal      0.124787  0.382707  0.276014  0.136750  0.011481  0.057441

          restecg   thalach     exang   oldpeak     slope        ca       hal
age      0.147193 -0.395204  0.098919  0.194405  0.153807  0.365356  0.124787
sex      0.031618 -0.060586  0.145444  0.104357  0.028328  0.093769  0.382707
cp       0.072291 -0.342089  0.375759  0.213564  0.171151  0.232361  0.276014
trestbps 0.147075 -0.049199  0.068578  0.189078  0.116556  0.099967  0.136750
chol     0.166298 -0.000058  0.058744  0.039676 -0.007164  0.115387  0.011481
fbs      0.061255 -0.008067  0.004878 -0.000472  0.029783  0.159755  0.057441
restecg  1.000000 -0.072474  0.084466  0.110482  0.128753  0.131828  0.016598
thalach -0.072474  1.000000 -0.384642 -0.348376 -0.392858 -0.268921 -0.275070
exang    0.084466 -0.384642  1.000000  0.292629  0.258355  0.146783  0.328979
oldpeak  0.110482 -0.348376  0.292629  1.000000  0.576984  0.297897  0.343520
slope    0.128753 -0.392858  0.258355  0.576984  1.000000  0.116398  0.277282
ca       0.131828 -0.268921  0.146783  0.297897  0.116398  1.000000  0.258398
hal      0.016598 -0.275070  0.328979  0.343520  0.277282  0.258398  1.000000
```

All correlation coefficients are close to zero to indicate that no correlation exists. The variables are many, so an immediate control of this trend is not easy. To overcome this inconvenience, we can plot a correlogram. A correlogram is a graph of a correlation matrix. It is very useful to highlight the most correlated variables in a data table. In this plot, correlation coefficients are colored according to the value:

```
plt.matshow(CorData)
plt.xticks(range(len(CorData.columns)), CorData.columns)
plt.yticks(range(len(CorData.columns)), CorData.columns)
plt.colorbar()
plt.show()
```

The correlogram is shown in the following diagram:

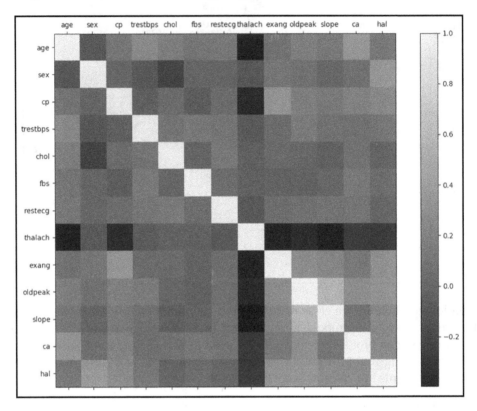

The cells are all dark, and according to the heatmap legend, this means that there is no specific correlation among the data.

Keras binary classifier

After exploring the dataset, it is time to build our classifier so that we can recognize a state of heart disease from the results of clinical tests. We prepare the data before proceeding. We split the starting data into two sets—a training set and a test set. The training set is used to train a classification model, and the test set to used to test model performance.

To split the data, the `scikit-learn` library has been used—more specifically, the `sklearn.model_selection.train_test_split()` function has been used. This function quickly computes a random split into training and test sets. Let's start by importing the function:

```
from sklearn.model_selection import train_test_split
```

Now, we have to split the two DataFrames:

```
Input_train, Input_test, Target_train, Target_test =
train_test_split(InputScaled, Target, test_size = 0.30, random_state = 5)
print(Input_train.shape)
print(Input_test.shape)
print(Target_train.shape)
print(Target_test.shape)
```

In the `train_test_split()` function, four parameters are passed: `InputScaled`, `Target`, `test_size`, and `random_state`. The `InputScaled` and `Target` parameters are inputs and target DataFrames. The `test_size` parameters could take the following types—`float`, `int`, or `None`, optional (default=0.25). If it is a `float`, the value should be between 0.0 and 1.0 and should represent the proportion of the dataset to include in the test split. If it is an `int`, the value represents the absolute number of test samples. If it is `None`, the value is set to the complement of the train size. By default, the value is set to 0.25. In our case, we set `test_size = 0.30`, which means that 30% of the data is divided up as test data. Finally, the `random_state` parameter is used to set the seed used by the random number generator. In this way, the repeatability of the splitting operation is guaranteed. The following results are returned:

```
(207, 13)
(89, 13)
(207, 1)
(89, 1)
```

So, the starting `InputScaled` DataFrame is splitted in two dataset having 207 rows (`Input_train`) and 89 rows (`Input_test`). A similar subdivision was made for the `Target`.

To perform a neural network classification analysis, we will use the Keras `Sequential` model. As we said in `Chapter 1`, *Getting Started with Keras*, to create a Keras `Sequential` model, we must follow these steps:

1. Import the `Sequential` class from `keras.models`
2. Stack the layers using the `.add()` method
3. Configure the learning process using the `.compile()` method
4. Train the model on the train dataset using the `.fit()` method

First, we have to load the libraries that are needed to run the analysis:

```
from keras.models import Sequential
from keras.layers import Dense
```

Three layer classes have been imported: `Sequential`, `Dense`, and `metrics`. The `Sequential` class is used to define a linear stack of network layers that make up a model. In the following code, we will use the `Sequential` constructor to create the model, which will then be enriched with layers by using the `add()` method. The `Dense` class is used to instantiate a `Dense` layer, which is the basic feedforward fully connected layer. Let's move on to building the model:

```
model = Sequential()
model.add(Dense(30, input_dim=13, activation='tanh'))
model.add(Dense(20, activation='tanh'))
model.add(Dense(1, activation='sigmoid'))
```

In the first row, we have set the type of the model as `Sequential`. Then, we have added the layers. We have already said that we will use a completely connected network structure with three levels. Fully connected levels are defined using the `Dense` class. The first is the most important because it is the level that defines the input—it must have the right number of inputs. This can be specified with the `input_dim` argument and set to 13 for the 13 input columns. We passed three parameters—30, `input_dim` = 13, and `activation` = '`tanh`'. 30 (units) is a positive integer representing the dimensionality of the output space, which denotes the number of neurons in the level. Finally, `activation='tanh'` is used to set the activation function (hyperbolic tangent activation function). The second layer has 20 neurons and the `tanh` activation function. Finally, the output layer has a single neuron (output) and the `sigmoid` activation function. Before training a model, you need to configure the learning process, which is done via the `compile()` method:

```
model.compile(optimizer='adam',loss='binary_crossentropy',metrics=['accurac
y'])
```

Three arguments are passed:

- The `adam` optimizer: An algorithm for first-order gradient-based optimization of stochastic objective functions, based on adaptive estimates of lower-order moments
- The `binary_crossentropy` loss function: We have used logarithmic loss, which for a binary classification problem is defined in Keras as `binary_crossentropy`
- The `accuracy` metric: A metric is a function that is used to evaluate the performance of your model during training and testing

To train the model, the `fit()` method is used, as follows:

```
model.fit(Input_train, Target_train, epochs=1000, verbose=1)
```

Four arguments are passed:

- `Input_train`: Array of input training data.
- `Target_train`: Array of target (label) data.
- `epochs=1000`: Number of epochs to train the model. An epoch is an iteration over the entire x and y data provided.
- `verbose=1`: An integer, either 0, 1, or 2. Verbosity mode: 0 = silent, 1 = progress bar, 2 = one line per epoch.

When the `fit()` function is used, the loss and the accuracy at the end of each training epoch is displayed, as shown in the following results:

```
Epoch 990/1000
207/207 [==============================] - 0s 101us/step - loss: 2.0041e-04 - acc: 1.0000
Epoch 991/1000
207/207 [==============================] - 0s 106us/step - loss: 1.9977e-04 - acc: 1.0000
Epoch 992/1000
207/207 [==============================] - 0s 97us/step - loss: 1.9886e-04 - acc: 1.0000
Epoch 993/1000
207/207 [==============================] - 0s 97us/step - loss: 1.9743e-04 - acc: 1.0000
Epoch 994/1000
207/207 [==============================] - 0s 97us/step - loss: 1.9678e-04 - acc: 1.0000
Epoch 995/1000
207/207 [==============================] - 0s 87us/step - loss: 1.9598e-04 - acc: 1.0000
Epoch 996/1000
207/207 [==============================] - 0s 97us/step - loss: 1.9558e-04 - acc: 1.0000
Epoch 997/1000
207/207 [==============================] - 0s 101us/step - loss: 1.9407e-04 - acc: 1.0000
Epoch 998/1000
207/207 [==============================] - 0s 82us/step - loss: 1.9327e-04 - acc: 1.0000
Epoch 999/1000
207/207 [==============================] - 0s 97us/step - loss: 1.9223e-04 - acc: 1.0000
Epoch 1000/1000
207/207 [==============================] - 0s 87us/step - loss: 1.9132e-04 - acc: 1.0000
```

To print a summary of the model, simply type the following:

```
model.summary()
```

The following results are given:

```
Layer (type) Output Shape Param #
===================================================================
dense_28 (Dense)  (None, 30)  420
_____
dense_29 (Dense)  (None, 20)  620
_____
dense_30 (Dense)  (None, 1)  21
===================================================================
Total params: 1,061
Trainable params: 1,061
Non-trainable params: 0
```

To evaluate the performance of the model we have just adapted, we must use the `evaluate()` function, as follows:

```
score = model.evaluate(Input_test, Target_test, verbose=0)
print('Keras Model Accuracy = ',score[1])
```

This function returns the loss value and metrics values for the model in test mode. Computation is done in batches. The following result is returned:

```
Keras Model Accuracy =  0.8089887673935193
```

To verify the model's capacity in classifying heart disease as a function of the thirteen variables assumed, we can display the predicted values against the current ones. To do this, we first perform the prediction on all the observations contained in the test dataset. We can use the `predict()` function for this, as follows:

```
Target_Classification = model.predict(Input_test)
Target_Classification = (Target_Classification > 0.5)
```

The second line has been added to obtain a binary result. Now, we can compare the results of the classification with the actual values. The best way to do this is to use a confusion matrix. In a confusion matrix, our classification results are compared with real data.

The strength of a confusion matrix is that it identifies the nature of the classification errors, as well as their quantities. In this matrix, the diagonal cells show the number of cases that were correctly classified; all the other cells show the misclassified cases. To calculate the confusion matrix, we can use the `confusion_matrix()` function that's contained in the `sklearn.metrics` package. Let's start by importing the function:

```
from sklearn.metrics import confusion_matrix
```

Then, we can use this function to print the confusion matrix:

```
print(confusion_matrix(Target_test, Target_Classification))
```

The following results are returned:

```
[[34  8]
 [ 9 38]]
```

72 observations of 89 were correctly classified by making 17 errors with an accuracy equal to 0.8089887673935193.

Summary

In this chapter, we have learned about the basic concepts of the classification problem. A classifier is a system that's able to identify the class of a new objective based on knowledge extracted from a series of samples. Different types of classification techniques have been explored—Naive Bayes, Mixture Gaussian, discriminant analysis, KNN, and SVM.

Then, we looked at Bayesian decision theory. Bayesian decision theory is an approach to statistical inference in which the probabilities are not interpreted as frequencies, proportions, or similar concepts, but rather as levels of confidence in the occurrence of a given event.

In the second part of this chapter, we dealt with a practical case where we used the concept for heart disease classification using Keras. The basic concepts of classification methods and how to implement them in the Keras environment has been learned.

In the next chapter, we will understand the basic concepts of prediction problems, discover multilayer neural networks, and how to implement them in the Keras environment. We will also understand how to train, test, and deploy a model. We will learn how to address a prediction problem to estimate the quality of concrete. We will also learn how to evaluate the model's performance. Finally, we will learn how to tune a model to improve the model's performance.

4
Concrete Quality Prediction Using Deep Neural Networks

Deep learning is the recent hot trend in machine learning and **Artificial Intelligence (AI)**. It's all about building advanced neural networks. By making multiple hidden layers work in a neural network model, we can work with complex nonlinear representations of data. We can create deep learning by using basic neural networks. **Artificial neural networks (ANNs)** are information-processing systems that try to simulate, within a computer system, the functioning of biological nervous systems that are made up of a large number of nerve cells, or neurons, connected to each other in a complex network. Each neuron is connected, on average, with tens or thousands of other neurons, with hundreds or billions of connections. Intelligent behavior emerges from the many interactions between these interconnected units. Deep learning has numerous use cases in real life. In this chapter, we'll address a prediction problem to estimate the quality of concrete.

The following are the topics that we'll be covering in this chapter:

- Basic concepts of ANNs
- Multilayer neural networks
- Implementing multilayer neural networks in Keras
- Keras deep neural network model
- Improving model performance by removing outliers

By the end of the chapter, we'll have learned the basic concepts of prediction problems and discovered multilayer neural networks and how to implement them in the Keras environment. We'll also have learned the following:

- How to train, test, and deploy a model
- How to prepare data

- How to create the model using a real-world example
- How to evaluate the model's performance
- How to tune a model to improve the model performance

Basic concepts of ANNs

ANNs are mathematical models thatare able to simulate the usual activities of the human brain such as image perception, pattern recognition, language comprehension, and sensory-motor coordination. These models are composed of a system of nodes, equivalent to the neurons of a human brain, which are interconnected by weighted connections, equivalent to the synapses between the neurons. The output of the network is iteratively changed from the link weights up to the convergence. The data to be analyzed is provided via the input level and the result provided by the network is returned from the output level. Input nodes represent the independent or predictive variables used to predict dependent variables, such as output neurons.

Modern computers and bundled software are very powerful tools for performing the tasks that require repetition of a series of well-defined operations where accuracy, reliability, and speed are the key features. These information-processing systems are very useful but are certainly not intelligent: the only element of intelligence in the whole process is the programmer who has analyzed the task and created the program. In order for an artificial system to be intelligent, it should at least be able to solve the problems that human beings find simple and commonplace.

ANNs try to simulate the functioning of biological nervous systems that are made up of a large number of nerve cells or neurons connected to each other in a complex network. Each neuron is connected on an average with tens or thousands of other neurons. Hence, there are hundreds of billions of connections. Intelligent behavior arises from the many interactions between interconnected units. Some of these units receive information from the environment, others emit responses in the environment, and some others only communicate with the units within the network: they are defined as input units, output units, and units hidden (hidden) respectively.

Each unit (neuron) performs a very simple operation, which consists of activating itself, if the total amount of signal it receives exceeds a certain threshold of activation. If a unit becomes active, it emits a signal that's transmitted along the communication channels to the other units to which it's connected; each connection point acts as a filter that transforms the received message into an inhibitory or excitatory signal, increasing or decreasing its intensity according to its own individual characteristics.

Architecture of ANNs

The units present in each layer and the connections between the units of the different layers define the architecture of an ANN, as shown in the following diagram:

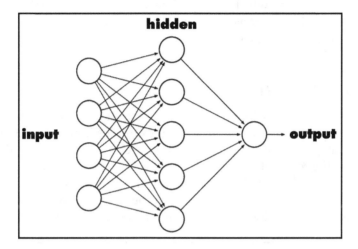

In the previous diagram we can identify three layers: input, hidden, and output. The layers exchange information with each other through connections. Each connection has a weight associated with it that can be tuned based on experience, making the ANNs adaptive to inputs and capable of learning. The input-output link, in other words, the network transfer function, isn't programmed but is simply obtained by a learning process based on empirical data obtained during the training phase. A neural network is structured using a layered approach, which is the same approach used by the Keras framework.

Learning paradigms

Learning consists of acquiring or changing knowledge, behaviors, abilities, and preferences. Human beings, animals, and plants possess this ability. The purpose of algorithms based on neural networks is to extend this feature to machines. Learning can be done by following different models depending on the feedback provided to the system. There are essentially two types of learning for neural networks, namely **supervised** and **unsupervised**.

By analogy, with human beings, we can learn from observations without any kind of target model (without supervision), or we can have a teacher who shows us the right model to follow (supervised). Halfway between supervised and unsupervised learning, there's semi-supervised learning, in which the teacher provides an incomplete dataset for training - that is, a set of training data among which there is data without the respective desired output. In Chapter 3, *Heart Disease Classification with Neural Networks*, we already introduced the topic. Let's go into the details of these concepts.

Supervised learning

In supervised learning, the algorithm generates a function that links input values to a desired output through the observation of a set of examples in which each data input has its relative output data, and that's used to construct predictive models. In this way, the machine can resolve the relevant tasks automatically. To do this, the input data is included in a set I, (typically vectors). Then, the set of output data is fixed as set O, and finally it defines a function f that associates each input with the correct answer. Such information is called a training set. The following diagram shows a generic supervised learning workflow:

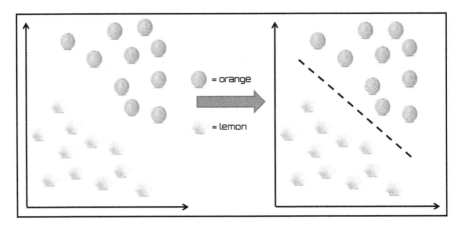

As you can see, a series of images of fruits characterized by different shapes and colors are supplied as input. In the input data, the images are also classified into two categories (**lemon** and **orange**). In this way, the neural network will be able to classify each new image provided correctly .

All supervised learning algorithms are based on the following thesis: if an algorithm provides an adequate number of examples, it'll be able to create a derived function B that'll approximate the desired function A.

If the approximation of the desired function is adequate, when the input data is offered to the derived function, this function should be able to provide output responses similar to those provided by the desired function that are acceptable. These algorithms are based on the following concept: similar input values correspond to similar output values.

Generally, in the real world, this assumption isn't valid; however, some situations exist in which it's acceptable. Clearly, the proper functioning of such algorithms depends significantly on the input data. If there are only a few training input values, the algorithm might not have enough experience to provide a correct output. Conversely, many input values may make it excessively slow since the derivative function generated by a large number of inputs could be very complicated.

Moreover, experience shows that this type of algorithm is very sensitive to noise; even a few pieces of incorrect data can make the entire system unreliable and lead to wrong decisions. In supervised learning, it's possible to split problems based on the nature of the data. If the output value is categorical, such as membership/non-membership of a certain class, it's a classification problem. If the output is a continuous real value in a certain range, then it's a regression problem.

Unsupervised learning

The aim of unsupervised learning is to extract information from databases automatically . This process occurs without prior knowledge of the contents to be analyzed. Unlike supervised learning, there's no information on membership classes of the examples or generally on the output corresponding to a certain input. The goal is to get a model that's able to discover interesting properties; groups with similar characteristics (clustering), for instance. Search engines are an example of an application of these algorithms. Given one or more keywords, they're able to create a list of links related to our search.

The validity of these algorithms depends on the usefulness of the information they can extract from the databases. These algorithms work by comparing data and looking for similarities or differences. Available data concerns only the set of features that describe each example. They show great efficiency with elements of numeric type, but are much less accurate with nonnumeric data. Generally, they work properly in the presence of data that contains an order or a clear grouping and is clearly identifiable.

The following diagram shows a generic unsupervised learning workflow:

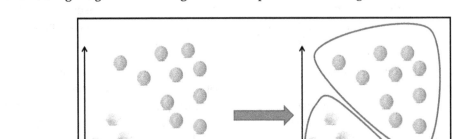

In the previous diagram, a series of images of fruits characterized by different shapes and colors are supplied as input. Nothing else is provided as input. The neural network will be able to group objects (images) on the basis of some common properties, which may be the color (yellow and orange) or the form (elliptical and rounded).

Semi-supervised learning

Halfway between the supervised and the non-supervised, partially supervised learning is based on mixed data in which a minimal part is already labeled and a very large majority consists of unlabeled data. This approach is used to improve the predictions made by the machine on unlabeled data and normally requires human intervention. The approach is mainly used in classification and clustering problems or in the description of the cause-effect relationships between variables.

Understanding the structure of neural networks

The atomic computational unit of a neural network is the artificial neuron. It simulates different basic functions of the biological neuron; it evaluates the intensity of each input, adds the different input values, and compares the result with an appropriate threshold. Finally, it determines what the value of the output is. The characteristic of the neuron to add algebraically the values of its input, represents the first function implemented by the artificial neuron; the **sum** function. The following diagram shows a scheme of a single neuron with the **threshold** of **activation**:

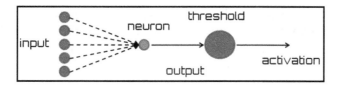

The values acquired as input subjected to an appropriate transformation are then returned as output, as a prediction of the result of the observation.

Weights and biases

In case of error in the simulation of the phenomenon, it's necessary to make an appropriate correction. To do this, each input must be assigned a weight—that is, a numerical value that modulates the impact that this input has on the total sum to determine the potential of the neuron. In other words, each input contributes more or less to determine the exceeding of the threshold value and the triggering of the potential.

The weight of a connection is a numerical value for which we multiply the value of the input. In this way, the input will have a greater or lesser effect on the total sum of the inputs according to the weight entity. The sum of the input values will now become the weighted sum of the input values. We can represent this process with the following equation:

$$Output = Input_1 * w_1 + Input_2 * w_2 + Input_3 * w_3 + \ldots + Input_n * w_n$$

Moreover, we can think of the input and the corresponding weight as vectors of the type $INPUT = (Input_1, Input_2, ..., Input_n)$ and $W = (w_1, w_2, ..., w_n)$. The total input signal to the neuron, what we have identified as the sum of the input values, will then be the scalar product of these two vectors ($INPUT \cdot W$). Each component of the INPUT vector is multiplied with the corresponding component of the vector W and all of the obtained products are added together. The result will be a scalar representing the weighted sum of the input values, as shown in the following formula:

$$Output = \sum_{i=1}^{n} Input_i * w_i$$

Geometrically, the scalar product of two vectors can be considered as a measure of their similarity. If the vectors have the same direction, the scalar product is maximum; if the vectors have opposite directions (180°), the scalar product is null. In the weighted sum, each entry participates in the sum proportionally to the weight entity.

Among the weights is a special weight named **bias**. It's not tied to any other unit of the network and it's as if it always had input equal to 1. The bias serves to make a translation on the axis of the abscissas to the output function. A new unitary input will be associated to the input values and an additional element b_i will be present in the weight vector, which will represent the weight referred to as the bias. On the basis of what has been said, the previous equation assumes the following form:

$$Output = \left(\sum_{i=1}^{n} Input_i * w_i \right) + b_i$$

The effect of the bias is to control the translation of the activation threshold with respect to the origin of the signals. Formally, the bias plays a role similar to that of the weights that act as regulators of the intensity of the signal emitted (or received).

Types of activation functions

The purpose of each node in the neural network is to accept input values and to enter an output value in the next layer. The input nodes insert the values of the variables in the hidden layer without modifying them. Each neuron adds the weighted values of all of the neurons connected to it and adds a bias value. To this result, an **activation function** is applied, which does nothing but transform the value mathematically before passing it to the next layer. In this way, the input values are propagated through the network up to the output neurons. The goal is to adjust weights and bias in order to achieve the desired result. The following diagram shows the scheme of a single neuron with the **activation function**:

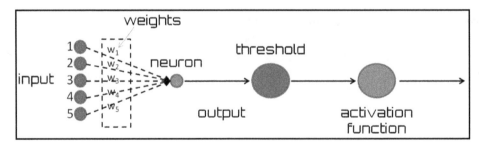

A neural network without an activation function is simply equivalent to a regression model; this means that it tries to approximate the distribution of data with a straight line (linear trend). On the contrary, the purpose of neural networks is to be able to approximate any function, and to do this it's necessary to introduce a non-linearity factor—this term is represented by the activation function.

The activation function must satisfy some criteria:

- It must have output values in the range {0, 1}
- It must provide an output value close to 1 when sufficiently stimulated (threshold effect), to propagate activity within the network

There're many activation functions available for a neural network to use. We'll try to analyze some of them.

Unit step activation function

A **unit step activation function** is a much-used feature in neural networks. The output assumes the value **0** for negative argument and **1** for positive argument. The function is as follows:

$$y = f(x) = \begin{cases} 0, & if \quad x < 0 \\ 1, & if \quad x \geq 0 \end{cases}$$

The range is between **(0,1)** and the output is binary in nature. These types of activation functions are useful for binary schemes. When we want to classify an input model in one of two groups, we can use a binary compiler with a unit step activation function. A unit step activation function is shown in the following screenshot:

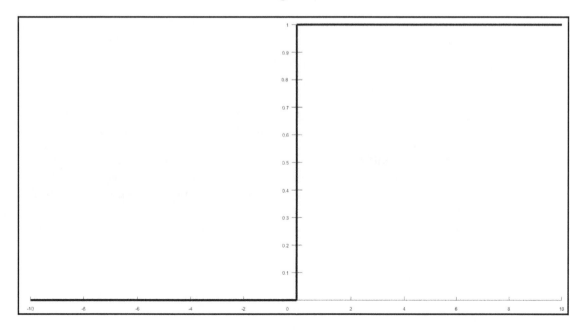

Sigmoid

The **sigmoid** function is a mathematical function that produces a sigmoidal curve—a characteristic curve known for its S shape. This is the earliest and often used activation function. This squashes the input to any value between **0** and **1** and makes the model logistic in nature. This function refers to a special case of logistic function, defined by the following formula:

$$y = f(x) = \frac{1}{1 + e^{-x}}$$

The following screenshot shows a sigmoid curve with an S shape:

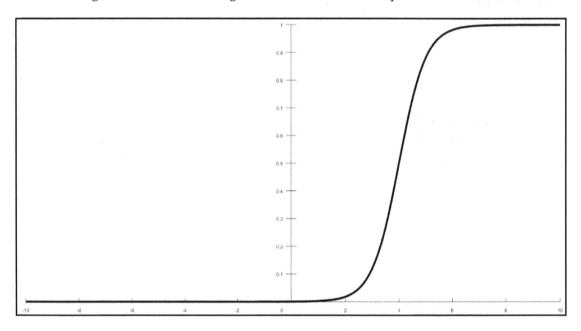

The sigmoid function is differentiable; this means that we can find the slope of the sigmoid curve at any point in its existence interval. This is a monotone function with a nonmonotonic derivative. The logistic sigmoid function is a sigmoid function as well as a softmax function, which is a more generalized logistic activation function that's used for multiclass classification.

Hyperbolic tangent

Another very popular and widely used activation feature is the **tanh** function. If you look at the screenshot that follows, you can notice that it looks very similar to sigmoid; in fact, it's a **scaled sigmoid function**. This is a nonlinear function, defined in the range of values **(-1, 1)**, so you need not worry about activations blowing up. One thing to clarify is that the gradient is stronger for tanh than sigmoid (the derivatives are more steep). The function is defined by the following formula:

$$y = f(x) = tanh(x) = \frac{1 - e^{-2x}}{1 + e^{-2x}}$$

The following figure shows a hyberbolic tangent activation function:

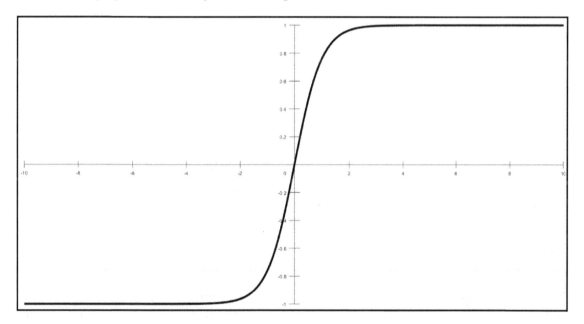

Deciding between sigmoid and tanh will depend on your gradient strength requirement. Like the sigmoid, tanh also has the missing slope problem.

Rectified linear unit

Rectified Linear Unit (ReLU) is the most used activation function since 2015. It's a simple condition and has advantages over the other functions. The function is defined by the following formula:

$$y = f(x) = \begin{cases} 0 & if \quad x < 0 \\ 1 & if \quad x \geq 0 \end{cases}$$

The following screenshot shows a ReLU activation function:

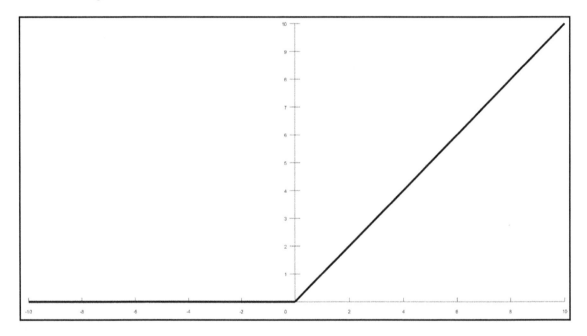

The range of output is between **0** and infinity. ReLU finds applications in computer vision and speech recognition using deep neural nets. There are various other activation functions as well, but we've covered the most important ones here.

Multilayer neural networks

The term multilayer neural networks denotes neural networks composed of many hidden levels (at least two) organized hierarchically. Hierarchical organization allows you to share and reuse information. Along the hierarchy, you can select specific features and discard unnecessary details in order to maximize the invariance. In multilevel machine learning, the deeper levels take inputs from the outputs of previous layers and perform more transformations and abstractions on them. This management of learning levels is inspired by the way in which a mammalian brain processes information and learns, responding to external stimuli. The following diagram shows a generic architecture of a multilayer neural network (with two hidden layers):

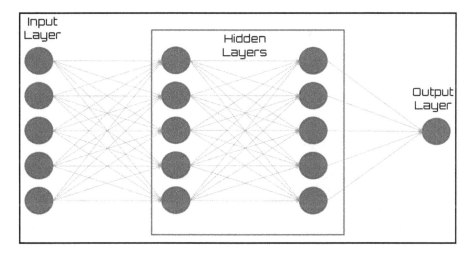

Multilayer neural networks have applications in many fields—speech recognition systems, pattern search, and image recognition. Thanks to the level-learning features, the network, step by step, concentrates its activity on specific areas of the vast input to be processed and classified.

So far, we've analyzed several examples of neural networks. In all cases it was a three-level network—an input level, a hidden layer, and an output level. Although the ability of a three-level neural network to distinguish between arbitrarily complex regions has been demonstrated, there are some advantages in using a multilayered architecture, which then exploits the depth of the network.

One of the main advantages, for example, is related to the number of nodes per layer; in fact, in a three-level network, the complexity of the region to be recognized is limited by the number of nodes for each level. As a result, there is a risk, limiting the depth, of needing a large number of nodes. Theoretical results show that there are situations in which the number of necessary nodes increases exponentially with the size of the input. An indiscriminate increase of nodes on the levels causes a high computational cost and a huge use of memory. For these reasons, it's essential to carry out a careful planning of the network architecture to be used.

The generic architecture of a multilayer network (feedforward multilayer) is defined by the following:

- M entry nodes, lacking processing capacity, associated with input values
- A set of neurons organized in $L >= 2$ layers (of which there are $L-1$ hidden layers and an output layer that supplies the output values of the network)
- A set of oriented and weighted arcs that establish the connections

There are no connections between the neurons of the same layer, nor connections in feedback.

The most widely used multilayer networks consist of a number of levels between 7 and 50. Deeper networks (100 levels and above) have shown that they can guarantee slightly better performance, but at the expense of efficiency. The depth of the network, represented by the number of levels, is only one of the factors of complexity. The number of neurons, connections, and weights also characterize the complexity of a multilayer network. The greater the number of weights (such as the parameters to be learned), the greater the complexity of the training. At the same time, a high number of neurons (and connections) makes the training operations more expensive, as the number of operations required increases.

There are many variations of multilayer neural networks:

- **Convolutional neural network (CNN)**: The layer of neurons that deals with the convolution divides the input data into various overlapping fragments, which are then analyzed to identify the particularities that characterize it, transferring the information to the following layer in the form of a feature map containing the relations between neurons and particularities.
- **Recurrent neural networks (RNN)**: It's a neural model in which a bidirectional flow of information is present. In other words, while the propagation of signals in feed-forward networks takes place only in a continuous manner in a direction from input values to output values, recurrent networks are different.

- **Deep belief network** (**DBN**): This is typically a feedforward network in which data flows from one layer to another without looping back. There's at least one hidden layer and there can be multiple hidden layers, increasing the complexity.
- **Restricted boltzmann machine** (**RBM**): This has a single hidden layer and there's no connection between nodes in a group. It's a simple **multilayer perceptron** (**MLP**) model of neural networks.

In the following chapters, we'll analyze the most common examples of deep networks, providing practical examples that will help us to understand the principles of how they function.

Implementing multilayer neural networks in Keras

We have gone through the theory of neural networks, we have learned about the activation functions and multilayer neural networks. We are now ready to implement our project on testing the quality of concrete using multilayer neural networks. Excited? Let's begin. Concrete is the most important material in civil engineering. Its compressive strength is a highly nonlinear function of age and ingredients. These ingredients include cement, blast furnace slag, fly ash, water, superplasticizer, coarse aggregate, and fine aggregate. The test to calculate compressive strength is carried out on either a concrete cube or cylinder through the use of a compression testing machine (2,000 kilonewtons). The test is destructive and takes a long time, so the possibility of predicting the compressive strength takes on significant importance. The following photograph shows a compressive strength test:

In this study, we want to create a model that allows us to calculate the compressive strength according to the ingredients used in the mixture. We begin, as always, by getting the data to be analyzed.

To get the data, we draw on the large collection of data available at the UCI Machine Learning Repository at the following link:
`http://archive.ics.uci.edu/ml/datasets/`
`concrete+compressive+strength`

To predict the compressive strength of concrete from the ingredients of the mixture, we can use the concrete compressive strength dataset containing eight quantitative input variables and one quantitative output variable.

The following shows all of the variables, followed by a brief description:

- `Cement` -- quantitative -- `kg in a` m³ `mixture`

- `Blast Furnace Slag` -- quantitative -- `kg in a` m³ `mixture`

- `Fly Ash` -- quantitative -- `kg in a` m³ `mixture`

- `Water` -- quantitative -- `kg in a` m³ `mixture`

- `Superplasticizer` -- quantitative -- kg in a m³

- `Coarse Aggregate` -- quantitative -- `kg in a` m³ `mixture`

- `Fine Aggregate` -- quantitative -- `kg in a` m³ `mixture`

- `Age` -- quantitative -- `Day (1~365)`

- `Concrete compressive strength` -- quantitative -- `MPa, megapascals`

This dataset contains the following instances and attributes:

- Number of instances: `1029`
- Number of attributes: `9` continuous attributes.

The data is available in a `.xlsx` file named `ConcreteData.xlsx` downloaded from the UCI dataset. To start, let's see how to import the data into Python. To do this, we'll use the `read_excel` module of the `pandas` library. The `read_ excel` method reads an Excel table into a `pandas` DataFrame.

The first thing to do is to import the library that we'll use:

```
import pandas as pd
```

The available data doesn't contain the header, so it's necessary to retrieve the names of the variables that are contained in another file, always available in the UCI archive. Let's put them in a list:

```
HDNames= ['Cement','BFS','FLA','Water','SP','CA','FA','Age','CCS']
```

Now, let's see how to import the data contained in the dataset in Python:

```
Data = pd.read_excel('ConcreteData.xlsx', names=HDNames)
```

Two parameters are passed: filename and the list of column names to use.

Exploratory analysis

Before starting with data analysis through the deep neural network algorithm, we conduct an exploratory analysis to understand how the data is distributed and extract preliminary knowledge.

To display the first 20 rows of the DataFrame imported, we can use the `head()` function as follows:

```
print(Data.head(20))
```

The first 20 rows are displayed, as shown in the following screenshot:

```
    Cement    BFS  FLA  Water   SP      CA     FA  Age        CCS
0   540.0    0.0   0.0  162.0  2.5  1055.0  676.0   28  61.887366
1   332.5  142.5   0.0  228.0  0.0   932.0  594.0  270  40.269535
2   332.5  142.5   0.0  228.0  0.0   932.0  594.0  365  41.052780
3   198.6  132.4   0.0  192.0  0.0   978.4  825.5  360  44.296075
4   266.0  114.0   0.0  228.0  0.0   932.0  670.0   90  47.029847
5   380.0   95.0   0.0  228.0  0.0   932.0  594.0  365  43.698299
6   380.0   95.0   0.0  228.0  0.0   932.0  594.0   28  36.447770
7   266.0  114.0   0.0  228.0  0.0   932.0  670.0   28  45.854291
8   475.0    0.0   0.0  228.0  0.0   932.0  594.0   28  39.289790
9   198.6  132.4   0.0  192.0  0.0   978.4  825.5   90  38.074244
10  198.6  132.4   0.0  192.0  0.0   978.4  825.5   28  28.021684
11  427.5   47.5   0.0  228.0  0.0   932.0  594.0  270  43.012960
12  190.0  190.0   0.0  228.0  0.0   932.0  670.0   90  42.326932
13  304.0   76.0   0.0  228.0  0.0   932.0  670.0   28  47.813782
14  380.0    0.0   0.0  228.0  0.0   932.0  670.0   90  52.908320
15  139.6  209.4   0.0  192.0  0.0  1047.0  806.9   90  39.358048
16  342.0   38.0   0.0  228.0  0.0   932.0  670.0  365  56.141962
17  380.0   95.0   0.0  228.0  0.0   932.0  594.0   90  40.563252
18  475.0    0.0   0.0  228.0  0.0   932.0  594.0  180  42.620648
19  427.5   47.5   0.0  228.0  0.0   932.0  594.0  180  41.836714
```

Now, the dataset is available in our Python environment; to extract some information, we can invoke the `info()` function, as follows:

```
print(Data.info())
```

This method prints a concise summary of a DataFrame, including the `dtype` index, `dtypes` column, `non-null` values, and `memory usage`. The following results are returned:

```
<class 'pandas.core.frame.DataFrame'>
RangeIndex: 1029 entries, 0 to 1028
Data columns (total 9 columns):
Cement 1029 non-null float64
BFS 1029 non-null float64
FLA 1029 non-null float64
Water 1029 non-null float64
SP 1029 non-null float64
CA 1029 non-null float64
FA 1029 non-null float64
Age 1029 non-null int64
CCS 1029 non-null float64
dtypes: float64(8), int64(1)
memory usage: 72.4 KB
None
```

Useful information is reported—the numbers of the entries (`1029`) and data columns (`9`). Essentially, the list of all features with the number of elements, the possible presence of missing data, and the type is returned. In this way, we can already get an idea of the type of variables we're about to analyze. In fact, analyzing the results obtained, we note that two types have been identified: `float64` (8) and `int64` (1).

To get a preview of the data contained in it, we can calculate a series of basic statistics. To do so, we'll use the `describe()` function in the following way:

```
summary = Data.describe()
print(summary)
```

The following results are returned:

```
              Cement          BFS          FLA        Water           SP    \
count    1029.000000  1029.000000  1029.000000  1029.000000  1029.000000
mean      280.914091    73.967298    54.239796   181.585374     6.206710
std       104.245542    86.290255    64.005258    21.357226     5.975279
min       102.000000     0.000000     0.000000   121.750000     0.000000
25%       192.000000     0.000000     0.000000   164.900000     0.000000
50%       272.800000    22.000000     0.000000   185.000000     6.350000
75%       350.000000   143.000000   118.270000   192.000000    10.160000
max       540.000000   359.400000   200.100000   247.000000    32.200000

                  CA           FA          Age          CCS
count    1029.000000  1029.000000  1029.000000  1029.000000
mean      972.853401   773.673712    45.679300    35.774912
std        77.763459    80.156602    63.198226    16.656880
min       801.000000   594.000000     1.000000     2.331808
25%       932.000000   732.600000     7.000000    23.696601
50%       968.000000   779.700000    28.000000    34.397958
75%      1029.400000   824.000000    56.000000    45.939786
max      1145.000000   992.600000   365.000000    82.599225|
```

The `describe()` function generates descriptive statistics that summarizes the central tendency, dispersion, and shape of a dataset's distribution, excluding `NaN` values. It analyzes both numeric and object series, as well as DataFrame column sets of mixed data types. The output will vary depending on what's provided.

Data visualization

By visualizing the data, it's possible to understand the meaning of the data by positioning it in a visual context. At first sight numerical analysis of data can hide patterns, trends, and correlations that instead represent the bases of data mining. These characteristics are highlighted instead through graphs and diagrams that describe the nature of the data under analysis.

The first task we can do is draw a data plot. In this way, we'll be able to highlight the characteristics we've already analyzed with the statistical data returned by the `describe()` function. A **boxplot** is a graphical representation used to describe the distribution of a sample by simple dispersion and position indexes. To draw a boxplot of a DataFrame, we can use the `seaborn` package. `seaborn` is a Python data visualization library based on `Matplotlib`. It provides a high-level interface for drawing attractive and informative statistical graphics and is closely integrated with pandas data structures.

seaborn offers many features that help us in the visual analysis of a data source. The most important are as follows:

- A dataset-oriented API for examining relationships between multiple variables
- Specialized support for using categorical variables to show observations or aggregate statistics
- Options for visualizing univariate or bivariate distributions and for comparing them between subsets of data
- Automatic estimation and plotting of linear regression models for different kinds of dependent variables
- Convenient views onto the overall structure of complex datasets
- High-level abstractions for structuring multiplot grids that let you easily build complex visualizations
- Concise control over Matplotlib figure styling with several built-in themes
- Tools for choosing color palettes that faithfully reveal patterns in your data

To start, we import the library:

```
import seaborn as sns
```

Remember, to import a library that isn't present in the initial distribution of Python, you must use the `pip install` command followed by the name of the library. This command should be used only once and not every time you run the code.

Then, we can draw the boxplot:

```
sns.set(style="ticks")
sns.boxplot(data = Data)
```

The first line sets the aesthetic style of the plots. This affects things such as the color of the axes, whether a grid is enabled by default, and other aesthetic elements. The following styles are available: `darkgrid`, `white grid`, `dark`, `white`, and `ticks`. The second line draws a boxplot to show distributions with respect to categories. In the following screenshot, the boxplots of all of the variables contained in the data frame are shown:

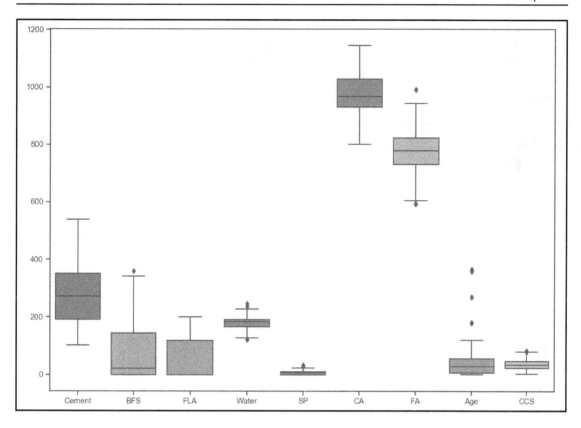

From the analysis of the previous screenshot, it's clear that the variables have distinctly different ranges of values. Moreover, some variables have possible outliers—that is, to say anomalous values that differ very much from the other observations.

Furthermore, by comparing the length of the whiskers and the heights of the rectangles with each other, information on the symmetry of the distribution is obtained: this is more symmetrical as the lengths of the whiskers are similar to each other and the heights of the two rectangles are similar.

Let's see now if we can get more information on the variables at our disposal and how these variables correlate with the target. To do this, we'll use the **scatter plot**. Through the scatter plots, we can have an idea of the shape and strength of the relationship between the variables. Deviations due to abnormal data, which are specific values that deviate from the general scheme or presence of different clusters, can also be highlighted:

```
sns.pairplot(data = Data)
```

`seaborn.pairplot()` plots pairwise relationships in a dataset. By default, this function will create a grid of axis so that each variable in data will by shared in the *y*-axis across a single row and in the *x*-axis across a single column. The diagonal axes are treated differently, drawing a plot to show the univariate distribution of the data for the variable in that column. The following screenshot shows a scatter plot matrix:

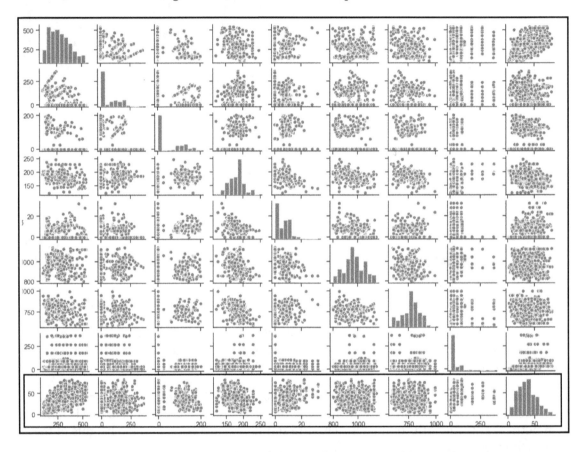

This graph shows all of the scatter plots of the two-by-two variables. At first glance, no particular trend is highlighted. But if we focus our attention on the last line of graphs (highlighted in the screenshot), it contains the scatter plots of the target of our **concrete compressive strength** (**CCS**) data compared to the predictors. Except for the first variable (**cement**), no other shows a particular trend. It follows that all of the variables are necessary to build the model.

Data scaling

Analyzing the graph with the boxplots, we've noted that the variables have different ranges. When the predictors have different ranges, the impact on response variables by the feature having a greater numeric range could be more than the one having a less numeric range, and this could, in turn, impact the prediction accuracy. Our goal is to improve predictive accuracy and not allow a particular feature to impact the prediction due to a large numeric value range. Hence, we may need to scale values under different features such that they fall under a common range. Through this statistical procedure, it's possible to compare identical variables belonging to different distributions and different variables or variables expressed in different units.

Remember, it's good practice to rescale the data before training a deep learning algorithm. With rescaling, data units are eliminated, allowing you to compare data from different locations easily.

In this case, we'll use the **min-max** method (usually called **feature scaling**) to get all of the scaled data in the range **[0, 1]**. The formula to achieve this is the following:

$$x_{scaled} = \frac{x - x_{min}}{x_{max} - x_{min}}$$

To perform feature scaling, we can use the preprocessing package available in the `sklearn` library. The `sklearn.preprocessing` package provides several common utility functions and transformer classes to modify the features available in a representation that best suits our needs. As always, we start by importing the package:

```
from sklearn.preprocessing import MinMaxScaler
```

To scaling features between a given minimum and maximum value, in our case between 0 and 1, so that the maximum absolute value of each feature is scaled to unit size, the `MinMaxScaler` function can be used. Let's start by defining `scaler`:

```
scaler = MinMaxScaler()
```

Now, just to have confirmation of what we're going to do, we print the parameters that we'll use for the next resizing:

```
print(scaler.fit(data))
```

The `fit` method computes the minimum and maximum to be used for later scaling. The result is as follows:

```
MinMaxScaler(copy=True, feature_range=(0, 1))
```

Now, we can scale the features:

```
DataScaled = scaler.fit_transform(Data)
```

The `fit_transform` method fits to data, then transforms it. A numPy array of shape is returned. It's advisable to report the results in the starting format (the `pandas` DataFrame), at least for comparison purposes. Let's do it:

```
DataScaled = pd.DataFrame(DataScaled, columns=BHNames)
```

To verify the transformation carried out, we print the basic statistics that we already calculated previously again:

```
summary = DataScaled.describe()
print(summary)
```

The following results are returned:

	Cement	BFS	FLA	Water	SP
count	1029.000000	1029.000000	1029.000000	1029.000000	1029.000000
mean	0.408480	0.205808	0.271063	0.477728	0.192755
std	0.238004	0.240095	0.319866	0.170517	0.185568
min	0.000000	0.000000	0.000000	0.000000	0.000000
25%	0.205479	0.000000	0.000000	0.344511	0.000000
50%	0.389954	0.061213	0.000000	0.504990	0.197205
75%	0.566210	0.397885	0.591054	0.560878	0.315528
max	1.000000	1.000000	1.000000	1.000000	1.000000

	CA	FA	Age	CCS
count	1029.000000	1029.000000	1029.000000	1029.000000
mean	0.499574	0.450762	0.122745	0.416646
std	0.226057	0.201095	0.173621	0.207517
min	0.000000	0.000000	0.000000	0.000000
25%	0.380814	0.347717	0.016484	0.266170
50%	0.485465	0.465881	0.074176	0.399491
75%	0.663953	0.577020	0.151099	0.543284
max	1.000000	1.000000	1.000000	1.000000

Now, every variable is included in a range between 0 and 1—all features have values between 0 and 1. We check the result by plotting the variable boxplots again:

```
sns.boxplot(data = DataScaled)
```

In the following screenshot, the boxplots of all of the scaled variables contained in the data frame are shown:

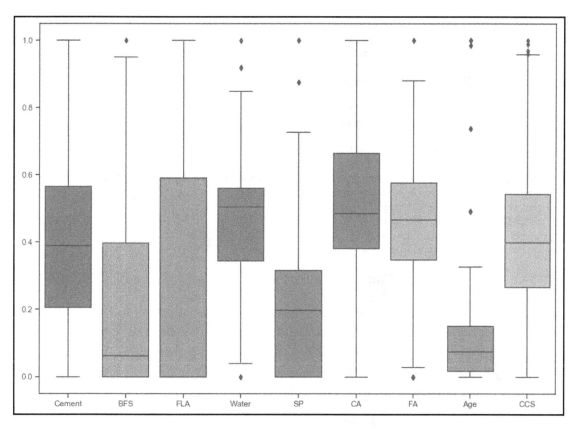

This chart makes visual analysis easier: now, everything is clearer. It's possible to make a comparison between the predictors; in fact, we can see which features have a greater variability in the data. In addition, the possible outliers (isolated points) are more highlighted.

Building a Keras deep neural network model

After exploring the dataset, it's time to build our deep neural network model, so as to predict the quality of concrete from the characteristics of its ingredients. We prepare the data before proceeding. We split the starting data into two sets: the **training set** and **test set**. The training set is used to train a classification model and the test set to test model performance.

To split the data, scikit-learn library has been used. More specifically, the `sklearn.model_selection.train_test_split()` function has been used. This function quickly computes a random split into training and test sets. Let's start by importing the function:

```
from sklearn.model_selection import train_test_split
```

Let's start by splitting the DataFrame into predictors and response:

```
Predictors = pd.DataFrame(DataScaled.iloc[:,:8])
Response = pd.DataFrame(DataScaled.iloc[:,8])
```

Now, we have to split the two DataFrames:

```
Pred_train, Pred_test, Resp_train, Resp_test = train_test_split(Predictors,
Response, test_size = 0.30, random_state = 1)
print(Pred _train.shape)
print(Pred _test.shape)
print(Resp _train.shape)
print(Resp _test.shape)
```

In the `train_test_split()` function, four parameters are passed: `Predictors`, `Response`, `test_size`, and `random_state`. `Predictors` and `Response` are the two DataFrames obtained from the scaled data. `test_size` could take the following types: `float`, `int` or `None`, and `optional` (default=0.25). If `float`, it should be between 0.0 and 1.0 and represent the proportion of the dataset to include in the test split. If `int`, it represents the absolute number of test samples. If `None`, the value is set to the complement the train size. By default, the value is set to 0.25. In our case, we set `test_size = 0.30`, which means that 30% of the data is divided up as test data. Finally, the `random_state` parameter is used to set the seed used by the random number generator. In this way, the repeatability of the splitting operation is guaranteed. The following results are returned:

```
(720, 8)
(309, 8)
(720, 1)
(309, 1)
```

So, at the start, the `Predictors` DataFrame is split into two datasets having `720` rows (`Pred_train`) and `309` rows (`Pred_test`); a similar subdivision was made for `Response`.

To build a deep neural network model, we'll use a Keras Sequential model. As we said in Chapter 1, *Getting Started with Keras*, to create a Keras Sequential model, follow these steps:

1. Import the `Sequential` class from `keras.models`

2. Stack layers using the `.add()` method

3. Configure the learning process using `.compile()` method

4. Train the model on train dataset using `.fit()` method

First, we have to load the libraries needed to run the analysis:

```
from keras.models import Sequential
from keras.layers import Dense
```

Two layer classes have been imported: `Sequential` and `Dense`. The `Sequential` class is used to define a linear stack of network layers that make up a model. In the following, we'll use the `Sequential` constructor to create the model, which will then be enriched with layers using the `add()` method. The `Dense` class is used to instantiate a `Dense` layer, which is the basic feedforward fully connected layer. Let's move on to build the model:

```
model = Sequential()
model.add(Dense(20, input_dim=8, activation='relu'))
model.add(Dense(10, activation='relu'))
model.add(Dense(10, activation='relu'))
model.add(Dense(1, activation='linear'))
```

In the first row, we've set the type of the model, `Sequential`. Then, we've added the layers. We'll use a completely connected network structure with four levels (two hidden layers). Fully connected levels are defined using the `Dense` class. The first is the most important because it's the level that defines the input; it must have the right number of input values. This can be specified with the `input_dim` argument and set to eight for the 8 input columns. We passed three parameters: `20`, `input_dim = 8`, and `activation = 'relu'`. `20` (units) is a positive integer representing the dimensionality of the output space and denotes the number of neurons in the level. `input_dim = 8` is the number of input variables. Finally, `activation = ' relu '` is used to set the activation function (rectified linear unit activation function).

The second layer has `10` neurons and `relu` activation function. The third layer has `10` neurons and `relu` activation function, again. Finally, the output layer has a single neuron (output) and `linear` activation function. Before training a model, you need to configure the learning process, which is done via the `compile()` method:

```
model.compile(optimizer='adam',loss='mean_squared_error',metrics=['accuracy'])
```

Three arguments are passed:

- `adam` **optimizer**: This is an algorithm for first-order, gradient-based optimization of stochastic objective functions, based on adaptive estimates of lower order moments.
- `mean_squared_error` **loss function**: **Mean squared error** (MSE) measures the average of the squares of the errors—that is, the average squared difference between the actual estimated values and what's to be estimated. MSE is a measure of the quality of an estimator—it's always non-negative and, the closer the values are to zero, the better.
- `accuracy` **metric**: A metric is a function that's used to evaluate the performance of your model during training and testing.

To train the model, the `fit ()` method is used as follows:

```
model.fit(Pred_train, Resp_train, epochs=1000, verbose=1)
```

Four arguments are passed:

- `Pred_train`: This is an array of predictors training data.
- `Resp_train`: This is an array of response data.
- `epochs=1000`: This is the number of epochs to train the model. An epoch is an iteration over the entire x and y data provided.
- `verbose=1`: This is an integer; 0, 1, or 2. Here the different verbosity modes represent the following; 0 = silent, 1 = progress bar, and 2 = one line per epoch.

When the `fit()` function is performed, `loss` and `accuracy` at the end of each training epoch are displayed, as shown in the following screenshot:

```
Epoch 990/1000
720/720 [==============================] - 0s 68us/step - loss: 0.0024 - acc: 0.0014
Epoch 991/1000
720/720 [==============================] - 0s 65us/step - loss: 0.0025 - acc: 0.0014
Epoch 992/1000
720/720 [==============================] - 0s 69us/step - loss: 0.0024 - acc: 0.0014
Epoch 993/1000
720/720 [==============================] - 0s 69us/step - loss: 0.0025 - acc: 0.0014
Epoch 994/1000
720/720 [==============================] - 0s 68us/step - loss: 0.0024 - acc: 0.0014
Epoch 995/1000
720/720 [==============================] - 0s 69us/step - loss: 0.0024 - acc: 0.0014
Epoch 996/1000
720/720 [==============================] - 0s 68us/step - loss: 0.0025 - acc: 0.0014
Epoch 997/1000
720/720 [==============================] - 0s 67us/step - loss: 0.0024 - acc: 0.0014
Epoch 998/1000
720/720 [==============================] - 0s 71us/step - loss: 0.0025 - acc: 0.0014
Epoch 999/1000
720/720 [==============================] - 0s 68us/step - loss: 0.0025 - acc: 0.0014
Epoch 1000/1000
720/720 [==============================] - 0s 67us/step - loss: 0.0025 - acc: 0.0014
```

To print a summary of the model, simply type the following:

```
model.summary()
```

The following are the results:

```
Layer (type) Output Shape Param #
=================================================================
dense_37 (Dense)  (None, 20)  180
_____
dense_38 (Dense)  (None, 10)  210
_____
dense_39 (Dense)  (None, 10)  110
_____
dense_40 (Dense)  (None, 1)  11
=================================================================
Total params: 511
Trainable params: 511
Non-trainable params: 0
```

To evaluate the performance of the model, we'll calculate the **coefficient of determination** (R-squared).

R-squared is a measure of how well a model can predict the data, and it lies between 0 and 1; the higher the value of the coefficient of determination, the better the model is at predicting the data. R-squared (also denoted as R^2) is defined as the proportion of variance in the dependent variable that's predictable from the independent variable.

To calculate the coefficient of determination, we can use the `r2_score()` function contained in the `sklearn.metrics` package. Let's start by importing the function:

```
from sklearn.metrics import r2_score
```

The `r2_score()` function calculates R^2 (coefficient of determination). The best possible score is 1.0 and it can be negative (because the model can be arbitrarily worse). A constant model that always predicts the expected value of y, disregarding the input features, would get an R^2 score of 0.0. To calculate R^2, we need ground truth target values and the estimated target values. We have to calculate the estimated target values:

```
Y_predKM = model.predict(Pred_test)
```

We've used the `predict()` function. This is a generic function for predictions from the results of various Keras models. Now we can calculate R^2:

```
print('Coefficient of determination of Keras Model')
print(r2_score(Resp_test, Y_predKM))
```

The following result is returned:

```
Coefficient of determination of Keras Model
0.8713463197672067
```

The better the model fits the data in comparison to the simple average, the closer the value of R^2 is to 1. The result (`0.8713463197672067`) is very close to 1, so the model fits the data very well.

Improving the model performance by removing outliers

In the *Data visualization* section, we saw that some predictors have outliers. Outliers are the values that, when compared to others, are particularly extreme. Outliers are a problem because they tend to distort data analysis results, in particular, in descriptive statistics and correlations. Outliers have a large influence on the fit, because squaring the residuals magnifies the effects of these extreme data points. For these reasons, it may be necessary to remove these values first to improve the performance of the model.

In some cases, you may be tempted to remove outliers that are influential or have an excessive impact on the synthesis measures you want to consider (such as the mean or the linear correlation coefficient). However, this way of proceeding isn't always cautious, unless the reasons for an abnormal observation have been identified and it can be assumed that it can be excluded from the analysis, as it's inconsistent with the reference collective. In other cases, it's not sensible to remove abnormal observations.

Treating or altering the outliers in a dataset isn't a standard operating procedure. However, it's essential to understand their impact on your predictive models. It's left to the best judgment of the reader to decide whether treating outliers is necessary and how to go about it.

There are different methods to detect outliers. We'll use **Tukey's** method, which uses the **interquartile range (IQR)** approach. This method isn't dependent on the distribution of the data and ignores the mean and the standard deviation, which are influenced by outliers.

As said before, to determine the outlier values, refer to the **IQR** given by the difference between the 25th percentile and the 75th percentile—that is, the amplitude of the range within which it falls. These 50% of observations occupy the central positions in the ordered series of data. An outlier is a value with positive deviation from the 75th percentile greater than two times the IQR or, symmetrically, a value with a negative deviation from the 25th percentile (in absolute value) greater than two times the IQR.

Practically, an outlier value is either of these two:

$$< (25th percentile) - (1.5 * IQR)$$

$$> (75th percentile) + (1.5 * IQR)$$

To calculate the percentiles, we'll use the `pandas.DataFrame.quantile()` function, which returns values at the given **quantile** over the requested axis:

$$Q1 = DataScaled.\,quantile(0.25)$$
$$Q3 = DataScaled.\,quantile(0.75)$$

IQR is given by the difference between the 25th percentile and the 75th percentile:

$$IQR = Q3 - Q1$$

Finally, we print the `IQR` for all columns in the dataset:

```
print(IQR)
```

The following are the results:

```
Cement     0.360731
BFS        0.397885
FLA        0.591054
Water      0.216367
SP         0.315528
CA         0.283140
FA         0.229303
Age        0.134615
CCS        0.277114
dtype: float64
```

Now, we have to remove the outliers from the scaled dataset:

```
DataScaledOut = DataScaled[~((DataScaled < (Q1 - 1.5 * IQR)) | (DataScaled
> (Q3 + 1.5 * IQR))).any(axis=1)]
DataScaledOut.shape
```

In the first line, we've created a new dataset (`DataScaledOut`) by inserting only the lines that don't respect the conditions included in brackets (outlier detection conditions). In the second row, the shape of the new dataset is displayed, as follows:

```
(925, 9)
```

It's changed from 1,029 rows to 925, so 104 rows have been removed. We evaluate the changes made by comparing the boxplots related to the two conditions, with outliers and without outliers:

```
import matplotlib.pyplot as plt
plt.figure(1)
plt.subplot(121)
sns.boxplot(data = DataScaled)plt.title("Data with outliers")
plt.subplot(122)
sns.boxplot(data = DataScaledOut)
plt.title("Data without outliers")
```

The graphs are shown in the following (the boxplot with outliers is on the left and the boxplot without outliers is on the right):

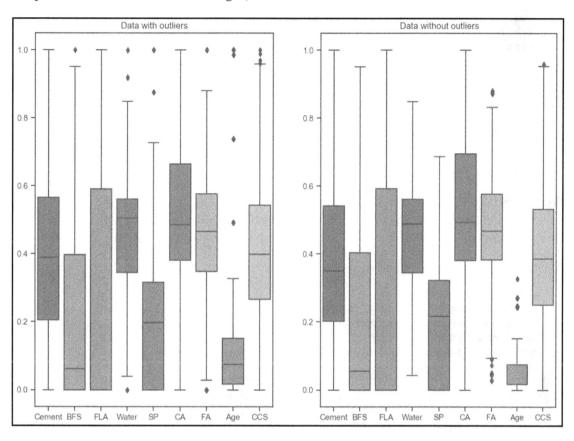

The graph on the left has a larger number of possible outliers, confirming that the removal operation of the outliers was successful. At this point, we can repeat the previous operations to build a new model, this time based on the data in which the outliers were removed. Let's start with the subdivision of the dataset into predictors and response:

```
Predictors2 = pd.DataFrame(DataScaledOut.iloc[:,:8])
Response2 = pd.DataFrame(DataScaledOut.iloc[:,8])
```

Now, we have to split the two DataFrames:

```
Pred_train2, Pred_test2, Resp_train2, Resp_test2 =
train_test_split(Predictors2,Response2, test_size = 0.30, random_state = 1)
print(Pred_train2.shape)
print(Pred_test2.shape)
print(Resp_train2.shape)
print(Resp_test2.shape)
```

The following results are returned:

```
(647, 8)
(278, 8)
(647, 1)
(278, 1)
```

So, the starting `Predictors2` DataFrame is split into two datasets, having 647 rows (`Pred_train2`) and 278 rows (`Pred_test2`); a similar subdivision was made for `Response2`.

Let's move on to build the model:

```
model = Sequential()
model.add(Dense(20, input_dim=8, activation='relu'))
model.add(Dense(10, activation='relu'))
model.add(Dense(10, activation='relu'))
model.add(Dense(1, activation='linear'))
```

The same architecture used in the *Keras deep neural network model* section were just adopted. Now, we need to configure the learning process through the `compile()` method:

```
model.compile(optimizer='adam',loss='mean_squared_error',metrics=['accuracy'])
```

To train the model, the `fit ()` method is used as follows:

```
model.fit(Pred_train, Resp_train, epochs=1000, verbose=1)
```

The following screenshot shows the `loss` and the `accuracy` at the end of each training epoch:

```
Epoch 990/1000
647/647 [==============================] - 0s 70us/step - loss: 0.0022 - acc: 0.0015
Epoch 991/1000
647/647 [==============================] - 0s 70us/step - loss: 0.0022 - acc: 0.0015
Epoch 992/1000
647/647 [==============================] - 0s 65us/step - loss: 0.0021 - acc: 0.0015
Epoch 993/1000
647/647 [==============================] - 0s 71us/step - loss: 0.0021 - acc: 0.0015
Epoch 994/1000
647/647 [==============================] - 0s 66us/step - loss: 0.0022 - acc: 0.0015
Epoch 995/1000
647/647 [==============================] - 0s 65us/step - loss: 0.0022 - acc: 0.0015
Epoch 996/1000
647/647 [==============================] - 0s 68us/step - loss: 0.0023 - acc: 0.0015
Epoch 997/1000
647/647 [==============================] - 0s 65us/step - loss: 0.0023 - acc: 0.0015
Epoch 998/1000
647/647 [==============================] - 0s 71us/step - loss: 0.0022 - acc: 0.0015
Epoch 999/1000
647/647 [==============================] - 0s 65us/step - loss: 0.0021 - acc: 0.0015
Epoch 1000/1000
647/647 [==============================] - 0s 63us/step - loss: 0.0022 - acc: 0.0015
```

To print a summary of the model, simply type the following:

```
model.summary()
```

The following are the results:

Layer (type)	Output Shape	Param #
dense_41 (Dense)	(None, 20)	180
dense_42 (Dense)	(None, 10)	210
dense_43 (Dense)	(None, 10)	110
dense_44 (Dense)	(None, 1)	11

Total params: 511
Trainable params: 511
Non-trainable params: 0

To evaluate the performance of the model, we'll calculate the coefficient of determination (R-squared) once again. First, we calculate the estimated target values:

```
Y_predKM2 = model.predict(Pred_test2)
```

Then, we calculate R-squared:

```
print('Coefficient of determination of Keras Model without outlier')
print(r2_score(Resp_test2, Y_predKM2))
```

The following result is returned:

```
Coefficient of determination of Keras Model without outlier
0.8938877269263837
```

Through the removal of the outliers, we obtained a performance improvement confirmed by the value of R-squared, which passed from 0.87 to 0.89 approximately. Finally, to appreciate the improvements obtained, we can compare the two models:

```
plt.figure(1)
plt.subplot(121)
plt.scatter(Resp_test,Y_predKM)
plt.plot([0, 1], [0, 1], linewidth=2)
plt.title("Data with outliers")
plt.subplot(122)
plt.scatter(Resp_test2, Y_predKM2)
plt.plot([0, 1], [0, 1], linewidth=2)
plt.title("Data without outliers")
```

In the following screenshot, the actual and predicted values are reported on the two axes; on analyzing ,it's possible to check how the data is arranged. To help with the analysis, the bisector of the quadrant has been traced:

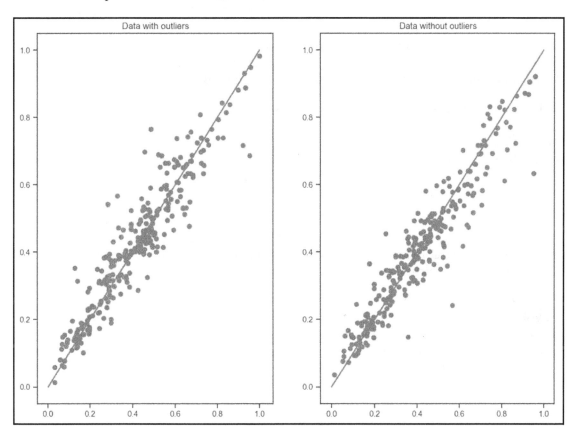

In our case, the difference between the two models is so slight that the differences can't easily be appreciated. The confirmation remains that the coefficient of determination has improved in the model without outliers.

Summary

In this chapter, we've learned the basic concepts of multilayer neural networks and how to implement it in them Keras environment. To begin, the essential elements of an artificial neural network were analyzed. ANNs are mathematical models able to simulate the usual activities of the human brain. A neural network is composed of layers; neurons and connections between the neurons are arranged in different layers. Changing the weights of these connections determines the learning ability of a neural network.

Multilayer neural networks are neural networks composed of many hidden levels (at least two) organized hierarchically. Hierarchical organization allows you to share and reuse information. Along the hierarchy, you can select specific features and discard unnecessary details in order to maximize the invariance. Many variations of multilayer neural networks were introduced: convolutional neural networks, recurrent neural networks, deep belief networks, and restricted Boltzmann machines.

Then, an example of a multilayered artificial network was addressed. We learned how to implement a model that allows us to calculate the compressive strength of the concrete according to the ingredients used in the mixture. Finally, we saw how to remove outliers to improve the performance of the model.

In the next chapter, we'll learn the basics of convolutional neural networks and discover convolution layer concepts. We'll learn the role of rectified linear units in the Keras network architecture and understand the use of pooling layers to reduce the spatial size. We'll also understand how convolutional neural networks continuously reduce the data step-by-step until you get a single result.

5
Fashion Article Recognition Using Convolutional Neural Networks

Object recognition is the ability to find a specific object in a sequence of images or videos. This task is performed automatically by human beings, even in particularly complex scenarios. For machines, it represents the challenges of the future. In convolutional neural networks, the fields of different neurons are partially overlapped so that they cover the entire field of view altogether. The response of a single neuron to stimuli taking place in its receptive field can be mathematically approximated by a convolution operation. A CNN is a particular type of ANN, which used above all other models for the analysis of images and the application of graphic filters. CNNs eliminate the need for the manual extraction of features, as these are learned directly from CNN. They produce state-of-the-art recognition results. They can be retrained for new recognition tasks, allowing preexisting networks to be exploited. In this chapter, a convolutional neural network will be trained so that it can solve pattern recognition problems. In this chapter, the following topics will be covered:

- Understanding computer vision concepts
- Convolutional neural networks
- Common CNN architecture
- Implementing a CNN for object recognition
- Using Keras in the CNN model
- Exploring the model's results

By the end of this chapter, we'll have learned about the basics of convolutional neural networks, including convolution layer concepts. We will also learn about the role of rectified linear units in the Keras network architecture, understand the use of pooling layers to reduce the spatial size of the output, and understand how convolutional neural networks continuously reduce data until a single result is obtained.

Understanding computer vision concepts

Vision is perhaps the most important sense for human beings. It allows you to interact with the three-dimensional world, allowing for the recognition and location of objects in a scene; more generally, it allows us to perceive the rapid changes that take place in our surrounding environment. Of all of our sensory abilities, vision is widely recognized as the one with the greatest potential. Our eyes collect a band of electromagnetic radiation, which is rebounded on different surfaces and comes from different light sources, while the brain processes this information by forming the picture of the scene as we perceive it.

Computer vision is a discipline that studies how to enable computers to understand and interpret visual information that's present in images or videos. It also deals with the analysis of numerical images on the computer. A computer processes images of a real scene that's been captured by one or more cameras to obtain useful information that will be used to make decisions automatically or semi-automatically. Through this technology, it is possible to construct systems that are capable of making decisions, starting from a description of the scene extrapolated from images/videos; inferring the 3D world from digital images; and recognizing objects, scenes, and context from digital images. Some examples of computer vision applications are as follows:

- Industrial automation and inspection
- Automobile traffic management
- Image retrieval based on content
- Automobile driver assistance
- Pedestrian tracking
- 3D city modeling from photos

A classic problem in artificial vision is to determine whether or not the image contains certain objects (object recognition) or activities. This problem can be solved effectively and without difficulty for specific objects in specific situations, for example, the recognition of specific geometric figures such as polyhedron, and the recognition of faces or handwritten characters. Things get complicated in the case of arbitrary objects in arbitrary situations.

Computer vision analyzes the environment from different viewpoints. This can be summarized into the following three fields:

- **Recognition**: One or more stored objects can be traced back to generic classes, usually together with their 2D or 3D position in the scene.
- **Identification**: A specific instance of a class is identified. This happens in identifying a face, fingerprint, or specific vehicle.

- **Detection**: The image is scanned until the identification of a specific condition is found, for example, in the identification of possible abnormal cells or tissues in medical images.

Another typical task is the reconstruction of a scenario: more 2D images try to reconstruct a 3D model of the scenario. In the simplest case, we are talking about a set of single points in a 3D space or entire surface. Generally, it is important to find the fundamental matrix that represents the common points coming from different images.

In general, the problems that computer vision seeks to solve concern the recognition and identification of people or objects. Supported by advanced machine learning techniques, its aim is to provide a complex representation of the acquired scenes and the recognition of specific patterns. The following diagram shows a computer vision system that's able to detect people on pedestrian crossings:

This sector, along with multiple application implications, has been the subject of rapid development in recent years, both in terms of acquisition techniques (optics, sensors, and scanners) and processing algorithms, which can rely on ever increasing computing power. Computer vision represents a technology that's characterized by great versatility, which is linked to the great amount of information that the images carry, and the possibility of extrapolating only necessary data for the specific application. Images store data that's coming from different directions, which is conveyed by the rays of light emitted or reflected by the people. On the other hand, the accuracy of the results can be strongly influenced by factors ranging from the resolution of the camera to the configuration of the algorithms.

Computer vision finds more and more space in the automation of industrial processes, in quality control, in military and aerospace applications, in building engineering, and in architecture and surveillance. Self-localization and environmental reconstruction are the themes of computer vision, and these present greater similarities with the functions of our visual apparatus. Given a sequence of frames of the same environment, which is made with continuity from a moving camera or camera, the self-tracking algorithm reproduces the trajectory of the device in the coordinates of an arbitrary reference.

Computer vision systems generally articulate on the following three levels of abstraction:

- **Low level**: Given an input image, a new one is produced (image reconstruction). It enhances some visual characteristics, in particular the extraction of geometric primitives, shape, depth, dimension, and contours of objects.
- **Medium level**: At this level, computer vision deals with the extraction of structural information from the image that was produced at a lower level and works on images to extract structural information.
- **High level**: Here, computer vision works on the information coming from the medium level vision to compose a semantic model of the scene. The aim of this level is to arrive at a form of understanding of the observed scene, such as the recognition of objects and spatial relations between objects.

The standard configuration of a computer vision model is represented with one or more cameras connected to a computer that must automatically interpret the images of a real scene, thus obtaining useful information for navigation, manipulation, and recognition.

Convolutional neural networks

As detailed in Chapter 4, *Concrete Quality Prediction Using Deep Neural Networks*, **artificial neural networks (ANNs)** are inspired from biological neural networks: starting from the mechanisms regulating natural neural networks, they intended to simulate human thinking. They are used to estimate or approximate functions that may depend on a large number of inputs, many of which are often unknown. ANNs are generally introduced as interconnected neuron systems, among which an exchange of messages takes place. Each connection has a related weight; the value of the weight is adjustable based on experience, and this makes neural networks an instrument that's adaptable to the various types of input and having the ability to learn, as depicted in the following diagram:

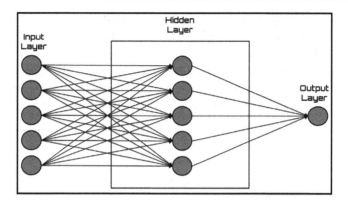

ANNs define the neuron as a central processing unit (CPU), which performs a mathematical operation to generate one output from a set of input values. The output of a neuron is a function of the weighted sum of the inputs plus the bias. Each neuron performs a very simple operation that involves activation if the total amount of signal received exceeds an activation threshold. In the preceding diagram, a simple ANN architecture is shown: essentially, **convolutional neural networks** (**CNNs**) are ANNs. In fact, just like the latter, CNNs are made up of neurons that are connected to one another by weighted branches (weight); the training parameters of the networks are once again the weight and the bias.

In CNNs, the connection pattern between neurons is inspired by the structure of the visual cortex in the animal world. The individual neurons that are present in this part of the brain (visual cortex) respond to certain stimuli in a narrow region of the observation, called the **receptive field**. The receptive fields of different neurons are partially overlapped to cover the entire field of vision. The response of a single neuron to stimuli taking place in its receptive field can be mathematically approximated by a convolution operation.

Everything related to the training of a neural network, that is, forward/backward propagation and updating the weight, also applies in this context; moreover, a whole CNN always uses a single function of differentiable cost. However, CNNs make a specific assumption that their input has a precise data structure, such as an image, and this allows them to take specific properties in their architecture to better process such data.

Normal neural networks are stratified with an **Fully Connected** (**FC**) architecture, where every neuron of each layer is connected to all the neurons of the previous layer (excluding bias neurons). In general, these do not scale well when there's an increase in the size of input data.

Let's look at a practical example: suppose we want to analyze an image to detect objects. To begin, let's see how the image is processed. As we already know, in the coding of an image, it is divided into a grid of small squares, each of which represents a pixel. At this point, to encode the color images, it will be enough to identify a certain number of shades and different color gradations for each square. Then, we can code each one by means of an appropriate sequence of bits. The following is a diagram of a simple image encoding:

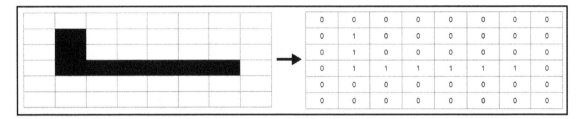

The number of squares in the grid defines the resolution of the image. For example, an image that is 1,600 pixels wide and 800 pixels high (1,600 x 800) contains (multiplied) 1,280,000 pixels, or 1.2 megapixels. Here, we must multiply the three color channels, finally obtaining 1,600 x 800 x 3 = 3,840,000. Therefore, each neuron that's completely connected in the first hidden layer would have 3,840,000 weights. This is only for a single neuron; considering the whole network, this would certainly become unmanageable!

CNNs are designed to recognize visual patterns in images – these are represented by pixels and require zero or very limited preprocessing. They are able to recognize extremely variable patterns, such as freehand writing and images representing the real world.

Typically, a CNN consists of several alternative convolution and subsampling levels (pooling), followed by one or more FC final levels in the case of classification. The following diagram shows a classic image processing pipeline:

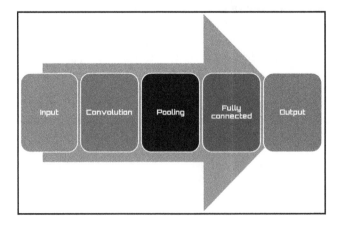

To solve problems in the real world, these steps can be combined and stacked as often as necessary. For example, you can have two, three, or even more layers of convolution. You can enter all the pooling you want to reduce the size of the data. As we stated previously, different types of levels are typically used in a CNN. Some of these have training parameters (weight and bias), while other layers simply implement a fixed function. In the following sections, the main ones will be covered.

Convolution layer

This is the main type of layer; the use of one or more of these layers in a CNN is essential. The parameters of a convolutional layer, in practice, relate to a set of workable filters. Unlike generic neural networks, convolutional layers have neurons organized in three dimensions, such as **width**, **height**, and **depth**. These are shown in the following diagram:

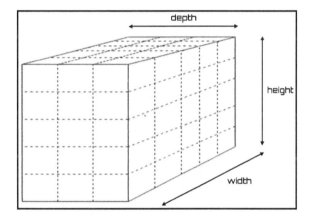

Each filter is spatially small (along the width and height dimensions), but it extends over the entire depth of the input volume to which it is applied.

During forward propagation, each filter is translated—or more precisely, convolved— with the width and height of the input volume, producing a two-dimensional activation map (or `feature map`) for that filter. As the filter is moved along the input area, a scalar product operation is performed between the values of the filter and those of the input portion to which it is applied.

Intuitively, the goal of the network will be to learn activated filters in the presence of some specific type of functionality in a given spatial region of the input. The queuing of all these feature maps (for all filters), and the depth dimension, form the output volume of a convolutional layer. Each element of this volume can be interpreted as the output of a neuron that observes only a small region of the input and which shares its parameters with the other neurons in the same feature map. This is because these values all come from the application of the same filter.

The mathematical steps for filtering are as follows:

1. Line up the feature and the image patch.
2. Multiply each image pixel by the corresponding feature pixel.
3. Add them up.
4. Divide each sum by the total number of pixels in the feature.

In summary, let's focus our attention on the following points:

- **Local receptive field**: Each neuron of a layer is (completely) connected to a small region of the input (called a local receptive field); each connection learns a weight.
- **Shared weights**: Since the interesting features (edge, blob, and so on) can be found anywhere in the image, the neurons of the same layer share the weights. This means that all of the neurons of the same layer will recognize the same feature, even if they have been placed at different points of the input.
- **Convolution**: The same weight map is applied to different positions. The convolution output is called a **feature map**.

Each filter captures a feature that's present in the previous layer. So, to extract different features, we need to train multiple convolutional filters. Each filter returns a feature map that highlights different characteristics.

Pooling layers

These layers are periodically inserted into a network to reduce the spatial size (width and height) of current representations, as well as volumes in a specific network stage; this serves to reduce the number of parameters and the computational time of the network. It also monitors overfitting. A pooling layer operates on each depth slice of the input volume independently to resize it spatially.

For each feature obtained in the convolutional step, we build up a matrix and now find the maximum in each chosen matrix to shrink the entire input. The steps are as follows:

1. Pick a window size (usually 2 or 3).
2. Pick a stride moving range of pixels (usually 2).
3. Slide the window across the filtered images.
4. For each window, we take the maximum value.

For example, this technique partitions an input image into a set of squares, and for each of the resulting regions, it returns the maximum value as output. CNNs also use pooling layers that are located immediately after the convolutional layers. A pooling layer divides input into regions and selects a single representative value (max pooling and average pooling).

The max pool layer selects the maximum number of features that have been detected by the convolution layers that precede it. The output checks whether a hypothetical feature is present in a region of the previous layers or not, but not exactly where. The idea is therefore to allow the successive layers to work on larger sections of the data. Max pooling allows for faster convergence rates, hence allowing us to select higher invariant features that improve generalization performance.

The use of a pooling layer has the following advantages:

- Reduces the calculations of subsequent layers
- Increases the robustness of the features with respect to spatial position

It is based on the concept that, once a certain feature has been identified, its precise position in the input is not as important as its approximate position in relation to the other features. In the typical CNN architecture, convolution layers and pooling layers are repeatedly alternated.

Rectified linear units

Rectified linear units (ReLUs) play the role of a neuronal activation function in neural networks. They are often used several times within the same network, usually after each convolutional layer. A ReLU layer is composed of neurons that apply the function $f(x) = max\ (0, x)$. These layers increase the non-linearity of the network and, at the same time, do not modify the receiving fields of convolution levels. The function of the ReLUs is preferred over others, such as the hyperbolic tangent or the `sigmoid` function since, in comparison to these, it leads to a much faster training process without significantly affecting the generalization accuracy.

In the following diagram, a ReLU function is shown:

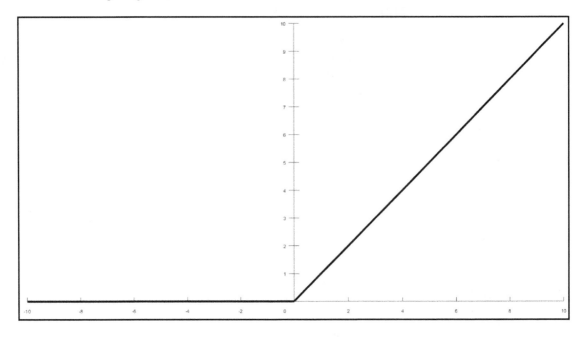

The ReLU layers allow you to train a network much faster and with similar performance. These types of layer have no settable parameter, so a fixed function is performed. In addition to having no settable parameters, these layers do not even have workable parameters. Layers without traversable parameters have a simpler backward propagation: the errors calculated up to that point, which arrive from the next layer, are passed back to the layer before the one that's considered.

Fully connected layer

This type of layer is exactly the same as any of the layers of a classical ANN with a FC architecture. In an FC layer, each neuron is connected to all the neurons of the previous layer, specifically to their activations.

This type of layer, unlike what has been seen so far in CNNs, does not use the property of local connectivity. An FC layer is connected to the entire input volume, and therefore, as you can imagine, there will be many connections. The only settable parameter of this type of layer is the number of K neurons that make it up. What basically defines an FC layer is as follows: connecting its K neurons with all the input volume and calculating the activation of each of its K neurons.

In fact, its output will be a single *1 x 1 x K* vector, containing the calculated activations. The fact that after using a single FC layer you switch from an input volume (organized in three dimensions) to a single output vector (in a single dimension) suggests that after applying an FC layer, no more convoluted layers can be used. The main function of FC layers in the context of CNNs is to carry out a sort of grouping of the information obtained up to that moment and expressing it with a single number (the activation of one of its neurons), which will be used in subsequent calculations for the final classification.

Structure of a CNN

After analyzing every component of a CNN in detail, it's time to see the general structure of a CNN as a whole. For example, starting from the images as input layers, there will be a certain series of convolutional layers interspersed with a ReLU layer and, when necessary, the standardization and pooling layers. Finally, there will be a series of FC layers before the output layer.

CNNs have the following two types of neurons:

- **Processing neurons**: These process a limited portion of the image through a convolution function. Their task is to extract features from input data.
- **Aggregation or pooling neurons**: These aggregate the input and reduces the volume by means of a subsampling in order to streamline the processing for the subsequent layers.

The set of output values of a layer allows you to reconstruct an intermediate image, which will serve as a basis for the next level.

Here is an example of a CNN architecture:

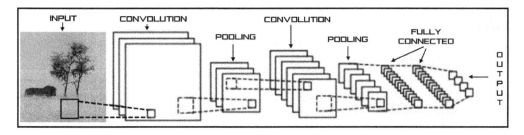

The basic idea is to start with a large image and continuously reduce the data step by step until you get a single result. The more convolution passages you have, the more the neural network will be able to understand and process complex functions.

The structure of a simple CNN can be summarized into the following elements:

- An input layer with the task of acquiring the input elements, such as images
- A series of convolutional layers, interspersed with a ReLU layer and, when necessary, by pooling layers
- A series of fully connected layers
- An output layer that returns the results

Recent studies have shown that the FC layers are not very essential, but for now it is assumed that this is the structure of a normal CNN.

Common CNN architecture

These networks have been widely used for various purposes; in the following sections, we will look at some common examples of the use of CNN networks in real-life cases.

LeNet-5

LeNet-5 is a convolutional network that was designed by Le Cun in the 1998 for handwritten and machine-printed character recognition. It was the first successful application of convolutional networks. This **CNN** classifies handwritten numbers, which is why it has been widely applied by banks around the world to recognize handwritten numbers on digitized bank checks in 32 x 32 pixel grayscale images.

The following diagram shows the LeNet-5 architecture, as published by the authors (LeCun, Y., Bottou, L., Bengio, Y., and Haffner, P., 1998. *Gradient-based learning applied to document recognition.* Proceedings of the IEEE, 86(11), pp.2,278-2,324.):

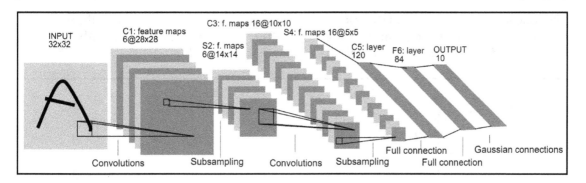

As we can see from the preceding diagram, it is a very simple architecture – in fact, it is used to teach people about CNNs. LeNet-5 consists of two groups of convolutional layers interspersed with pooling layers, then a flattened convolutional layer, two completely connected layers, and finally the output state.

AlexNet

AlexNet is a convolutional network with eight layers; the first five are convolutional layers, some of which are followed by maximum levels of pooling, and the last three are completely connected layers. It uses the ReLU activation function, which, as mentioned previously, shows better training performance compared to `tanh` and `sigmoid`. AlexNet was originally written with Compute Unified Device Architecture (CUDA) to work with GPU support.

AlexNet won the **ImageNet Large-Scale Visual Recognition Challenge (ILSVRC)**, an international competition in the field of computer vision based on the ImageNet dataset, which contains more than a million images, accompanied by labels and designed specifically for benchmarking. After obtaining this prestigious award, he began the trend of the extensive use of CNNs in the computer vision field. 2012 was the first year in which victory went to an architecture based on CNN. In addition to the victory itself, the one that made the most noise in the computer vision community was the result achieved on the top five error, that is, the probability that, given an image, the correct label is not found among the five value predictions. AlexNet scored a 15.5% top five error, with a good 10.6 percentage point gap on the runner up, standing at 26.2%.

The following diagram shows the AlexNet architecture, as published by the authors (Krizhevsky, A., Sutskever, I. and Hinton, G.E., 2012. Imagenet classification with deep CNNs. In *Advances in neural information processing systems* (pp. 1,097-1,105)):

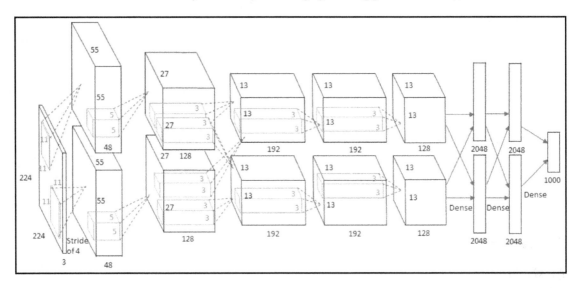

Compared to today's networks, AlexNet presents a relatively simple structure. As we've already mentioned, it consists of five convolution levels, pooling and dropout, and three fully connected levels.

ResNet

The **Residual Network** (**ResNet**) represents an architecture that, through the use of new and innovative types of blocks (known as **residual blocks**) and the concept of residual learning, has allowed researchers to reach depths unthinkable with the classic feedforward model due to the problem of the degradation of the gradient.

The following diagram shows the ResNet architecture, as published by the authors (He, K., Zhang, X., Ren, S. and Sun, J., 2016. Deep residual learning for image recognition. In *proceedings of the IEEE conference on computer vision and pattern recognition* (pp. 770-778)):

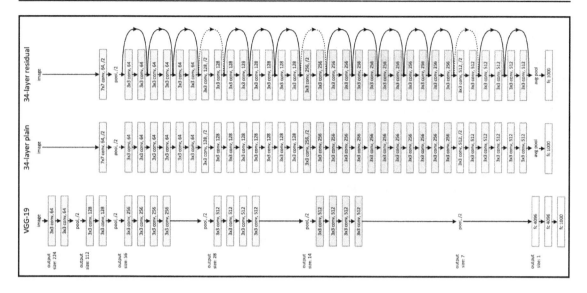

There are implementations with different depths, of which the deepest, in fact, counts as many as 152 levels. There is also a prototype with 1,202 levels, but it has achieved worse results due to overfitting. This architecture won ILSVRC 2015, with an error of 3.6%. To understand the value of this result, just think that the error generally achieved by a human being is around 5-10%, based on their skills and knowledge. Thanks to these results, the ResNet model is currently the state of the art in the field of computer vision.

VGG Net

Visual Geometry Group (VGG) Net represents a CNN architecture that was realized in 2014 and is characterized by a very simple but at the same time very deep structure. It contains no less than 19 levels, where only 3 x 3 convolutions are used with unit stride and padding, along with 2 x 2 pooling with stride two and three fully connected final levels. It has different configurations, of which the one with the best results has recorded a minimum error of 7.3% on the ImageNet dataset. The most important result that this network has brought in the field of CNN is to have shown that the key point for the improvement of performance is not represented by the increase in complexity of the network, but by the greater depth of it.

GoogleNet

GoogLeNet was built by overlaying inception layers to create a deep convolutional neuronal network. It is a parallel combination of convolutional filters, such as 1 x 1, 3 x 3, and 5 x 5. It is based on the assumption that 1 x 1 convolutions reduce the number of parameters. GoogLeNet won ILSVRC 2014.

 For further reference you can check the ResNet architecture, as published by the authors (Szegedy, C., Liu, W., Jia, Y., Sermanet, P., Reed, S., Anguelov, D., Erhan, D., Vanhoucke, V., and Rabinovich, A., 2015. Going deeper with convolutions. In *proceedings of the IEEE conference on computer vision and pattern recognition* (pp. 1-9)).

The idea of the inception layer is to cover a larger area, but also to maintain a fine resolution for small image information. Therefore, the idea is to convey in parallel different sizes from the most accurate detail (1 x 1) to a larger one (5 x 5).

Implementing a CNN for object recognition

Object recognition is the ability to find a specific object in a sequence of images or videos. Human beings are able to recognize different objects in images with little effort, despite the fact that the image of objects may vary. Furthermore, objects can be recognized, even when they are partially out of view. This task is still a challenge for computer vision in general.

For each object in an image, there are many interesting characteristics. These can be extracted so as to provide a description of the object. This description can then be used to identify this object when trying to locate it in a test image containing multiple objects. It is important that the set of characteristics extracted from the sample image is insensitive to image scale variations, disturbances, illumination, and geometric distortions, in order to make the recognition reliable. CNNs are particularly suited to this task by offering algorithms that can recognize objects with excellent performance.

`fashion-mnist` is a dataset of Zalando article images—consisting of a training set of 60,000 examples and a test set of 10,000 examples. Each example is a 28 x 28 grayscale image, associated with a label from 10 classes. It shares the same image size and structure of training and testing splits.

The `fashion-mnist` dataset was presented by the authors in the following paper: Xiao, H., Rasul, K. and Vollgraf, R., 2017. *fashion-mnist—a novel image dataset for benchmarking machine learning algorithms.* arXiv preprint arXiv:1708.07747.

The `fashion-mnist` dataset is freely available at the following URL: `https://github.com/zalandoresearch/fashion-mnist`.

There are 10 categories to classify in the `fashion-mnist` dataset, as follows:

Label	Description
0	T-shirt/top
1	Trouser
2	Pullover
3	Dress
4	Coat
5	Sandal
6	Shirt
7	Sneaker
8	Bag
9	Ankle boot

The following diagram shows a sample of images from the `fashion-mnist` dataset:

As anticipated, these are 28 x 28 pixel miniatures in grayscale. The different classes of images are already identifiable by sight. Now, we have to build an algorithm that allows the machine to do this too.

Exploratory analysis

The `fashion-mnist` dataset is already available in the `keras` library. Just load the appropriate library and then load the data:

```
from keras.datasets import fashion_mnist
```

At this point, we will load the data. The data is divided into input (*X*) and output (*Y*); the data was also split into the data we will use for `train` (training) so that we can test the model (test):

```
(XTrain, YTrain), (XTest, YTest) = fashion_mnist.load_data()
```

The following tuples are returned:

- XTrain, XTest: uint8 array of grayscale image data with shape (num_samples, 28, 28)
- YTrain, YTest: uint8 array of labels (integers in range 0-9) with shape (num_samples)

Now, let's check the size of the imported data by executing the following line:

```
print("X train shape:", XTrain.shape, "Y train shape:", YTrain.shape)
print("X test shape:", XTest.shape, "Y test shape:", YTest.shape)
```

The following results are returned:

```
X train shape: (60000, 28, 28) Y train shape: (60000,)
X test shape: (10000, 28, 28) Y test shape: (10000,)
```

As we've already mentioned, 60,000 examples are available for the training phase and 10,000 are available for the testing phase.

Let's check the contents of the numpy.ndarray objects that have been returned. We print an image and then read the class associated with it. To print the contents of a training data record, we use the imshow() function of the matplotlib library, as follows:

```
import matplotlib.pyplot as plt
plt.imshow(XTrain[5])
```

The following screenshot is printed:

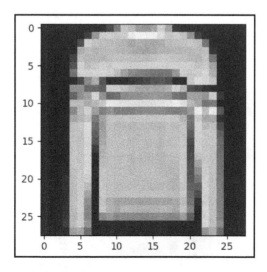

Now, we will print the class associated with that image:

```
print(YTrain[5])
```

The following result is printed:

```
2
```

The label-description table shows that class 2 corresponds to pullover, which the one is shown in the previous image. The procedure that we've just followed is quite complicated; we will try to simplify it by printing both the image of the object and a label, as indicated in the label-description table that we saw previously. To do this, we start by creating a dictionary that contains the label-description pair according to this table, as follows:

```
LabelData = {
    0: 'T-shirt',
    1: 'Trouser',
    2: 'Pullover',
    3: 'Dress',
    4: 'Coat',
    5: 'Sandal',
    6: 'Shirt',
    7: 'Sneaker',
    8: 'Bag',
    9: 'AnkleBoot',
}
```

Now, we simply have to reprint the object by adding the label as the chart title:

```
plt.imshow(XTrain[5])
plt.title("(Object: " + str(LabelData[YTrain[5]]) + ")")
```

The following screenshot shows the result:

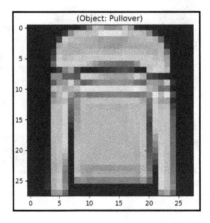

In this way, controlling the selected image and the associated label is easier. In fact, we immediately notice that it is a pullover. All of this will be useful when we perform automatic object recognition.

Before proceeding with the construction of the model, we must analyze the contents of the starting dataset. We have said that these are images of articles of clothing and accessories offered for sale by the Zalando online store. Let's try and see how the different classes are represented in the data – namely, we count the occurrences of each class in the data. We will do this for both the training and testing data, as follows:

```
import numpy as np
unique, counts = np.unique(YTrain, return_counts=True)
```

To obtain the count of the occurrences of each class, we used the numpy.unique () function. This function finds the unique elements of an array and returns the sorted unique elements of an array. There are three optional outputs in addition to the unique elements, such as the indices of the input array that give the unique values, the indices of the unique array that reconstruct the input array, and the number of times each unique value comes up in the input array. The return_counts parameter has been used: this is a boolean parameter (True, or False). If True, it also returns the number of times each unique item appears in the data. The following two values are returned:

- unique(ndarray): The sorted unique values
- counts(ndarray): The number of times each of the unique values comes up in the original array

To print a list with the number of occurrences for each class, we will use the dict() and zip() functions, as follows:

```
dict(zip(unique, counts))
```

The dict() function create a new dictionary. The zip() function make an iterator that aggregates elements from each of the iterables. This returns an iterator of tuples, where the ith tuple contains the ith element from each of the argument sequences or iterables. The iterator stops when the shortest input iterable is exhausted. The following result is returned (the XTrain data):

```
{0: 6000,
 1: 6000,
 2: 6000,
 3: 6000,
 4: 6000,
 5: 6000,
 6: 6000,
```

```
   7: 6000,
   8: 6000,
   9: 6000}
```

In the same way, we will proceed with the XTest dataset, as follows:

```
unique, counts = np.unique(YTest, return_counts=True)
print (dict(zip(unique, counts)))
```

The following result is returned (the XTest data):

```
{0: 1000,
 1: 1000,
 2: 1000,
 3: 1000,
 4: 1000,
 5: 1000,
 6: 1000,
 7: 1000,
 8: 1000,
 9: 1000}
```

By doing this, we have verified that the 10 classes are equally represented both in the data that we will use for the training and in those that we will use for the testing.

Data scaling

We said that the data at our disposal represents grayscale images: what do we find if we open a single record? For example, referring once again to the record number 5 (training data), we obtain the following matrix:

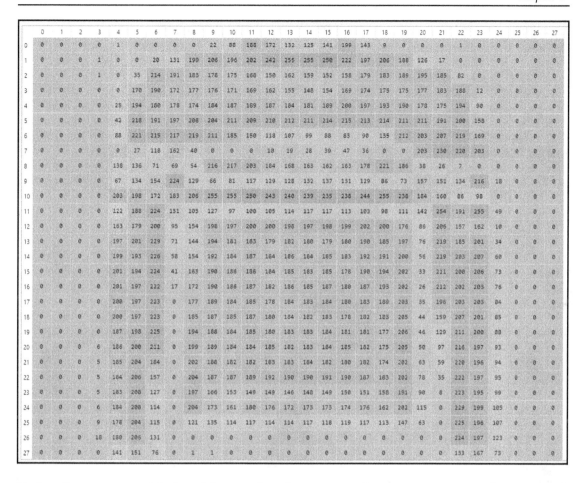

Each cell represents a pixel and the number that we can glimpse at represents the gray level in a range from 0 (black) to 255 (white). The data should be scaled.

Remember, it is a good practice to rescale the data before training a deep learning algorithm. With rescaling, data units are eliminated, allowing you to easily compare data from different locations.

In this case, we will use the min-max method (usually called **feature scaling**) to get all the scaled data in the range [0, 1]. The formula to achieve this is as follows:

$$x_{scaled} = \frac{x - x_{min}}{x_{max} - x_{min}}$$

In this case, the task is greatly simplified as it results in $x_{min} = 0$, and $x_{max} = 255$. So, to scale the data, just divide the data by `255.0`, as follows:

```
XTrain = XTrain / 255.0
XTest = XTest / 255.0
```

The information contained in the data remained unchanged; we only contained the differences between the different values. For further confirmation, we will show the first 20 images that are contained in the data for the training:

```
plt.figure(figsize=(10,10))
for i in range(20):
    plt.subplot(5,5,i+1)
    plt.xticks([])
    plt.yticks([])
    plt.grid(False)
    plt.imshow(XTrain[i], cmap=plt.cm.binary)
    plt.xlabel(LabelData[YTrain[i]])
```

The following screenshot shows the results:

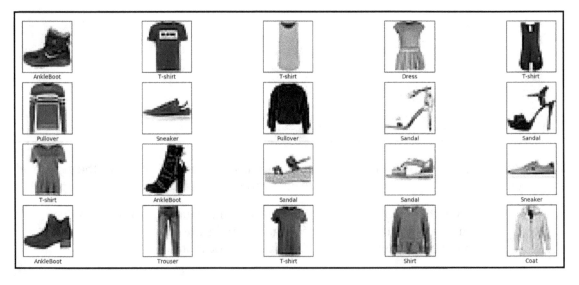

Now, we can focus on building the model.

Using Keras in the CNN model

After exploring the dataset, it's time to build the CNN model so that it can recognize the articles of clothing and accessories offered for sale by the Zalando online store from images recorded in the dataset. We have just prepared the data. We split the starting data into two sets: **training set** and **test set**. The training set will be used to train a classification model and the test set will be used to test the model's performance. To build a model, we will use the Keras `Sequential` model. Let's start by importing the necessary libraries, as follows:

```
from keras.models import Sequential
from keras.utils import np_utils
from keras.layers import Flatten
from keras.layers import Dense, MaxPool2D, Conv2D
from keras.initializers import Constant
```

The functionality of these libraries will be deepened when we use them in the continuation of the discussion. However, one last action needs to be performed on the data. Our aim is to set up a convolutional model, which, as mentioned in *Convolution layer* section, unlike generic neural networks, have neurons organized into three dimensions such as width, height, and depth. It is therefore necessary to transform the dataset into four dimensions, such as the number of samples, depth, width, and height, as follows:

```
XTrain = XTrain.reshape(XTrain.shape[0], 1, 28, 28)
XTest = XTest.reshape(XTest.shape[0], 1, 28, 28)
```

Then, we have to convert one-dimensional class arrays (output) into 10-dimensional class matrices:

```
YTrain = np_utils.to_categorical(YTrain, 10)
YTest = np_utils.to_categorical(YTest, 10)
```

Now, we can really work on the model. We will use the `Sequential` model here, which is a linear stack of layers. We can create a `Sequential` model by passing a list of layer instances to the constructor. To start, we must set the model type, as follows:

```
CNNModel = Sequential()
```

As indicated in the preceding line, the first layer we are going to add will be a convolutional layer, as follows:

```
CNNModel.add(Conv2D(32, kernel_size=(2, 2),
        padding='same',
        bias_initializer=Constant(0.02),
        kernel_initializer='random_uniform',
        input_shape=(1, 28, 28)
    )
)
```

`Conv2D` adds a 2D convolution layer (spatial convolution over images). This layer creates a convolution kernel that is convolved with the layer input to produce a tensor of outputs. When using this layer as the first layer in a model, provide the `input_shape` keyword argument to load the input data. The following arguments are passed:

- 32: Filters – the dimensionality of the output space (the number of output filters in the convolution).
- `kernel_size = (2, 2)`: This is an integer or tuple/list of two integers, specifying the height and width of the 2D convolution window.
- `padding='same'`: This is one of `valid` or `same`. The `same` padding means the size of output feature-maps are the same as the input feature maps.
- `bias_initializer=Constant(0.02)`: This is the initializer for the bias vector. A constant initializer generates tensors that have been initialized to a constant value (0.02).
- `kernel_initializer='random_uniform'`: This is the initializer for the kernel weights matrix. `random_uniform` generates tensors with a uniform distribution.
- `input_shape=(1, 28, 28)`: The 4D tensor with shape: (batch, channels, rows, cols). It is the shape of the image that's presented to the CNN.

The layer output is a 4D tensor with shape: (batch, filters, `new_rows`, `new_cols`).

We previously stated that in a CNN there are a series of convolutional layers, interspersed by pooling layers. This is because it is necessary to add layers that process a limited portion of the image through a convolution function, and layers with the task of aggregating the input and reducing the volume by means of a subsampling in order to streamline the processing for the subsequent layers. Now, we will add a ReLu layer, as follows:

```
CNNModel.add(Activation('relu'))
```

ReLU plays the role of a neuronal activation function in neural networks and is used several times within the same network, often after each convolutional layer. So, after the first convolutional layer, it is necessary to add a pooling layer, as follows:

```
CNNModel.add(MaxPool2D(padding='same'))
```

MaxPooling2D is a max pooling operation that's used for spatial data. Only the padding parameter has been passed. We will now add a further convolutional layer:

```
CNNModel.add(Conv2D(64,kernel_size=(2, 2),
        padding='same',
        bias_initializer=Constant(0.02),
        kernel_initializer='random_uniform'
    )
)
```

The same structure for the previous convolutional layer was adopted, except for the value of the filters, which has changed. Let's add an activation layer again, as follows:

```
CNNModel.add(Activation('relu'))
```

Activation can either be used through an Activation layer, or through the activation argument, which is supported by all forward layers. Let's add another pooling layer, as follows:

```
CNNModel.add(MaxPool2D(padding='same'))
```

We will now add a Flatten() layer, as follows:

```
CNNModel.add(Flatten())
```

The Flatten layer flattens the input: it does not affect the batch size. It is used without parameters. The use of this layer is necessary so that we can use completely connected layers after some convolutional layers. Fully connected layers do not have a local limitation such as convolutional levels. Therefore, it is possible to combine all the local features found in the previous convolutional layers. This operation is performed by the Flatten layer, which flattens input data into a vector. Now, we can add the fully connected layer, as follows:

```
CNNModel.add(Dense(128,
        activation='relu',
        bias_initializer=Constant(0.02),
        kernel_initializer='random_uniform',
    )
)
```

Fully connected layers are defined using the `Dense` class. Here, we passed the following four parameters:

- `128`: 128 (units) is a positive integer representing the dimensionality of the output space. This denotes the number of neurons in the level.
- `activation = ' relu '`: This parameter is used to set the activation function (the ReLU activation function).
- `bias_initializer=Constant(0.02)`: This is the initializer for the bias vector. A constant initializer generates tensors that have been initialized to a constant value (`0.02`).
- `kernel_initializer='random_uniform'`: This is the initializer for the `kernel` weights matrix. `random_uniform` generates tensors with a uniform distribution.

Let's add the final layer, as follows:

```
CNNModel.add(Dense(10, activation='softmax'))
```

This is a fully connected layer, and the following parameters are passed:

- `10`: This parameter represents the number of classes.
- `activation = 'softmax'`: This is an activation function for the final layer. The `softmax` activation is used, which is a standard for multiclass classification.

To print a summary of the CNN model, simply type the following line:

```
model.summary()
```

The preceding line generates the following results:

```
Layer (type)                 Output Shape              Param #
=================================================================
conv2d_20 (Conv2D)           (None, 1, 28, 32)         3616
_____
activation_6 (Activation)    (None, 1, 28, 32)         0
_____
max_pooling2d_14 (MaxPooling (None, 1, 14, 32)         0
_____
conv2d_21 (Conv2D)           (None, 1, 14, 64)         8256
_____
activation_7 (Activation)    (None, 1, 14, 64)         0
_____
max_pooling2d_15 (MaxPooling (None, 1, 7, 64)          0
_____
flatten_7 (Flatten)          (None, 448)               0
_____
dense_13 (Dense)             (None, 128)               57472
_____
dense_14 (Dense)             (None, 10)                1290
=================================================================
Total params: 70,634
Trainable params: 70,634
Non-trainable params: 0
```

The structure of the CNN has finally been set: we can proceed.

Exploring the model's results

Before training a model, you need to configure the learning process. This is done via the `compile()` method, as follows:

```
CNNModel.compile(optimizer='adam',loss='categorical_crossentropy',metrics=[
'accuracy'])
```

The following three arguments are passed:

- `optimizer='adam'`: An algorithm for first-order gradient-based optimization of stochastic objective functions, based on adaptive estimates of lower-order moments.
- `loss='categorical_crossentropy'`: We have used the `categorical_crossentropy` argument here. When using `categorical_crossentropy`, your targets should be in categorical format (we have 10 classes; the target for each sample must be a 10-dimensional vector that is all-zeros except for a one at the index corresponding to the class of the sample).
- `metrics=['accuracy']`: A metric is a function that is used to evaluate the performance of your model during training and testing.

To train the model, the `fit()` method is used, as follows:

```
CNNModel.fit(XTrain, YTrain, epochs=1000,batch_size=32, verbose=1)
```

The following five arguments are passed:

- `XTrain`: This is an array of input training data.
- `YTrain`: This is an array of target (label) data.
- `epochs=1000`: This is the number of epochs to train the model. An epoch is an iteration over the entire x and y data provided.
- `batch_size=32`: This is the number of samples per gradient update.
- `verbose=1`: This is an integer, either 0, 1, or 2. Verbosity mode: 0 = silent, 1 = progress bar, 2 = one line per epoch.

When the `fit()` function is used, the loss and the accuracy at the end of each training epoch are displayed, as shown in the following screenshot:

```
Epoch 990/1000
60000/60000 [==============================] - 17s 275us/step - loss: 0.0200 - acc: 0.9955
Epoch 991/1000
60000/60000 [==============================] - 17s 277us/step - loss: 0.0220 - acc: 0.9951
Epoch 992/1000
60000/60000 [==============================] - 17s 277us/step - loss: 0.0231 - acc: 0.9949
Epoch 993/1000
60000/60000 [==============================] - 16s 275us/step - loss: 0.0220 - acc: 0.9949
Epoch 994/1000
60000/60000 [==============================] - 17s 276us/step - loss: 0.0248 - acc: 0.9944
Epoch 995/1000
60000/60000 [==============================] - 17s 276us/step - loss: 0.0177 - acc: 0.9958
Epoch 996/1000
60000/60000 [==============================] - 17s 276us/step - loss: 0.0230 - acc: 0.9946
Epoch 997/1000
60000/60000 [==============================] - 16s 275us/step - loss: 0.0242 - acc: 0.9950
Epoch 998/1000
60000/60000 [==============================] - 16s 275us/step - loss: 0.0261 - acc: 0.9944
Epoch 999/1000
60000/60000 [==============================] - 17s 275us/step - loss: 0.0208 - acc: 0.9954
Epoch 1000/1000
60000/60000 [==============================] - 17s 276us/step - loss: 0.0245 - acc: 0.9948
```

To evaluate the performance of the model we have just adapted, we can use the `evaluate()` function, as follows:

```
Scores = CNNModel.evaluate(XTest,YTest, verbose=1)
```

This function returns the loss value and metrics values for the model in test mode. Computation is done in batches. Let's print the loss and accuracy, as follows:

```
print('Test loss:', Scores[0])
print('Test accuracy:', Scores[1])
```

The following results are printed:

```
Test loss: 0.026746396384239
Test accuracy: 0.9792
```

The accuracy that's obtained confirms that a convolutional network is able to recognize images of articles of clothing and accessories offered for sale by the Zalando online store with excellent results.

Summary

In this chapter, we have learned about the basics of CNNs. To begin with, the basic concepts of computer vision were analyzed. Computer vision is the discipline that studies how to enable computers to understand and interpret visual information that's present in images or videos. This also deals with the analysis of numerical images.

Then, the architecture of convolutional network models was explored. A CNN consists of a series of layers such as input, convolutional, ReLU, pool, and fully connected layers. Each identify as a level of the CNN. The convolutional layer is the main level of the network. Its goal is to identify patterns, such as curves, angles, circumferences, or squares that have been depicted in an image with high accuracy. The ReLU layer aims to erase negative values that have been obtained in previous levels, and it is usually placed after convolutional levels. The pool layer allows to identify whether the study characteristic is present in the previous level. The fully connected layer connects all of the neurons of the previous level in order to establish the various identification classes displayed in the previous levels according to a given probability.

To understand how these levels must be put together, a problem that was derived from real life was given. A CNN Keras model to recognize images of articles of clothing and accessories offered for sale by the Zalando online store was implemented.

In the next chapter, we will learn how to identify the expression of opinions in a specific context, discover word embedding techniques, and how to implement them using neural networks. We will also understand recurrent neural network basics, learn how to train the model, and how to improve the model's performance. We will also learn how to implement an RNN to classify the sentiment of sentences from movie reviews.

6
Movie Reviews Sentiment Analysis Using Recurrent Neural Networks

A recurrent neural network is a neural model in which a bidirectional flow of information is present. In other words, while the propagation of signals in feedforward networks takes place only in a continuous manner in one direction, from inputs to outputs, recurrent networks are different. In recurrent networks, this propagation can also derive from a neural layer following the current one, between neurons belonging to the same layer, or even between a neuron and itself. The set of natural language processing techniques, text analysis, and computational linguistics that are used to identify and extract subjective information in written or spoken text sources is called **sentiment analysis**. In this chapter, a recurrent neural network is used to classify sentiment in movie reviews.

The following topics are covered in this chapter:

- Sentiment analysis basic concepts
- Lexicon and semantics analysis
- Recurrent neural networks
- Classifying sentiment in movie reviews using recurrent neural networks

In this chapter, we will learn how to identify expressions of opinions in a specific context. We will discover word-embedding techniques and how to implement them using neural networks. We will gain an understanding of recurrent neural network basics, and learn how to train a model and improve its performance. Finally, we will implement an RNN to classify the sentiment of sentences from movie reviews.

Sentiment analysis basic concepts

The term **sentiment analysis** refers to the use of natural language processing techniques, text analysis, and computational linguistics to identify and extract subjective information in written or spoken text sources. If this subjective information is taken from large amounts of data, and, therefore, from the opinions of large groups of people, sentiment analysis can also be called **opinion mining**.

To define this term in more detail, we will refer to the Oxford Dictionary published by Oxford University Press, the largest university press in the world. Here, sentiment analysis is defined as follows:

> *The process of computationally identifying and categorizing opinions expressed in a piece of text, especially in order to determine whether the writer's attitude towards a particular topic or product is positive, negative, or neutral.*

This type of analysis has clear and important applications in the political, social, and economic fields. For example, a company might be interested in knowing the opinions of consumers about their products. Also, potential buyers of a particular product or service might be interested in knowing the opinion and experience of someone who has already bought or used the product. On the other hand, a public figure might be interested in knowing what people think of them.

Identifying, extracting, and classifying all the opinions expressed by people is a very challenging activity if done by human beings; an automatic process seems to be the best solution. Unfortunately, because of the inherent complexity of human language, modeling a language automatically is a long and expensive process and, moreover, the procedure to be followed is not the same for all languages.

The most difficult part in this analysis is determining the orientation of opinion (polarity), because the polarity classification of any text is often a very subjective activity—a sentence can be labeled positive by some but neutral by others, on the basis of a scale of entirely personal values.

The widespread use of social media has fueled an interest in sentiment analysis. With the proliferation of opinions, judgments, advice, and other forms of online expression, this field has turned into a great opportunity for companies looking to market their products, identify new opportunities, and manage their reputation.

The main problems in using these techniques are due to the fact that most sentiment analysis algorithms use simple terms to express an opinion about a product or service. However, cultural factors, linguistic differences, and various contexts make it extremely difficult to turn a string of written text into a simple positive or negative feeling.

The advanced analysis of sentiment seeks to identify moods, such as happy, sad, and angry. For example, you can tackle the task of classifying a review of a song as positive or negative to predict the score on a numeral scale, or take a detailed analysis of hotel reviews, providing the score for various aspects of the hotel, such as comfort, noise levels, and design.

It is possible to classify a given text into one of two classes: objective or subjective. A text can in fact contain objective information, such as a news article, or can be subjective, such as the political opinions expressed in an interview. The subjectivity of sentences may depend on their context and an objective document may contain subjective phrases, for example, quotations. The extraction of the subjective or objective is often more difficult than the classification of polarity as it depends on the context in which the text is placed.

Sentiment analysis techniques

Sentiment analysis can be tackled through different approaches. The most commonly used can be grouped into four macro-categories (*A Study and Comparison of Sentiment Analysis Methods for Reputation Evaluation* by Collomb. A., Costea. C., Joyeux. D., Hasan. O., and Brunie. L., 2014):

- **Lexicon-based methods**: These detect emotional keywords, and assign arbitrary words affinity likely to represent particular emotions.
- **Rule-based methods**: These classify texts using emotional categories, based on the presence of unambiguous emotional words, such as happy, sad, and bored.
- **Statistical methods**: Here, we try to identify the owner of a sentiment, that is, who the subject is, and the objective, or the object to which the sentiment is felt. To measure opinion in context and to find the characteristic that has been judged, grammatical relations of words used are used. Relationships of grammatical dependence are obtained through a thorough scan of the text.
- **Machine learning methods**: These use different learning algorithms to determine sentiment by having a dataset classified (supervised methods). The learning process is not immediate, in fact, models have to be built that associate a polarity to different types of comments and, if necessary, a topic for analysis purposes.

To date, the greatest limitation of sentiment analysis, and in particular automatic sentiment analysis, is attributable to the fact that any tool or platform that records posts and comments and attributes polarity is not able to grasp complex emotional concepts such as irony.

The next challenges for sentiment analysis

Like any evolving technology, sentiment analysis is also subject to improvements and reinforcements over time. Let's see what we expect in the near future:

- The current sentiment analysis tools operate mostly on English language texts. This is mainly due to the large availability of texts written in this language and the fact that the main studies of this type of analysis come from countries where this language is spoken. However, the growing importance of sentiment analysis requires multi-language support—an understanding of texts written in languages other than English.
- The right understanding of the text is a key element to obtaining the information required in various fields: market research, customer experience, product launch analysis, and much more. Machine learning and the various machine learning algorithms provide increasingly reliable results, allowing machines to identify the sense of a phrase even if expressed in the language spoken on the street. Furthermore, techniques for recognizing the real meaning of a word are gradually being refined, as these terms can take on different meanings in different contexts. To support the comprehension of the text, improvements in the fields of semantics, lexicon and syntax will be made, which will ensure greater precision in the analysis and implementation of new methods of classification.
- The use of emojis and emoticons is increasingly common. Rather than using words, one's mood is conveyed with small round faces and other symbols, useful for communicating one's message in a quick and enjoyable way.
- The analysis of sentiment and emotions about an an item cannot be limited to text analysis—attitudes, inclinations, moods, and opinions can, in fact, accompany any multimedia element, be it an image, a video, audio or a text. A further, increasingly important, step is the analysis of images and videos.

Machine learning techniques will provide valuable help in the evolution of this technology and will allow us to record the necessary improvements in order to make sentiment analysis more and more valid.

Lexicon and semantics analysis

Semantic and lexical language analysis can help us to improve the performance of opinion classification systems. In addition to opinion words, there are other language features that can be considered in an opinion mining system. Opinion words are words, terms, and idioms belonging to the natural language that usually indicate feelings, opinions, and moods. Let's look at some of the available features in detail:

- **Parts of speech**: Some parts of speech can be excellent indicators of opinion. For example, adjectives, which are often an important indicator of opinion, can be treated as special features. Also, the ways of saying (opinion phrases) of a particular language are evidently useful for the detection of sentiment.
- **Negations and conjunctions**: Denial clauses are very important because, usually, they express a change in orientation to that expressed by the opinion word. The opinion word detected (nice) expresses, without a doubt, a positive sentiment, but the application of the negation changes, or reverses, the sentiment expressed by the word and, consequently, the sentence.
- **Sentiment consistency**: In a complex period, it is often possible that more opinions will be expressed in agreement and against. The theory of sentiment consistency states that in a period in which two opinions are expressed, separated by a clause or juxtaposition clause, it is sufficient to single out a single opinion to understand the meaning of the second. The junction clause expresses the maintenance of opinion, for example, in the phrase, my home is beautiful and comfortable, the positive opinion persists before and after the clause. But in the phrase, my home is beautiful but small, the positive opinion turns into negative after the clause.

In the following sections, we will apply the concepts learned to identify the expression of opinions in a specific context.

Recurrent neural networks

Feedforward neural networks are based on input data that is powered to the network and converted into output. If it is a supervised learning algorithm, the output is a label that can recognize the input. Basically, these algorithms connect raw data to specific categories by recognizing patterns. Recurrent networks, on the other hand, take as input not only the current input data that is powered to the network, but also what they have experienced over time.

A **recurrent neural network** (**RNN**) is a neural model in which a bidirectional flow of information is present. In other words, while the propagation of signals in feedforward networks takes place only in a continuous manner in one direction from inputs to outputs, recurrent networks are different. In recurrent networks, this propagation can also occur from a neural layer following a previous one, between neurons belonging to the same layer, or even between a neuron and itself.

> A decision made by a recurrent network at a specific instant affects the decision it will reach immediately afterward. So, recurrent networks have two input sources—the present and the recent past—which combine to determine how to respond to new data, just as people do in life everyday.

Recurrent networks are distinguished from feedforward networks thanks to the feedback loop linked to their past decisions, thus accepting their output momentarily as inputs. This feature can be emphasized by saying that recurrent networks have memory. Adding memory to neural networks has a purpose: there is information in the sequence itself and recurrent networks use it to perform the tasks that feedforward networks cannot.

Access to memory occurs through the content rather than by address or location. One approach to this is that the memory content is the pattern of activations on the nodes of an RNN. The idea is to start the network with an activation scheme that is a partial or noisy representation of the requested memory content and that the network stabilizes on the required content.

An RNN is a class of neural network where there is at least one feedback connection between neurons that form a directed cycle. A typical RNN with connections between the output layer and the hidden layer is represented in the following diagram:

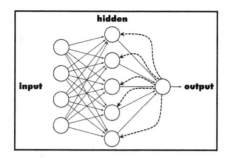

In the recurring network shown in the preceding diagram, both the input level and the output level are used to define the weights of the hidden level. Ultimately, we can think of RNNs as a variant of ANNs: these variants can be characterized on a different number of hidden levels and different trends of the data flow. RNNs are characterized by different trends in the flow of data, in fact, the connections between the neurons form a cycle. Unlike feedforward networks, RNNs can use internal memory for their processing. RNNs are a class of ANNs that feature connections between hidden layers that are propagated over time in order to learn sequences.

The way the data is kept in memory and flows at different time periods makes RNNs powerful and successful. RNNs are used in the following fields:

- Image captioning
- Stock market predictions
- Weather forecasts
- Language translation
- Time-series based forecasts
- Handwritten digit recognition
- Speech recognition
- Robotics action sequencing
- Audio or video processing

Recurrent networks are designed to recognize patterns as a sequence of data and are helpful in prediction and forecasting. They can work on text, images, speech, and time series data.

RNNs are among the more powerful ANNs and represent the biological brain, including memory with processing power.

Recurrent networks take inputs from the current input (like a feedforward network) and the output that was calculated previously. In the following diagram, we compare a single neuron operating scheme for both a feedforward neural network and an RNN:

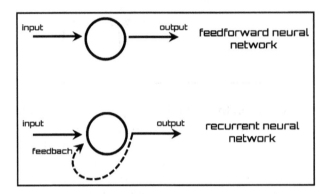

As you can see in the preceding simple single-neuron scheme, the feedback signal is added to the input signal in the RNN. Feedback is a considerable and significant feature. A feedback network is more likely to update and has more computing capacity than a simple network limited to one-way signals from input to output. Feedback networks show phenomena and processes not revealed by one-way networks.

To understand the differences between ANNs and RNNs, we consider an RNN as a network of neural networks, and the cyclic nature is unfolded in the following manner: the state of a neuron is considered at different time periods (*t-1, t, t+1*, and so on) until convergence, or until the total number of epochs is reached.

The network learning phase can be performed using gradient descent procedures similar to those leading to the backpropagation algorithm for feedforward networks. At least this is valid in the case of simple architectures and deterministic activation functions. When activations are stochastic, simulated annealing approaches may be more appropriate.

RNN architectures can have many different forms. There are more variants in the way data flows backward, as follows:

- Fully recurrent
- Recursive
- Hopfield
- Elman networks
- LSTM
- Gated recurrent unit

- Bidirectional
- Recurrent MLP

In the following sections, we will analyze the architecture of some of these networks.

Fully recurrent neural networks

A fully RNN is a network of neurons, each with a directed (one-way) connection to every other neuron. Each neuron has a time-varying, real-valued activation. Each connection has a modifiable real-valued weight. Input neurons, output neurons, and hidden neurons are expected. This type of network is a multilayer perceptron, with the previous set of hidden unit activations feeding back into the network along with the inputs, as shown in the following screenshot:

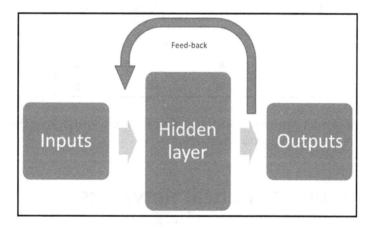

At each step, each non-input unit calculates its current activation as a nonlinear function of the weighted sum of activations of all units that connect to it.

Recursive neural networks

A recursive network is just a generalization of a recurrent network. In a recurrent network, the weights are shared and dimensionality remains constant along the length of the sequence. In a recursive network, the weights are shared and dimensionality remains constant—but at every node. The following figure shows what a recursive neural network looks as follows:

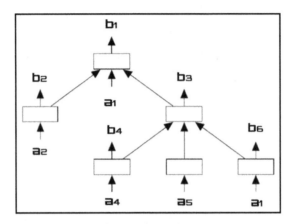

Recursive neural networks can be used for learning tree-like structures. They are highly useful for parsing natural scenes and language.

Hopfield recurrent neural networks

In 1982, physicist John J. Hopfield published a fundamental article in which a mathematical model commonly known as the Hopfield network was introduced (*Neural networks and physical systems with emergent collective computational abilities* by John J. Hopfield, 1982). Hopfield recurrent neural networks highlighted new computational capabilities deriving from the collective behavior of a large number of simple processing elements. A Hopfield network is a form of recurrent ANN.

According to Hopfield, every physical system can be considered as a potential memory device if it has a certain number of stable states, which act as an attractor for the system itself. On the basis of this consideration, he formulated the thesis that the stability and placement of such attractors represented spontaneous properties of systems consisting of considerable quantities of mutually interacting neurons.

Structurally, the Hopfield network constitutes a recurrent symmetrical neural network (therefore, with a synaptic weights matrix that is symmetric), one that is completely connected and in which each neuron is connected to all the others, as shown in the following diagram:

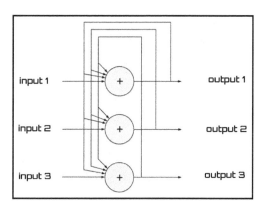

As already mentioned, a recurrent network is a neural model in which a flow of bidirectional information is present—in other words, while in feedforward networks the propagation of the signals takes place only in a continuous manner in the direction that leads from the inputs to the outputs in the recurrent networks. This propagation can also occur from a neural layer following the current one, between neurons belonging to at the same layer (Hopfield network), or even between a neuron and itself.

The dynamics of a Hopfield network are described by a nonlinear system of differential equations and the neuron update mechanism can be one of the following:

- **Asynchronous**: One neuron is updated at a time
- **Synchronous**: All neurons are updated at the same time
- **Continuous**: All the neurons are continually updated

Elman neural networks

An Elman neural network is a feedforward network in which the hidden layer, besides being connected to the output layer, forks into another identical layer, called the context layer, to which it is connected with weights equal to one. At each moment of time (each time the data is passed to the neurons of the input layer), the neurons of the context layer maintain the previous values and pass them to the respective neurons of the hidden layer.

The following figure shows an Elman network scheme:

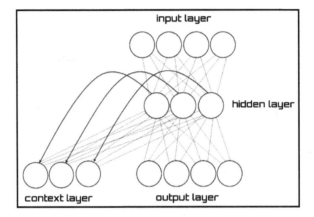

Like feedforward networks, Elman's RNNs can be trained with an algorithm called **Backpropagation Through Time (BPTT)**, a variant of backpropagation created specifically for RNNs. Substantially, this algorithm unrolls the neural network transforming it into a feedforward network, with a number of layers equal to the length of the sequence to be learned; subsequently, the classic backpropagation algorithm is applied.

Alternatively, it is possible to use global optimization methods, such as genetic algorithms, especially with RNN topologies on which it is not possible to apply BPTT.

Long short-term memory network

A **Long short-term memory network (LSTM)** is a particular architecture of RNN, originally conceived by Hochreiter and Schmidhuber in 1997. This type of neural network has been recently rediscovered in the context of deep learning because it is free from the problem of the vanishing gradient, and in practice, it offers excellent results and performance.

The vanishing gradient problem affects the training of ANNs with gradient-based learning methods. In gradient-based methods such as backpropagation, weights are adjusted proportionally to the gradient of the error. Because of the way in which the aforementioned gradients are calculated, we obtain the effect that their module decreases exponentially, proceeding towards the deepest layers. The problem is that in some cases, the gradient will be vanishingly small, effectively preventing the weight from changing its value. In the worst case, this may completely stop the neural network from further training.

LSTM-based networks are ideal for the prediction and classification of time sequences, and they are supplanting many classic machine learning approaches. In fact, in 2012, Google replaced its voice recognition models, passing from Hidden Markov Models (which represented the standard for over 30 years) to deep learning neural networks. In 2015, it switched to RNNs LSTM combined with **connectionist temporal classification (CTC)**.

> A **CTC** is a type of neural network output and associated scoring function for training **RNNs**.

This is due to the fact that LSTM networks are able to consider long-term dependencies between data, and in the case of speech recognition, this means managing the context within a sentence to improve recognition capacity.

An LSTM network consists of cells (**LSTM blocks**) linked together. Each cell is in turn composed of three types of ports: input gate, output gate, and forget gate. They respectively implement the write, read, and reset functions on the cell memory. The ports are not binary but analogical (generally managed by a sigmoid activation function mapped in a range (0, 1), where zero indicates total inhibition and 1 indicates total activation), as they are multiplicative. The presence of these ports allows the LSTM cells to remember information for an indefinite amount of time. In fact, if the input gate is below the activation threshold, the cell will maintain the previous state, while if it is enabled, the current state will be combined with the input value. As the name suggests, the forget gate resets the current state of the cell (when its value is brought to zero), and the output gate decides whether the value inside the cell must be taken out or not.

The following figure shows an LSTM unit:

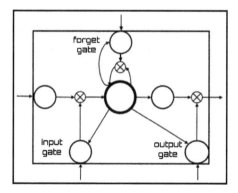

The approaches based on neural networks are very powerful, as they allow the capture of the characteristics and relationships between the data. In particular, it has also been seen that LSTM networks, in practice, offer high performance and excellent recognition rates. One disadvantage is that the neural networks are black box models, so their behavior is not predictable, and it is not possible to trace the logic with which they process the data.

Classifying sentiment in movie reviews using an RNN

Reviews are now an integral part of the policy of any successful business sector. We're talking about the review of products, or in-depth feedback written by customers after purchasing an item, or reviews of the service offered by the company. While on the one hand, reviews can help those looking to read up before buying, on the other hand, they provide sellers with good ideas on how to improve and make themselves more attractive to customers. But above all, they feed the interaction between users, and consequently the digital word of mouth that can greatly increase a company's ranking on both social and search engines. Getting good reviews online has become crucial if you want to carry on a profitable business, big or small.

In recent years, the online reviews mechanism has radically changed the buying habits of consumers around the world. The decision-making process that leads to the purchase of a product or service has been distorted by the advent of social networks and the web. A further step in the decision-making process has led the potential buyer to search for content and information on a network before making a purchase. Word of mouth is no longer enough; consumers are more autonomous and less directly influenced, pondering their purchases well.

People search for prices and promotions by comparing products, services, or the features offered. They are informed about the brand, the seller, shipping methods, the services included, guarantees, returns management, and types of payments. It follows that the opinions left by consumers contain important information that can guide potential buyers to make a purchase, but at the same time, they can help companies to modify their offers according to the general sentiment on the web.

In the past, the quality of a film was judged only and exclusively by expert and competent staff through so-called criticism. This product assumed a form of pedagogy of cultural consumption: it helped the cinema enthusiast to identify the most interesting films of the season. In this sense, the critic could educate the tastes of consumers, contributing to the development of their critical sense; even though this risked orienting choices in an overly authoritarian way, even replacing the direct experience of the consumer. In recent years, the opinion of experts in the sector has been joined by that of consumers, overtaking critics in terms of importance, becoming the most appreciated judgment by potential viewers/users.

All this underlines the importance of assessing the sentiment of users when launching a new film product. In this section, we will analyze a database containing movie reviews to classify users' opinions.

IMDB Movie reviews dataset

To predict the sentiment of movie reviews as either positive or negative, we will use the `IMDB Movie reviews` dataset. This is a dataset for binary sentiment classification containing 50,000 highly polarized reviews from the `Internet Movie` Database. The dataset was split into a set of 25,000 highly polar movie reviews for training, and 25,000 for testing. There is additional unlabeled data for use as well. Raw text and already processed bag of word formats are provided.

The dataset was presented by the authors in the following publication: Maas, A.L., Daly, R.E., Pham, P.T., Huang, D., Ng, A.Y. and Potts, C., 2011, June, *Learning word vectors for sentiment analysis,* during the proceedings of the 49th annual meeting of the association for computational linguistics: *Human language technologies-volume 1* (pp. 142-150), Association for Computational Linguistics.

The dataset is already contained in the Keras distribution, where there is also a detailed description of its content, as shown in the following section (`https://keras.io/datasets/`).

The dataset contains 50,000 movies reviews from IMDB, labeled by sentiment (positive/negative). The reviews have been preprocessed, and each review is encoded as a sequence of word indexes (integers). For convenience, words are indexed by their overall frequency in the dataset, so that, for instance, the integer 3 encodes the third most frequent word in the data. This allows quick filtering operations such as: only consider the top 10,000 most common words, but eliminate the top 20 most common words. As a convention, 0 does not stand for a specific word, but instead is used to encode any unknown word.

To import the `imdb` dataset in a Python environment, the following code must be used:

```
from keras.datasets import imdb
(XTrain, YTrain), (XTest, YTest) =
                    imdb.load_data(path="imdb.npz",
                    num_words=None,
                    skip_top=0,
                    maxlen=None,
                    seed=113,
                    start_char=1,
                    oov_char=2,
                    index_from=3)
```

Here, the parameters passed are as follows:

- `path`: If you do not have the data locally at the `~/.keras/datasets/` path, it will be downloaded to this location
- `num_words`: An integer or none. The top most frequent words to consider. Any less frequent words will appear as `oov_char` value in the sequence data.
- `skip_top`: An integer. The top most frequent words to ignore (they will appear as `oov_char` value in the sequence data).
- `maxlen`: `int`. Maximum sequence length. Any longer sequences will be truncated.
- `seed`: `int`. Seed for reproducible data shuffling.
- `start_char`: `int`. The start of a sequence will be marked with this character. Set to 1 because 0 is usually the padding character.
- `oov_char`: `int`. Words that were cut out because of the `num_words` or `skip_top` limit will be replaced with this character.
- `index_from`: `int`. Index actual words with this index and higher.

The following data is returned:

- XTrain, XTest: A list of sequences, which are lists of indexes (integers). If the num_words argument is specified, the maximum possible index value is num_words-1. If the maxlen argument is specified, the largest possible sequence length is maxlen.
- YTrain, YTest: list of integer labels (1 or 0).

The label contained in the output (YTrain, and YTest) is an integer value of either 0 or 1, where 0 stands for a negative review, and 1 stands for a positive review.

Exploratory analysis

As anticipated, the dataset is already available in the keras library. So, we have loaded the appropriate library and then loaded the data. The following information is returned:

```
Downloading data from
https://s3.amazonaws.com/text-datasets/imdb.npz17465344/17464789
[==============================] - 14s 1us/step
```

Amazon S3 is a web storage service offered by **Amazon Web Services** (**AWS**). Objects to be archived can be files, HTML pages, or images. Amazon launched this service in 2006 in the United States. Amazon offers users the same infrastructure they use for international online sales portals. Amazon S3 allows, first of all, scalability, like all AWS services, and reliability as the service is guaranteed to have uptime of 99.999999999% and will resist the simultaneous loss of an object on two nodes of the structure. You can also activate an option that allows you to reduce the price of the service, if you are willing to lose a little reliability and go from 99.999999999% to only 99.99% uptime, and resistance to the loss of an object in a single node instead of two.

Now, let's check the contents of the four objects we imported. First, we get the type of such objects. To do this, we will use the built-in type() function, as follows:

```
print('XTrain class = ',type(XTrain))
print('YTrain class = ',type(YTrain))
print('XTest shape = ',type(XTest))
print('YTest shape = ',type(YTest))
```

The `type()` function follows the principle that, if a single argument (object) is passed, the type of the given object is returned. If three arguments (name, bases, and dict) are passed, a new type object is returned. The following results are obtained:

```
XTrain class =  <class 'numpy.ndarray'>
YTrain class =  <class 'numpy.ndarray'>
XTest shape =  <class 'numpy.ndarray'>
YTest shape =  <class 'numpy.ndarray'>
```

So, four `numpy.ndarray` objects are returned. An array object represents a multidimensional, homogeneous array of fixed-size items. An associated datatype object describes the format of each element in the array (its byte-order, how many bytes it occupies in memory, whether it is an integer, a floating point number, or something else, and so on). Now, we extract the number of elements contained in each array:

```
print('XTrain shape = ',XTrain.shape)
print('XTest shape = ',XTest.shape)
print('YTrain shape = ',YTrain.shape)
print('YTest shape = ',YTest.shape)
```

The `shape` attribute for arrays returns the dimensions of the array. The following results are obtained:

```
XTrain shape =   (25000,)
XTest shape =   (25000,)
YTrain shape =   (25000,)
YTest shape =   (25000,)
```

As we anticipated, the 50,000 items in the database were divided into 25,000 items for training and 25,000 items for testing. We previously said that the data output is represented by a dichotomous datum, which indicates the polarity of the review (positive = 1 or negative = 0). We are looking for confirmation of this assumption:

```
import numpy as np
print('YTrain values = ',np.unique(YTrain))
print('YTest values = ',np.unique(YTest))
```

To extract the output values, the `numpy.unique()` function was used, which finds the unique elements of an array. This function returns the sorted unique elements of an array. There are three optional outputs in addition to the unique elements—the indices of the input array that give the unique values, the indices of the unique array that reconstruct the input array, and the number of times each unique value comes up in the input array. The following results are returned:

```
YTrain values =   [0 1]
YTest values =   [0 1]
```

In this way, we have confirmed that the data output is represented by a dichotomous datum that indicates the polarity of the review (positive = 1 or negative = 0). It may be useful to analyze the distribution of the two values in the available arrays. To start, we count the number of occurrences:

```
unique, counts = np.unique(YTrain, return_counts=True)
print('YTrain distribution = ',dict(zip(unique, counts)))
unique, counts = np.unique(YTest, return_counts=True)
print('YTrain distribution = ',dict(zip(unique, counts)))
```

The `numpy.unique` function was once again applied: in this case, the `return_counts` attribute was added, which, if set to `True`, also returns the number of times a unique item appears. Then, the `dict()` function was applied, which creates a new dictionary, while the `zip()` function makes an iterator that aggregates elements from each of the iterables, and returns an iterator of tuples, where the i-th tuple contains the i-th element from each of the argument sequences or iterables. The iterator stops when the shortest input iterable is exhausted. The following results are shown:

```
YTrain distribution =   {0: 12500, 1: 12500}
YTrain distribution =   {0: 12500, 1: 12500}
```

It is clear that the two polarities are equally represented in the data. We can also see this in a graph:

```
import matplotlib.pyplot as plt
plt.figure(1)
plt.subplot(121)
plt.hist(YTrain, bins='auto')
plt.xlabel("Classes")
plt.ylabel("Number of occurrences")
plt.title("YTrain data")

plt.subplot(122)
plt.hist(YTest, bins='auto')
plt.xlabel("Classes")
plt.ylabel("Number of occurrences")
plt.title("YTest data")
plt.show()
```

To visualize the number of occurrences of the two classes, a histogram has been adopted. A histogram is a graphical representation of a numerical distribution, showing the shape of a distribution. It consists of adjacent rectangles (bins), whose bases are aligned on an axis oriented and equipped with a unit of measure (the axis assumes the unit of measure of the character and can be safely understood as the X axis). The adjacency of the rectangles reflects the continuity of the character. Each rectangle has a base length equal to the width of the corresponding class; the height is calculated as a frequency density, so it is equal to the ratio between the frequencies (absolute) associated with the class and the amplitude of the class. To plot a histogram in Python, use the `hyst()` function of the matplotlib library. This function plots a histogram—it essentially computes and draws the histogram of specific data. The return value is a tuple (n, bins, patches) or ([n_0, n_1, ...], bins, [$patches_0$, $patches_1$,...]) if the input contains multiple data. Multiple data can be provided as a list of datasets of potentially different lengths ([x_0, x_1, ...]), or as a 2-D ndarray in which each column is a dataset. The following arguments were passed:

- `YTrain`, `YTest`: An array or sequence of arrays. For input values, this takes either a single array or a sequence of arrays that are not required to be of the same length.
- `bins`: `Int` or `sequence` or `str`, optional. With Numpy 1.11 or newer, you can alternatively provide a string describing a binning strategy, such as `auto`, `sturges`, `fd`, `doane`, `scott`, `rice`, or `sqrt`. In our case the `auto` option was selected.

To compare the results obtained on both output datasets (`YTrain`, `YTest`), two histograms were traced side by side, as shown in the following figure:

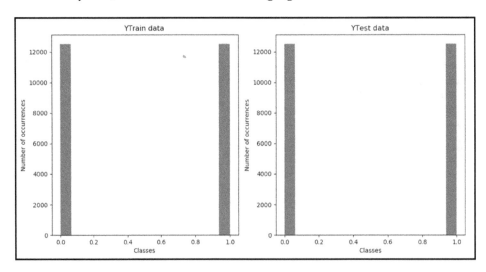

As previously verified, the classes are equally represented in both datasets (12,500 samples). Now let's see what's inside the data. We print the first record of the data we will use for the training:

```
print(XTrain[0])
```

The following result is returned:

```
[1, 14, 22, 16, 43, 530, 973, 1622, 1385, 65, 458, 4468, 66, 3941, 4, 173, 36, 256, 5,
25, 100, 43, 838, 112, 50, 670, 22665, 9, 35, 480, 284, 5, 150, 4, 172, 112, 167, 21631,
336, 385, 39, 4, 172, 4536, 1111, 17, 546, 38, 13, 447, 4, 192, 50, 16, 6, 147, 2025, 19,
14, 22, 4, 1920, 4613, 469, 4, 22, 71, 87, 12, 16, 43, 530, 38, 76, 15, 13, 1247, 4, 22,
17, 515, 17, 12, 16, 626, 18, 19193, 5, 62, 386, 12, 8, 316, 8, 106, 5, 4, 2223, 5244,
16, 480, 66, 3785, 33, 4, 130, 12, 16, 38, 619, 5, 25, 124, 51, 36, 135, 48, 25, 1415,
33, 6, 22, 12, 215, 28, 77, 52, 5, 14, 407, 16, 82, 10311, 8, 4, 107, 117, 5952, 15, 256,
4, 31050, 7, 3766, 5, 723, 36, 71, 43, 530, 476, 26, 400, 317, 46, 7, 4, 12118, 1029, 13,
104, 88, 4, 381, 15, 297, 98, 32, 2071, 56, 26, 141, 6, 194, 7486, 18, 4, 226, 22, 21,
134, 476, 26, 480, 5, 144, 30, 5535, 18, 51, 36, 28, 224, 92, 25, 104, 4, 226, 65, 16,
38, 1334, 88, 12, 16, 283, 5, 16, 4472, 113, 103, 32, 15, 16, 5345, 19, 178, 32]
```

What do all these numbers mean? As we specified at the beginning of the section, the dataset contains users' reviews of some successful movies. These reviews represent strings of text. Before being able to use them as input for a model based on neural networks, it is necessary to transform them into a compatible format. This work has already been done by the creators of the dataset, who replaced the words with integers that indicate the absolute popularity of the words in the dataset. The sequence of integers returned by the previous command then represents the sequence of words contained in the first review. This sequence was obtained according to rules established a priori.

The users' reviews are different in content but also in length (the number of words). Let's see, for example, how many words are contained in the first review—the one we just printed:

```
len(XTrain[0])
```

The following result is obtained:

218

This means that 218 words are contained in the first review. To confirm the different lengths of the reviews, we print the length of the first ten reviews:

```
for i in XTrain[0:10]:
    print(len(i))
```

This will give the following result:

218
189

```
141
550
147
43
123
562
233
130
```

To understand how the dataset has been encoded, we follow a backward path—from a coded review, we try to get the original review. To do this, we need the list containing the pairs—word, integer index. This information is included in the original dataset; we only need to load it into our environment:

```
WordIndex = imdb.get_word_index()
```

First, we analyze the type of data that we have loaded:

```
print(type(WordIndex))
```

The following result is obtained:

```
<class 'dict'>
```

So, it is a dictionary. Dictionaries are associative arrays, hence objects that are substantially similar to arrays but that use different indices. In fact, unlike lists that use only whole numbers, dictionaries can adopt any Python objects as indices as long as they are immutable, that is, strings, tuples, and also numbers. In them, a value is specified by a key and the value associated with it and the correspondence between the two elements will be indicated by the: (colon) symbol; all enclosed in braces. To recall a value from a dictionary, simply refer to its key. Let's see how many words have been coded:

```
print(len(WordIndex))
```

The following result is obtained:

```
88584
```

So, `88584` words are contained in the dictionary. The values returned from the first record of the training dataset (`XTrain`) represent the values of the dictionary. So, to get the words associated with this integer index, we will have to extract the key associated with it from the dictionary. To do this we can use the `items()` method, as follows:

```
for keys, values in WordIndex.items():
    if values == 88283:
        print(keys)
```

The `items()` method returns a view object that displays a list of dictionary's (`key`, `value`) tuple pairs. To decode a word from the first training data record, which, as seen previously, was represented by the integer index = `88283`, we looked for the value 88283 out of all the values and extracted the key. In the following code block, the result is shown:

```
philadelphia
```

So, the second word of the first review is the word `philadelphia`. This procedure will be useful for decoding the entire first review. To print the entire dictionary we can use the following command:

```
print(WordIndex.items())
```

In the following diagram, the first part of the dictionary is returned:

```
dict_items([('fawn', 34701), ('tsukino', 52006), ('nunnery', 52007), ('sonja', 16816), ('vani', 63951), ('woods', 1408),
('spiders', 16115), ('hanging', 2345), ('woody', 2289), ('trawling', 52008), ("hold's", 52009), ('comically', 11307),
('localized', 40830), ('disobeying', 30568), ("'royale", 52010), ("harpo's", 40831), ('canet', 52011), ('aileen', 19313),
('acurately', 52012), ("diplomat's", 52013), ('rickman', 25242), ('arranged', 6746), ('rumbustious', 52014),
('familiarness', 52015), ("spider'", 52016), ('hahahah', 68804), ("wood'", 52017), ('transvestism', 40833),
("hangin'", 34702), ('bringing', 2338), ('seamier', 40834), ('wooded', 34703), ('bravora', 52018), ('grueling', 16817),
('wooden', 1636), ('wednesday', 16818), ("'prix", 52019), ('altagracia', 34704), ('circuitry', 52020), ('crotch', 11585),
('busybody', 57766), ("tart'n'tangy", 52021), ('burgade', 14129), ('thrace', 52023), ("tom's", 11038), ('snuggles', 52025),
('francesco', 29114), ('complainers', 52027), ('templarios', 52125), ('272', 40835), ('273', 52028), ('zaniacs', 52130),
('275', 34706), ('consenting', 27631), ('snuggled', 40836), ('inanimate', 15492), ('uality', 52030), ('bronte', 11926),
('errors', 4010), ('dialogs', 3230), ("yomada's", 52031), ("madman's", 34707), ('dialoge', 30585), ('usenet', 52033),
('videodrome', 40837), ("kid'", 26338), ('pawed', 52034), ("'girlfriend'", 30569), ("'pleasure", 52035), ("'reloaded'", 52036)
('mailings', 52038), ('brainwashed', 11927), ('mcanally', 16819), ("tom''", 52039), ('kurupt', 25243), ('affiliated', 21905),
('babaganoosh', 52040), ("noe's", 40840), ('quart', 40841), ('kids', 359), ('uplifting', 5034), ('controversy', 7093),
('kida', 21906), ('kidd', 23379), ("error'", 52041), ('neurologist', 52042), ('spotty', 18510), ('cobblers', 30570),
('projection', 9878), ('fastforwarding', 40842), ('sters', 52043), ("eggar's", 52044), ('etherything', 52045),
('gateshead', 40843), ('airball', 34708), ('unsinkable', 25244), ('stern', 7180), ("cervi's", 52046), ('dnd', 40844),
('dna', 11586), ('insecurity', 20598), ("'reboot'", 52047), ('trelkovsky', 11037), ('jaekel', 52048), ('sidebars', 52049),
("sforza's", 52050), ('distortions', 17633), ('mutinies', 52051), ('sermons', 30602), ('7ft', 40846), ('boobage', 52052),
("o'bannon's", 52053), ('populations', 23380), ('chulak', 52054), ('mesmerize', 27633), ('quinnell', 52055), ('yahoo', 10307),
('meteorologist', 52057), ('beswick', 42577), ('boorman', 15493), ('voicework', 40847), ("ster'", 52058),
('blustering', 22922), ('hj', 52059), ('intake', 27634), ('morally', 5621), ('jumbling', 40849), ('bowersock', 52060),
("'porky's'", 52061), ('gershon', 16821), ('ludicrosity', 40850), ('coprophilia', 52062), ('expressively', 40851),
("india's", 19500), ("post's", 34710), ('wana', 52063), ('wang', 5283), ('wand', 30571), ('wane', 25245), ('edgeways', 52321),
('titanium', 34711), ('pinta', 40852), ('want', 178), ('pinto', 30572), ('whoopdedoodles', 52065), ('tchaikovsky', 21908),
('travel', 2103), ("'victory'", 52066), ('copious', 11928), ('gouge', 22433), ("chapters'", 52067), ('barbra', 6702),
('uselessness', 30573), ("wan'", 52068), ('assimilated', 27635), ('petiot', 16116), ('most\x85and', 52069),
('dinosaurs', 3930), ('wrong', 352), ('seda', 52070), ('stollen', 52071), ('sentencing', 34712), ('ouroboros', 40853),
('assimilates', 40854), ('colorfully', 40855), ('glenne', 27636), ('dongen', 52072), ('subplots', 4760), ('kiloton', 52073),
('chandon', 23381), ("effect'", 34713), ('snugly', 27637), ('kuei', 40856), ('welcomed', 9092), ('dishonor', 30071),
```

Then, check the correctness of the procedure followed—we print the key relative to the value `16115`, which, as we can see from the figure, corresponds to the `spiders` key (the first pair of the second line):

```
for keys, values in WordIndex.items():
    if values == 16115:
        print(keys)
```

The following result is returned:

```
spiders
```

We have explained how a dictionary is made in Python, and we have also highlighted the meaning of the key value pair. In particular, in the dictionary associated with the reviews, the words represent the keys and the integer indices the values. To decode a review, it is necessary to reverse this correspondence so that the keys are the integer indices and the values the words. This is because once the sequence of integer indices is known, it will be possible to reconstruct the review. To reverse these pairs, we will proceed as follows:

```
ReverseIndex = dict([(value, key) for (key, value) in WordIndex.items()])
```

Now, to rebuild the review, we have to extract the key values and join the results:

```
DecodedReview = " ".join( [ReverseIndex.get(i - 3, "!") for i in XTrain[0]]
)
```

Analyzing the code just proposed, you can see that the indices have been offset by 3 because 0, 1, and 2 are reserved indices for padding, start of sequence, and unknown. At this point, we just have to print the first review contained in the training dataset:

```
print(DecodedReview)
```

In the following figure, the original review is shown:

```
! this film was just brilliant casting location scenery story direction everyone's really suited the part they
played and you could just imagine being there robert redford's is an amazing actor and now the same being
director norman's father came from the same scottish island as myself so i loved the fact there was a real
connection with this film the witty remarks throughout the film were great it was just brilliant so much
that i bought the film as soon as it was released for retail and would recommend it to everyone to watch
and the fly fishing was amazing really cried at the end it was so sad and you know what they say if you
cry at a film it must have been good and this definitely was also congratulations to the two
little boy's that played the part's of norman and paul they were just brilliant children are
often left out of the praising list i think because the stars that play them all grown up are
such a big profile for the whole film but these children are amazing and should be praised
for what they have done don't you think the whole story was so lovely because it was
true and was someone's life after all that was shared with us
```

Now, the content of the dataset is clear enough and we can focus on building the model.

Keras recurrent neural network model

After exploring the dataset, it is time to build the RNN model to predict the sentiment of movie reviews from data recorded in the dataset. Before proceeding, it is necessary to prepare the data appropriately. This is a question of solving the problem of how words can be coded to process textual information automatically, in a similar way to what is done on images, as we saw in Chapter 5, *Fashion Article Recognition using Convolutional Neural Networks*.

One possible solution is represented by word embeddings, a set of tools, language models, and machine learning techniques that allow the representation of words and phrases through the use of real-component vectors. Keras provides a special layer to perform this operation. This is the embedding layer, which turns positive integers (indexes) into dense vectors of a fixed size. This layer can only be used as the first layer in a model. We'll see later how it will be used.

In the *Exploratory analysis* section, we saw that the dictionary contains 88584 words. Many of these appear a few times and therefore are superfluous. We'd better focus our attention on the most important ones. To do this, we can use the num_words attribute when loading the dataset. We limit the number of words in the dictionary to 10,000, of course, the most frequent. So, we load the dataset again with this limitation:

```
(XTrain, YTrain),(XTest, YTest) = imdb.load_data(num_words=10000)
```

Let's check if the dictionary is actually limited to 10,000 words:

```
print(max([max(sequence) for sequence in Xtrain]))
```

The following result is returned:

9999

To indicate that now, in the XTrain dataset, there are just 10,000 integer indexes (9999 because we start from 0).

Before focusing on the model, it is necessary to convert the arrays of integers (reviews) into tensors. This is because, as we specified in Chapter 1, *Getting started with Keras*, Keras relies on a specialized, well-optimized tensor manipulation library, serving as the backend engine.

The tensor we will use will have the length of the review in one dimension, and the number of reviews in the other. But in the *Exploratory analysis* section, we saw that the reviews have different lengths. To solve this problem, we can truncate the reviews so that they are the same length. To do this, we will use the `keras.preprocessing.sequence.pad_sequences()` function, as follows:

```
from keras.preprocessing.sequence import pad_sequences
XTrain= pad_sequences(XTrain, maxlen=100)
XTest = pad_sequences(XTest, maxlen=100)
```

The `pad_sequences()` function pads `num_samples` sequences to the same length. This function transforms a list of sequences into a 2D Numpy array of shape (`num_samples`, `num_timesteps`). Sequences that are shorter than `num_timesteps` are padded with value at the end. Sequences longer than `num_timesteps` are truncated so that they fit the desired length. The position where padding or truncation happens is determined by the arguments padding and truncating, respectively. Two arguments are passed:

- `Xtrain`,`XTest`: List of lists, where each element is a sequence

- `maxlen=100`: Integer, maximum length of all sequences

Now all the reviews have the same length (100 words). Let's check this:

```
for i in XTrain[0:10]:
    print(len(i))
```

In this way, we print the length of the first 10 reviews, obtaining the following result:

```
100
100
100
100
100
100
100
100
100
100
```

To get an idea of how a review has changed, let's analyze a shorter review of the length we set. For example, XTrain [5], which we saw earlier, had a length of 43, thus less than the 100 words we set as a limit. Let's print the content to see what happened:

```
print(XTrain[5])
```

In the following figure, the results are shown:

```
[   0    0    0    0    0    0    0    0    0    0    0    0    0    0
    0    0    0    0    0    0    0    0    0    0    0    0    0    0
    0    0    0    0    0    0    0    0    0    0    0    0    0    0
    0    0    0    0    0    0    0    0    0    0    0    0    0    0
    0    1  778  128   74   12  630  163   15    4 1766 7982 1051    2
   32   85  156   45   40  148  139  121  664  665   10   10 1361  173
    4  749    2   16 3804    8    4  226   65   12   43  127   24    2
   10   10]
```

A series of zeroes were added in the first part of the review to get the desired length. So, we will pass these fixed-length vectors to an embedding layer capable of handling this form as the first level in our network. We have just split the starting data into two sets: a training set (XTrain) and a test set (XTest). The training set will be used to train the model and the test set to test the model's performance. To build a model, we will use Keras' Sequential model. Let's start importing the libraries:

```
from keras.models import Sequential
from keras.layers.embeddings import Embedding
from keras.layers import SimpleRNN
from keras.layers import Dense
from keras.layers import Activation
```

Five layer classes have been imported: Sequential, Embedding, SimpleRNN, Dense, and Activation. The Sequential class is used to define a linear stack of network layers that make up a model. In the following, we will use the Sequential constructor to create the model, which will then be enriched with layers using the add () method. The Embedding layer is used to turn positive integers (indexes) into dense vectors of a fixed size. This layer can only be used as the first layer in a model. The SimpleRNN layer is used to add a fully connected RNN where the output is to be fed back to the input. The Dense class is used to instantiate a Dense layer, which is the basic feedforward fully connected layer.
The Activation layer is used to add an activation function to the sequence of layers. To start, we must set the model type:

```
RNNModel=Sequential()
```

As indicated in the preceding code block, the first layer we are going to add will be an Embedding layer:

```
RNNModel.add(Embedding(10000, 32, input_length=100))
```

The `Embedding` layer takes as input a 2D tensor with shape (`batch_size`, `sequence_length`), where each entry is a sequence of integers. A 3D tensor with shape (`batch_size, sequence_length, output_dim`) is returned. The following parameters are passed:

- `10000`: input dimension (*int > 0*). The size of the vocabulary, that is, the maximum integer *index + 1*.

- `32`: output dimension (*int >= 0*). The dimension of the dense embedding.

- `input_length=100`: Length of input sequences, when it is constant. This argument is required if you are going to connect Flatten then Dense layers upstream (without it, the shape of the dense outputs cannot be computed).

Now we can insert an RNN layer:

```
RNNModel.add(SimpleRNN(32, input_shape=(10000, 100),
return_sequences=False))
```

The `SimpleRNN` layer adds a fully connected RNN where the output is to be fed back to the input. The following parameters are passed:

- `32`:Positive integer, the dimensionality of the output space.

- `input_shape=(10000, 100)`: This is a shape tuple (a tuple of integers or None entries, where None indicates that any positive integer may be expected. 10,000 is the dictionary dimension (the number of words), and 100 is the length of the reviews (the limit we imposed).

- `return_sequences=False`: A Boolean. Whether to return the last output in the output sequence, or the full sequence.

Now, we will add a fully connected dense layer to create one dimensional output:

```
RNNModel.add(Dense(1))
```

Finally, an `Activation` layer must be added:

```
RNNModel.add(Activation('sigmoid'))
```

A `sigmoid` activation function is used, which produces a sigmoidal curve; a characteristic curve characterized by its S shape. This is the earliest and most often used activation function. This squashes the input to any value between 0 and 1, and makes the model logistic in nature. This activation function is particularly suited to our case because the output will be dichotomous, having only two values (1 and 0).

To print a summary of the CNN model, simply type:

```
model.summary()
```

In the following figure, the results are shown:

```
Layer (type)                    Output Shape              Param #
=================================================================
embedding_15 (Embedding)        (None, 100, 32)           320000
_____
simple_rnn_15 (SimpleRNN)       (None, 32)                2080
_____
dense_22 (Dense)                (None, 1)                 33
=================================================================
Total params: 322,113
Trainable params: 322,113
Non-trainable params: 0
```

The structure of the RNN has finally been set and we can proceed.

Exploring model results

Before training a model, you need to configure the learning process, which is done via the `compile()` method:

```
RNNModel.compile(loss='binary_crossentropy', optimizer='rmsprop',
metrics=['accuracy'])
```

Three parameters are passed:

- The `binary_crossentropy` loss function: We have used logarithmic loss, which for a binary classification problem is defined in Keras as `binary_crossentropy`.

- The `RMSProp` optimizer: It is recommended to leave the parameters of this optimizer at their default values (except the learning rate, which can be freely tuned). This optimizer is usually a good choice for recurrent neural networks.

- The `accuracy` metric: A metric is a function that is used to evaluate the performance of your model during training and testing.

To train the model, the `fit()` method is used as follows:

```
RNNModel.fit(XTrain, YTrain, validation_data=(XTest, YTest), epochs=3,
batch_size=64, verbose=1)
```

This function trains the model for a given number of epochs (iterations on a dataset). Six parameters are passed, as follows:

- `Xtrain`: An array of input training data

- `Ytrain`: An array of target (label) data

- `validation_data=(XTest, Ytest)`: Tuple on which to evaluate the loss and any model metrics at the end of each epoch. The model will not be trained on this data.

- `epochs=3`: The number of epochs to train the model. An epoch is an iteration over the entire Xtrain and Ytrain data provided.

- `batch_size=64`: The number of samples per gradient update.

- `verbose=1`: An integer with the following values-0, 1, or 2. Verbosity mode are: 0 = silent, 1 = progress bar, 2 = one line per epoch.

When the `fit()` function is performed, the loss and the accuracy at the end of each training epoch are displayed, as shown in the following figure:

```
Train on 25000 samples, validate on 25000 samples

Epoch 1/3
25000/25000 [==============================] - 13s 538us/step - loss: 0.5606 - acc: 0.6901
- val_loss: 0.4697 - val_acc: 0.7800

Epoch 2/3
25000/25000 [==============================] - 12s 465us/step - loss: 0.3440 - acc: 0.8558
- val_loss: 0.3983 - val_acc: 0.8194

Epoch 3/3
25000/25000 [==============================] - 12s 470us/step - loss: 0.2659 - acc: 0.8933
- val_loss: 0.3938 - val_acc: 0.8435
```

To evaluate the performance of the model we have just adapted, we use the `evaluate()` function as follows:

```
scores = RNNModel.evaluate(XTest, YTest, verbose=1)
```

The `evaluate()` function returns the loss value and metrics values for the model in test mode. Computation is done in batches. Let's print the loss and accuracy:

```
print("Accuracy: %.2f%%" % (scores[1]*100)
```

The following results are printed:

```
25000/25000 [==============================] - 4s 170us/step
Accuracy: 84.35%
```

The accuracy obtained confirms that an RNN is able to predict the sentiment of movie reviews.

Summary

In this chapter, we have learned how to identify the sentiment of opinions in a specific context. To start, the basic concepts of sentiment analysis were covered. Sentiment analysis refers to a set of natural language processing techniques, text analysis, and computational linguistics that are used to identify and extract subjective information in written or spoken text sources. Different sentiment analysis techniques were explored. Then, the next challenges for sentiment analysis were analyzed. So, we have seen how semantic and lexical linguistic analysis can help us improve the performance of opinion grading systems.

In the second part of the chapter, the basics of RNN were addressed. In an RNN, a bidirectional flow of information is present. In contrast with the propagation of signals in feedforward networks, which takes place only in a continuous manner in one direction from inputs to outputs, in recurrent networks this propagation can also occur from a neural layer following the current one, between neurons belonging to the same layer, or even between a neuron and itself. We analyzed the architecture of some of these networks: fully recurrent neural networks, recursive neural networks, Hopfield recurrent neural networks, Elman neural networks, and long short-term memory networks.

Finally, an RNN model was set up to classify sentiment in movie reviews. We learned how to train a model and how to evaluate the model's performance.

In the next chapter, we will learn the basic concepts of forecasting techniques, discover time-series analysis, gain an understanding of LSTM basics, learn how to set the embedding layer and the tensor sizes of a network, and also learn how to implement an LSTM model to forecast stock volatility.

7
Stock Volatility Forecasting Using Long Short-Term Memory

Human beings have always tried to predict the future. Forecasting has been, therefore, one of the most studied techniques over time. Forecasts cover several fields—weather forecasts, economic and political events, sports results, and more. Since we try to predict so many different events, there are a variety of ways in which predictions can be developed.

A **time series** is a sequence of observations ordered with respect to time (for example, monthly turnover, the daily prices of shares, the weekly interest rate, the annual profits, and so on). The purpose of the analysis of time series consists of the study of the past evolution of the phenomenon with respect to time, in order to predict the future trend of the phenomenon. The forecast is obtained by hypothesizing that such behavioral regularities will repeat in the future.

Long short-term memory (LSTM) is a particular architecture of RNN, originally conceived by Hochreiter and Schmidhuber in 1997. This type of neural network has been recently rediscovered in the context of deep learning because it is free from the problem of the vanishing gradient and, in practice, it offers excellent results and performance. LSTM thanks to the blocks of memory that are connected through the levels can be used to deal with difficult sequence problems such as those provided by the time series.

In this chapter, along with short-term memory, a network will be used to forecast stock volatility. We will learn about the basic concepts of forecasting techniques, discover time series analysis, understand long short-term memory basics, learn how to set the embedding layer and the tensor sizes of the network, and learn how to implement the LSTM model to forecast stock volatility by covering the following topics:

- The basics of forecasting
- Time series analysis
- Time series models
- Long short-term memory in Keras
- Implementing LSTM to forecast stock volatility

The basics of forecasting

Forecasting the data and information related to the evolution of variables is of crucial importance for the setting of plans for the policies of any activity. For example, to plan the production of a company, it is not enough to know that the demand for products or services is increasing or decreasing, but it is essential to predict the trend of future demand for products, prices, and raw material costs. All of these factors are considered influential in production activity.

Forecasts play a central role that lies at the heart of the entire decision-making process. Inaccurate and inadequate forecasts risk, therefore, invalidating the conclusions reached through the difficult implementation and resolution of a decision model. The term "forecasting process" refers to that of complex activities, which are more or less explicit, that lead to the formulation of a forecast.

"Forecast" and "prediction" are often used as synonyms: It's always a good idea to make a distinction between the meanings of these two terms. Forecasting allows you to associate the probability of occurrence with future events, or to specify confidence intervals to estimate the size that will be observable and measurable in the future. Prediction, on the other hand, consists of identifying the specific value that a measurable quantity will assume in the future. It is, therefore, easy to associate the corresponding forecasts to the predictions thus formulated, using classical instruments of the inferential statistics to derive the relative confidence intervals.

The main objective of all forecasting models is to find out an estimate of the expected value, together with an estimate of the error that the forecast model can produce.

Forecast horizon

The **forecast horizon** is a factor that significantly characterizes the forecast process. The forecasts can concern an immediate future of up to 12 months, where the forecasts represent support for operational decisions. It could be the case of a demand for a product for the next two months or aimed at medium-term planning, between 12 and 24 months, where forecasts are built to support decisions regarding production plans.

Lastly, they may have as their objective a broad extension in the future, beyond 24 months, where forecasts are formulated to support managerial decisions regarding company development plans. In the three situations described, characterized by a short, medium, and long horizon of prediction, respectively, the objectives of the decision makers wishing to use the forecasts are very different, as is the degree of accuracy and detail required by the corresponding forecasts.

Forecasting methods

Forecasting methodologies differ mainly on the basis of the characteristics and objectives of the decisions for which they will be used. The length of the time horizon, the availability and the homogeneity of a wide historical database, and the characteristics of the product to which the forecasts refer, such as the life cycle stage, are some of the factors that influence the choice of a method.

Essentially, we can divide forecasting methods into two large families—quantitative methods and qualitative methods.

Quantitative methods

We talk about quantitative methods when quantitative information is adequately available. It is used to predict future data based on past data. These methods are usually applied to short or intermediate decisions. Examples of quantitative prediction methods are as follows:

- **Time series**: The phenomenon to be expected is treated like a black box because it does not try to identify the phenomena that can influence it. The goal of this approach is to identify the past evolution of the phenomenon and to extrapolate the past to obtain prediction. In other words, the phenomenon to be predicted is modeled with respect to time and not with respect to an explanatory variable (consider sales trends, GDP trends, and so on).

- **Explanatory methods**: This assumes that the variable to be predicted can be related to one or more independent or explanatory variables. For example, the demand for consumer goods of a family depends on the income received, the age of the components, and so on.

Such forecasting techniques employ regression methods, and therefore, the main phase of the analysis consists in specifying and estimating a model that relates the variable to be predicted (response) and the explanatory variables (for example, effects on sales of advertising and/or price promotion).

These methods can be used in the following hypotheses:

- Sufficient information is available on the past evolution of the phenomenon.
- This information can be quantified.
- It can be assumed that the characteristics of the past evolution continue to exist in the future in order to make the forecast.

Ultimately, quantitative methods are used when adequate quantitative information is available.

Qualitative methods

Qualitative methods are based primarily on judgements and therefore depend on the opinion and judgement of consumers and experts. They are used when there is limited or no quantitative information, but sufficient qualitative information exists. The following are some examples of the application of qualitative methods:

- **Assessments of the sales department**: Each sales agent estimates the future demand for its territory for the next period. The hypothesis underlying this method is that the people closest to the client know their future needs better than anyone else. This information is then aggregated to arrive at global forecasts for each geographic area or product family.
- **Market surveys**: Companies often turn to firms specialized in market surveys to make this type of forecast. Information is obtained directly from customers or more often from a representative sample of them. This type of investigation, however, is mainly used to look for new ideas, to like or dislike existing products, to find out which are the favorite brands of a given product, and so on.

- **Expert panels**: The forecasts are developed by a small group of experts from the various functional areas of the company (marketing, finance, and production) that interact directly with each other. The forecast is developed through meetings with exchanges of ideas and information between managers at all levels. However, there is the problem that lower level employees are overlooked by those at the highest level, and for this reason their opinions are not taken into account.

- **Delphi method**: To prevent the problems of the expert panel, the anonymity of those taking part in the study is guaranteed so that everyone has the same weight. A questionnaire is drawn up and distributed to the participants. The answers are aggregated and, based on these, a new set of questions are prepared that are presented to the group.

Ultimately, qualitative methods are used when adequate quantitative information is not available but qualitative knowledge exists.

Time series analysis

A time series constitutes a sequence of observations on a phenomenon that's carried out in consecutive instants or time intervals that are usually, even if not necessarily, evenly spaced or of the same length. The trend of commodity prices, stock market indices, the BTP/BUND spread, and the unemployment rate are just a few examples of times series.

Contrary to what happens in classical statistics, where it is assumed that independent observations come from a single random variable, in a time series, it is assumed that there are n observations coming from as many dependent random variables as possible. The inference of the time series is thus configured as a procedure that attempts to bring the time series back to its generating process.

The time series can be of two types:

- **Deterministic**: If the values of the variable can be exactly determined on the basis of the previous values
- **Stochastic**: If the values of the variable can be determined on the basis of the previous values, but only partially

The majority of time series are stochastic, and therefore it is impossible to draw up forecasts without errors. It is generally assumed that an observed time series is the result of the composition of these two meaning. The two sequences are not individually observable, but must be determined on the basis of a sample.

We can indicate the series as the sum of these two contributions, as shown in the following equation:

$$Y_t = f(t) + w(t)$$

According to the classical approach to time series, it is assumed that there exists a law of temporal evolution of the phenomenon, represented by $f(t)$. The random component $w(t)$ is assumed to represent the set of circumstances, each of negligible entities, which we do not want or cannot consider in Y_t.

Therefore, the residual part of Y_t, which is not explained by $f(t)$, is imputed to this case and assimilated to a set of accidental errors. This is equivalent to hypothesizing that the stochastic component $w(t)$ is generated by a white noise process, that is, by a sequence of independent and identically distributed random variables of zero mean and constant variance.

In summary, in the classic approach, attention is concentrated on $f(t)$, *and* $w(t)$ is considered a process with uncorrelated components and therefore negligible.

Denoting the time with $t = 1.... T$, we will indicate this sequence, y_t; time is the parameter that determines the sequence of events that cannot be neglected, so we also need to know the position of observation along the temporal dimension. Generally, it is used to represent the pair of values (t, y_t) on a Cartesian diagram with a continuous line graph as if the phenomenon were detected continuously. This graph is called a **time series** plot.

In the following graph, we can see a time series plot of the flow of the river Nile at Aswan from **1871** to **1970** (Cobb(1978), Table 1, p.249):

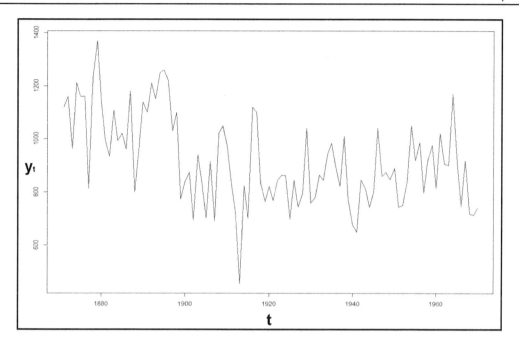

A time series plot immediately reveals trends or regular oscillations, and other systematic trends over time. The previous graph shows annual data in a systematically decreasing trend over a long period of time. In particular, it has a zigzag pattern; since the data is monthly, there is the phenomenon called seasonality. It can be noted that high peaks are always recorded in those months, when rain is expected.

The univariate analysis of the time series proposes to interpret the dynamic mechanism that generated the series and to foresee future realizations of the phenomenon. In these operations, the information that is exploited regards only the couple $(t; y_t)$, where $t = 1,..., T$. The fundamental point is that the past and the present contain relevant information to predict the future evolution of the phenomenon.

It can be considered that univariate analysis is too restrictive; we usually have information on phenomena related to the one to be forecast, which should be appropriately incorporated to improve the performance of the model of revision. Nonetheless, it is a useful benchmark that allows for the validation of more sophisticated alternatives.

In a time series plot, four types of patterns can be identified with respect to time:

- **Horizontal pattern**: In this case, the series oscillates around a constant value (series average). This series is called stationary on average. This is the typical case that occurs in quality control when the process is kept under control with respect to the average.
- **Seasonal pattern**: This exists when the series is influenced by seasonal factors (for example, monthly, semi-annual, quarterly, and so on). Products such as ice cream, soft drinks, and electricity consumption are subject to the seasonal phenomenon. The series influenced by seasonality are also called periodic series since the seasonal cycle repeats itself in a fixed period. In the annual data, seasonality is not present.
- **Cyclic pattern**: This type of trend is present when the series has increases and decreases that are not of a fixed period. This is the main difference between cyclical and seasonal fluctuations. Moreover, the amplitude of cyclical oscillations is generally larger than that due to seasonality. In economic series, the cyclical pattern is determined by the expansions and contractions of the economy due to conjectural phenomena.
- **Trend**: This is characterized by an increasing or decreasing long-term trend. The series of the population of the world is an example of an increasing trend; the series of monthly beer sales, on the other hand, does not show any trend. It has a horizontal background pattern.

Many series highlight a combination of these patterns. It is precisely this kind of complexity that makes the forecasting operation extremely interesting. The forecasting methods, in fact, must be able to recognize the various components of the series in order to reproduce them in the future, in the hypothesis that the past pattern continues to repeat itself in its evolutionary characteristics also in the future.

The classic approach to time series is based on the decomposition of the deterministic part of the series into a set of signal components (which express the structural information of the series) with respect to the negligible part of noise. In practice, we will try to identify some of the patterns that we previously listed in the time series trend.

The following diagram shows a time series with some components identified:

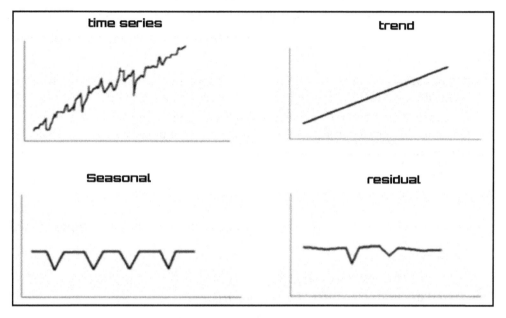

In the previous diagram, the components we have identified are as follows:

- **Trend**: This is the underlying trend of the phenomenon considered, referring to a long period of time.
- **Seasonal**: This consists of movements of the phenomena during the year. Due to the influence of climatic and social factors, they tend to repeat themselves in a similar way in the same period (for example, month, quarter, and so on).
- **Residual**: In the time series models, there is never a perfect relationship between the variable under observation and the different components. The accidental component takes this into account, as well as the unpredictable behavior of economic agents, social factors, and so on.

Finally, we can say that by adopting this approach, a time series can be seen as the sum of the three components that we've just analyzed (additive method).

The classical approach to time series

So far, we have dealt with time series according to a classical approach to the topic. From this perspective, the classical models that try to simulate the phenomenon can be of two types:

- **Composition models**: The elementary components are known, and, by assuming a certain form of aggregation, the resulting series is obtained.
- **Decomposition models**: When an observed series is hypothesized, the existence of some elementary trends, which we want to establish the characteristics of, are obtained.

The decomposition models are the most used in practice, and, for this reason, we will analyze them in detail.

The components of a time series can be aggregated according to different types of methods:

- **Additive method**: $Y(t) = \tau(t) + C(t) + S(t) + r(t)$
- **Multiplicative method**: $Y(t) = \tau(t) * C(t) * S(t) * r(t)$
- **Mixed method**: $Y(t) = \tau(t) * C(t) + S(t) * r(t)$

In these formulas, the factors are defined as follows:

- $Y(t)$ represents the time series
- $\tau(t)$ represents the trend component
- $C(t)$ represents the cyclic component
- $S(t)$ represents the seasonality component
- $r(t)$ represents the residual component

The multiplicative model can be traced back to the additive model through a logarithmic transformation of the components of the series:

$$Y(t) = \tau(t) * C(t) * S(t) * r(t)$$

This formula, by applying the logarithm function to all factors, becomes the following:

$$ln(Y(t)) = ln(tau(t)) * ln(C(t)) * ln(S(t)) * ln(r(t))$$

Now, the model is additive again.

Estimation of the trend component

Estimation of the trend component can occur in two different modes, depending on the linear/nonlinear characteristic. If the series trend is linear or linearizable in the parameters through a logarithmic transformation, then these trends can be estimated through the procedures derived from linear regression. We can hypothesize a polynomial trend that can be represented by the following equation:

$$\tau(t) = \alpha_0 + \alpha_1 t_1 + \alpha_2 t_2 + \dots + \alpha_q t_q + \epsilon t$$

In this formula, q represents the degree of the polynomial.

Depending on the value assumed by q, the following cases can be represented:

q	Cases
0	A constant trend is obtained.
1	We obtain a linear trend.
2	We obtain a parabolic trend.

On the contrary, the presence of a nonlinear trend makes it difficult, if not impossible, to identify a known functional form *f(t)* with which to express the trend component. In these cases, the AM operation is used. **AM** stands for **arithmetic mean** (simple or weighted), and moves to each new iteration (at any time, *t*) from the beginning to the end of the data sequence.

Suppose we have n data terms, as follows:

$$a_1, a_2, a_3, \dots, a_{(n-1)}, a_n$$

The following procedure is adopted:

1. First, we calculate the average of the first three terms and substitute the average value for the central data term.
2. Then, we repeat the procedure with the second three terms.
3. The procedure is exhausted when there is no more data available.

In this case, the AM is composed of only three terms. The AM order can be extended to 5, 7, 9, and so on. For it to be centered with respect to the available data, the order must be odd.

Estimating the seasonality component

The study of the seasonality of a historical series can have the following purposes:

- Simply estimating the seasonal component
- Eliminating it from the general course, once it has been estimated

If you have to compare several time series with different seasonality, the only way to compare them is by a seasonal adjustment of them.

There are several ways to estimate the seasonal component. One of these is the use of a regression model using dichotomous auxiliary variables (dummy variables).

Suppose an additive model without a trend component exists:

$$Y(t) = S(t) + r(t)$$

And suppose we have measured the series on a monthly basis. The dummy variables can be defined in the following way:

- $d_j(t)$: 1 if the observation t is relative to the jth month of the year
- $d_j(t)$: 0 otherwise

Once the periodic dummy variables have been created, the seasonal component can be estimated using the following regression model:

$$Y(t) = \beta_1 D_1 + \beta_2 D_2 + \dots + \beta_n D_n + \epsilon(t)$$

The remaining $\varepsilon(t)$ part of the model represents the part of the series that's not explained by seasonality. If a trend component is present in the series, it will coincide precisely with $\varepsilon(t)$.

Time series models

In the previous section, *Time series analysis*, we explored the basics behind time series. To perform correct predictions of future events based on what happened in the past, it is necessary to construct an appropriate numerical simulation model.

Choosing an appropriate model is extremely important as it reflects the underlying structure of the series. In practice, two types of models are available: linear or nonlinear. These can be selected based on whether the current value of the series is a linear or nonlinear function of past observations.

The following are the most widely used models for forecasting time series data:

- **AR (autoregressive)**
- **MA (moving average)**
- **ARMA (autoregressive moving average)**
- **ARIMA (autoregressive integrated moving average)**

Autoregressive models

Autoregressive (AR) models are useful to tackle the prediction problem in relation to a time series. A strong correlation between consecutive values of a series is often observed.

In this case, we speak of autocorrelation of the first order when we consider adjacent values, of the second order if we refer to the relation between the values of the series after two periods, and in general of the *pth* order if the values considered have *p* periods between them. AR models allow you to exploit these bonds to obtain useful forecasts of the future behavior of the series.

AR is a linear predictive modeling technique. This model tries to predict the time series based on the previous values assumed using the AR parameters as coefficients. The number of samples used for the forecast determines the order of the model (*p*). As the name indicates, it is a regression of the variable against itself; that is, a linear combination of the past values of the variables is used to forecast the future value. The AR model of *p* order is defined as follows:

$$Y_t = c + \sum_{i=1}^{p} \phi_i * Y_{t-i} + \epsilon_t$$

In the previous formula, the terms are defined as follows:

- Y_t is the actual value at time period t
- c is a constant
- ϕ_i ($i = 1,2,..., p$) are model parameters
- Y_{t-i} is the past value at time period t-i
- ε_t is the random error at time period t (white noise)

It may happen that the constant term is omitted; this is done to make the model as simple as possible.

Moving average models

The **moving average** (**MA**) model specifies that the output variable depends linearly on the past and current past values of a stochastic term (imperfectly predictable). The MA model should not be confused with the MA we saw in previous sections. This is an essentially different concept, although some similarities are evident. Unlike the AR model, the finished MA model is always stationary.

Just as a model, AR(*p*), regresses with respect to the past values of the series, an MA(*q*) model uses past errors as explanatory variables.

The MA model of *q* order is defined as follows:

$$Y_t = \mu + \sum_{i=1}^{q} \theta_i * \epsilon_{t-i} + \epsilon_t$$

In the previous formula, the terms are defined as follows:

- Y_t is the actual value at time period *t*
- μ is the mean of the series
- θ_i (*i* = 1,2,..., *q*) are model parameters
- ε_{t-i} is the past random error at time period *t-i*
- ε_t is the random error at time period *t* (white noise)

The MA model is essentially a finite impulsive response filter applied to white noise, with some additional interpretations placed on it.

Autoregressive moving average model

Autoregressive moving average (**ARMA**) is a type of linear mathematical model that provides an output value based on the previous input and output values, instant by instant. The system is seen as an entity that, instant by instant, receives an input value (input) and generates an output (output), calculated on the basis of internal parameters that, in turn, vary according to linear laws.

Each internal parameter, therefore, will be at each instant place, equal to a linear combination of all internal parameters of the previous instant and the incoming value. The output value, in turn, will be a linear combination of internal parameters, and, in rare cases, also of the incoming one.

Much more simply, ARMA can be seen as an effective combination of the AR and MA models to form a general and useful class of time series models.

The model is generally defined as the ARMA model (p, q), where p is the order of the AR part and q is the order of the part of the MA. The ARMA model is defined by the following formula:

$$Y_t = c + \sum_{i=1}^{p} \phi_i * Y_{t-i} + \sum_{i=1}^{q} \theta_i * \epsilon_{t-i} + \epsilon_t$$

In the previous formula, the terms are defined as follows:

- Y_t is the actual value at time period t
- c is again a constant
- ϕ_i (i = 1,2,..., p) are AR model parameters
- Y_{t-i} is the past value at time period t-i
- θ_i (i = 1,2,..., q) are MA model parameters
- ε_{t-i} is the past random error at time period t-i
- ε_t is the random error at time period t (white noise)

In general, once the order (p, q) has been chosen, the parameters of an ARMA model (p, q) can be estimated through the maximum likelihood estimator, for example. As for the AR model, the choice of the model's order must respond to the opposing needs of a good adaptation to the data and parsimony in the number of parameters to be estimated.

Autoregressive integrated moving average models

The **autoregressive integrated moving average** (**ARIMA**) model is a generalization of the ARMA model. ARIMA models are applied in cases where data shows a clear tendency to nonstationarity. In these cases, to eliminate nonstationarity, an initial differentiation step is added to the ARMA algorithm (corresponding to the integrated part of the model), which is then applied one or more times.

This algorithm is, therefore, essentially composed of three parts:

- The part of AR that determines a regression on its own delayed (that is, previous) values to the evolving variable of interest
- The MA part indicates that the regression error is actually a linear combination of error terms whose values have occurred simultaneously and at various times in the past
- The integrated part indicates that the data values have been replaced with the difference between their current values and the previous values (this differentiation process may have been performed more than once)

The purpose of each of these features is to make the model suitable for data in the best possible way.

To formulate the representative equation of the ARIMA model, we start from the ARMA model equation:

$$Y_t = c + \sum_{i=1}^{p} \phi_i * Y_{t-i} + \sum_{i=1}^{q} \theta_i * \epsilon_{t-i} + \epsilon_t$$

Simply move the AR part to the right-hand side of the equation to obtain the following equation (less than the constant c):

$$Y_t - \sum_{i=1}^{p'} \phi_i * Y_{t-i} = \sum_{i=1}^{q} \theta_i * \epsilon_{t-i} + \epsilon_t$$

By introducing the lag operator (L), we can rewrite this equation as follows:

$$\left(1 - \sum_{i=1}^{p'} \phi_i L^i\right) Y_t = \left(1 + \sum_{i=1}^{q} \theta_i L^i\right) \epsilon_t$$

Remember: The lag operator (L) operates on an element of a time series to produce the previous element, with the meaning that $LYt = Yt\text{-}1$.

Thus, we are assuming the following:

$$\left(1 - \sum_{i=1}^{p'} \phi_i L^i\right) = \left(1 - \sum_{i=1}^{p'-d} \phi_i L^i\right)(1 - L)^d$$

This precisely expresses the factoring procedure of order *d* that was previously carried out to eliminate nonstationarity. Based on this assumption and setting $p = p'-d$, we can write the following equation to represent the mathematical formulation of the ARIMA *(p,d,q)* model using lag polynomials:

$$\left(1 - \sum_{i=1}^{p} \phi_i L^i\right)(1 - L)^d Y_t = \left(1 + \sum_{i=1}^{q} \theta_i L^i\right)\epsilon_t$$

The *d* parameter controls the level of differentiating. Generally, *d=1* is enough in most cases.

Long short-term memory in Keras

As we said in Chapter 6, *Movie Reviews Sentiment Analysis Using Recurrent Neural Networks,* LSTM is a particular architecture of RNN.

RNNs are based on the need to preserve a memory of past events; this behavior is not possible with normal networks, and that is why RNNs are used in areas where the classic networks do not produce results, such as the prediction of time series (weather, quotations, and so on) that refer to previous data.

An LSTM network consists of cells (LSTM blocks) that are linked together. Each cell is, in turn, composed of three types of ports: input gate, output gate, and forget gate. They implement the write, read, and reset functions on the cell memory, respectively.

So, the LSTM modules are able to regulate what is stored and deleted. This is possible thanks to the presence of various elements called gates, which are composed of a sigmoid neural layer and a pointwise product.

The output of each gate is in the range (0,1), representing the percentage of information that flows inside it.

The first part of the LSTM module decides what information is deleted from the cell. The gate takes the inputs and returns a value between 0 and 1 for each state of the cell. The gate output can take two values:

- **0**: Complete reset of the cell status
- **1**: Total storage of the cell value

Data storage is divided into two phases:

- The first is entrusted to one sigmoid layer called the **input gate layer**; it carries out an operation that establishes which values will need to be updated.
- The second phase is instead entrusted to a tanh layer that creates a vector of values intended to be updated. To create an updated set of values, the outputs of the two layers are combined.

Finally, the result will be given by a sigmoid layer, which decides on which parts of the cell will contribute to the output and from the current state of the cell, filtered through a tanh function to obtain a range from -1 to 1.

The result of this operation is multiplied by the value of the sigmoid layer so that only the desired outputs are output.

To add an LSTM layer in Keras, we must use the following syntax:

```
keras.layers.LSTM(units, activation='tanh',
recurrent_activation='hard_sigmoid',use_bias=True,
kernel_initializer='glorot_uniform', recurrent_initializer='orthogonal',
bias_initializer='zeros', unit_forget_bias=True, kernel_regularizer=None,
recurrent_regularizer=None, bias_regularizer=None,
activity_regularizer=None, kernel_constraint=None,
recurrent_constraint=None, bias_constraint=None, dropout=0.0,
recurrent_dropout=0.0, implementation=1, return_sequences=False,
return_state=False, go_backwards=False, stateful=False, unroll=False)
```

Read through the following list to understand the arguments used in the preceding code block:

- `units`: This is a positive integer and the dimensionality of the output space.
- `activation`: The activation function to use. The default is the hyperbolic tangent (`tanh`). If you pass None, no activation is applied.
- `recurrent_activation`: The activation function to use for the recurrent step. The default is the hard sigmoid (`hard_sigmoid`). If you pass None, no activation is applied.

- `use_bias`: This is a Boolean that decides whether the layer uses a bias vector.
- `kernel_initializer`: This is an initializer for the kernel weights matrix, and is used for the linear transformation of the inputs.
- `recurrent_initializer`: This is an initializer for the `recurrent_kernel` weights matrix, and is used for the linear transformation of the recurrent state.
- `bias_initializer`: This is initializer for the bias vector.
- `unit_forget_bias`: Boolean. If True, add 1 to the bias of the forget gate at initialization. Setting it to true will also force `bias_initializer="zeros"`.
- `kernel_regularizer`: A regularizer function that's applied to the kernel weights matrix.
- `recurrent_regularizer`: A regularizer function that's applied to the `recurrent_kernel` weights matrix.
- `bias_regularizer`: A regularizer function that's applied to the bias vector.
- `activity_regularizer`: A regularizer function that's applied to the output of the layer.
- `kernel_constraint`: A constraint function that's applied to the kernel weights matrix.
- `recurrent_constraint`: A constraint function that's applied to the `recurrent_kernel` weights matrix.
- `bias_constraint`: A constraint function that's applied to the bias vector.
- `dropout`: A float between 0 and 1. This indicates the fraction of the units to drop for the linear transformation of the inputs.
- `recurrent_dropout`: A float between 0 and 1. This indicates the fraction of the units to drop for the linear transformation of the recurrent state.
- `implementation`: Implementation mode, either 1 or 2. Mode 1 will structure its operations as a larger number of smaller dot products and additions, whereas Mode 2 will batch them into fewer, larger operations. These modes will have different performance profiles on different hardware and for different applications.
- `return_sequences`: This is a Boolean that decides whether to return the last output in the output sequence, or the full sequence.
- `return_state`: This is a Boolean that decides whether to return the last state in addition to the output.

- `go_backwards`: Boolean (its default value is False). If True, process the input sequence backwards and return the reversed sequence.
- `stateful`: Boolean (its default is False). If True, the last state for each sample at index i in a batch will be used as the initial state for the sample of index i in the following batch.
- `unroll`: Boolean (its default is False). If True, the network will be unrolled, otherwise a symbolic loop will be used. Unrolling can speed up an RNN, although it tends to be more memory-intensive. Unrolling is only suitable for short sequences.

In the next section, we will deep dive into an applicative example of LSTM model using the Keras library.

Implementing an LSTM to forecast stock volatility

The stock market forecast has always been a very popular topic: this is because stock market trends involve a truly impressive turnover. The interest that this topic arouses is clearly linked to the opportunity to get rich through good forecasting by a stock market title. A positive difference between the purchased stock price and that of the sold stock price entails a gain on the part of the investor. But, as we know, the performance of the stock market depends on multiple factors.

In this section, we'll look at how the LSTM model can be applied to predict the future stock price of a very popular company: I refer to Amazon, the US e-commerce company, based in Seattle, Washington, which is the largest internet company in the world.

Amazon has been listed on Wall Street since 1997 with the AMZN symbol; its title is included in the NASDAQ index, which gathers companies in technology and IT sectors. Founded in the 1990s, Amazon was one of the first major companies to sell products using the internet; its business strategy has been set with a long-term perspective, with the proviso from the beginning that it wouldn't generate profits for several years and instead focus on a rapid expansion of the business and the conquest of new market areas.

To analyze the performance of Amazon stock prices, we will use the data relating to the stock prices in the time interval from 2000-06-05 to 2018-06-05 on the NASDAQ GS stock quote (it is possible to set a different interval from the one displayed by default).

This data was downloaded from the Yahoo! Finance website at `https://finance.yahoo.com/quote/AMZN/history/`.

The following screenshot shows the Yahoo! Finance website:

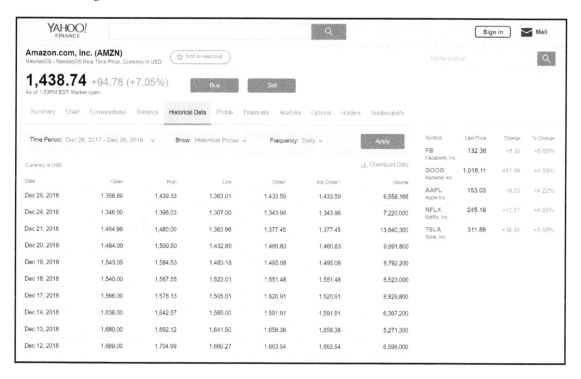

This file (in `.csv` format) contains the following features:

- **Date**: Date of quote
- **Open**: Open price
- **High**: High price
- **Low**: Low price
- **Close**: Close price adjusted for splits
- **Adj Close**: Close price adjusted for both dividends and splits
- **Volume**: Exchange volume

The data that's available in the CSV file is named `AMZN.csv`. To start, let's look at how we can import this data into Python. The first thing to do is import the library that we will use:

```
import pandas as pd
```

With this code, we import the pandas library. Now, let's look at how we can import the data contained in the dataset in Python:

```
Data = pd.read_csv('AMZN.csv',header=0, usecols=['Date',
        'Close'],parse_dates=True,index_col='Date')
```

To import the dataset, we used the `read_csv` module of the pandas library. The `read_csv` method loads the data in a pandas DataFrame, which we named dataset. The following arguments are used:

- `header`: The row number(s) used as the column names and the start of the data. The default behavior is to infer the column names; if no names are passed, the behavior is identical to header=0, and the column names are inferred from the first line of the file. If the column names are passed explicitly, then the behavior is identical to `header=None`.
- `usecols`: This returns a subset of the columns. If list-like, all elements must either be positional (that is, integer indices into the document columns) or strings that correspond to column names, provided either by the user in names or inferred from the document header row(s). In our case, we have collected only two columns (Date and Close).
- `parse_dates`: This is a Boolean. If True, try parsing the index.
- `index_col`: This is the column to use as the row labels of the DataFrame. If a sequence is given, a MultiIndex is used.

Once the data that's necessary for the simulation has been correctly imported, we can proceed with our analysis.

Exploratory analysis

Before starting with data prediction using the LSTM method, we will conduct an exploratory analysis to understand how the data is distributed and extract preliminary knowledge. To extract preliminary information about the imported dataset, we can invoke the `info()` function:

```
print(Data.info())
```

This function prints information about a DataFrame, including the index and column dtypes, non-null values, and memory usage. The following results are returned:

```
<class 'pandas.core.frame.DataFrame'>
DatetimeIndex: 4529 entries, 2000-11-21 to 2018-11-21
Data columns (total 1 columns):
Close     4529 non-null float64
dtypes: float64(1)
memory usage: 70.8 KB
None
```

From the analysis of the results that have been obtained, we can see that the dataset contains 4529 observations of Amazon stock prices in the period from 2000-11-21 to 2018-11-21. To display the first five rows of the imported DataFrame, we can use the head() function, as follows:

```
print(Data.head())
```

This function returns the first *n* rows for the object based on position. It is useful for quickly testing if your object has the right type of data in it. By default (if n is omitted), the first five rows are displayed. The following results are returned:

```
               Close
Date
2000-11-21    24.2500
2000-11-22    25.1875
2000-11-24    28.9375
2000-11-27    28.0000
2000-11-28    25.0312
```

To get a preview of the data contained in it, we can calculate a series of basic statistics. To do so, we will use the describe() function in the following way:

```
print(Data.describe())
```

This function generates descriptive statistics that summarize the central tendency, dispersion, and shape of a dataset's distribution, excluding **NaN** (**not a number**) values. It analyzes both numeric and object series, as well as DataFrame column sets of mixed data types. The output will vary depending on what is provided. The following results are returned:

```
               Close
count    4529.000000
mean      290.353723
std       407.211585
min         5.970000
```

```
25%        39.849998
50%       117.889999
75%       327.440002
max      2039.510010
```

From an initial analysis of the results that have been obtained, we can see that Amazon stock prices have made a noticeable change over the last 18 years. In fact, the minimum value is equal to $5.97, while the maximum value is equal to $2039.51. To confirm this, the standard deviation values are high, indicating a high volatility: the value of the examined data deviates significantly from its average.

After having taken a look at the content of the dataset, we are going to perform an initial visual exploratory analysis. To do so, we will use the matplotlib library:

```
import matplotlib.pyplot as plt
```

By doing this, the pyplot module is imported from the matplotlib library, and we just have to draw the graph:

```
plt.figure(figsize=(10,5))
plt.plot(Data)
plt.show()
```

Three functions have been used here: figure(), plot(), and show().

Let's analyze these operations in detail. The first one, figure(), creates a new figure, which is empty for now. We need to set the size of the frame that will contain it. In fact, we used the figsize parameter, which sets the width and height in inches. Then, the plot() function was used, which plots the dataset, and finally the show() function was used to display the plot. The show() function, when running in IPython in PyLab mode, displays all figures and returns to the IPython prompt.

In noninteractive mode, it displays all figures and blocks until the figures have been closed; in interactive mode, it has no effect unless figures were created prior to a change from noninteractive to interactive mode (not recommended). In this case, it displays the figures, but does not block. In the following graph, Amazon stock prices from 2000-11-21 to 2018-11-21 are shown:

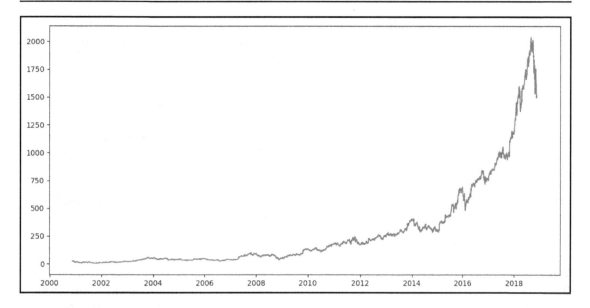

From the analysis of the previous graph, we can see that prices have increased considerably over time. In particular, starting from 2015, this increase has shown an exponential trend.

Now, let's try to obtain a deeper understanding of the change that Amazon stock has recorded over time. It is interesting to study the evolution of a phenomenon, not only through the graph of its time series, but also by making comparisons between the intensity of the phenomenon at different times, that is, calculating the variations of intensity from one period to another. Furthermore, it can be interesting to analyze the trend of the variations of the phenomenon that occurred between adjoining periods of time.

We indicate a time series with $Y_1, ..., Y_t, ..., Y_n$. As we said in the *Time series analysis* section, time series is the chronological recording of experimental observations of a variable, such as price trends, stock market indices, spreads, and unemployment rates. It is therefore a succession of data ordered over time from which we want to extract information for the characterization of the phenomenon under observation, and for the prediction of future values.

The variation that occurs between two different times (let's indicate them with t and $t + 1$) can be measured using the following ratio:

$$\frac{Y_{t+1} - Y_t}{Y_t}$$

This index is a percentage ratio and is called a percentage change. In particular, this is the percentage rate of variation of the phenomenon *Y* of the time *t + 1*, with respect to the previous time, *t*. The percentage change method gives a more precise description as to how the data has changed over a period of time.

This method is used both to track the prices of individual securities and of large market indices, as well as comparing the values of different currencies. Balance sheets with comparative financial statements will generally include the prices of specific assets at different points in time, along with the percentage changes over the accompanying periods of time.

To calculate percentage changes in Python, we will use the `pct_change()` function. This function returns percentage changes over a given number of periods:

```
DataPCh = Data.pct_change()
```

What we have just calculated coincides with the concept of return: why do we want to use the returns instead of prices? The benefit of using returns, versus prices, is normalization: measuring all variables in a comparable metric, hence enabling evaluation of analytic relationships among two or more variables, despite originating from a price series of unequal values. This is a requirement for many multidimensional statistical analysis and machine learning techniques.

In particular, we will calculate the logarithm of returns. Also, in this case, we have clear benefits:

- **Log-normality**: If we assume that prices are distributed log normally, then *log(1 + r)* is conveniently normally distributed.
- **Approximate raw-log equality**: When returns are very small results, *log(1 + r)* is roughly equal to *r*.
- **Logarithmic returns**: These are additive over time.

To calculate the logarithm of returns, we will use the `log()` function from numpy. First, we will import the numpy library:

```
import numpy as np
```

Then, we will apply the `log` function:

```
LogReturns = np.log(1 + DataPCh)
```

To get a preview of what we've got, let's `print` the tail:

```
print(LogReturns.tail(10))
```

The `tail()` function returns the last *n* rows from the object, based on position. It is useful for quickly verifying data, for example, after sorting or appending rows. The following values are returned (the last 10 rows of the `LogReturns` object):

```
                Close
Date
2018-11-08  -0.000330
2018-11-09  -0.024504
2018-11-12  -0.045140
2018-11-13  -0.003476
2018-11-14  -0.019913
2018-11-15   0.012696
2018-11-16  -0.016204
2018-11-19  -0.052251
2018-11-20  -0.011191
2018-11-21   0.014123
```

Now, we will draw a diagram with the logarithm of the returns we have calculated:

```
plt.figure(figsize=(10,5))
plt.plot(LogReturns)
plt.show()
```

As we have done previously, we first set the dimensions of the graph, then we plot the graph, and finally we visualize it. The following graph shows the logarithm of the returns:

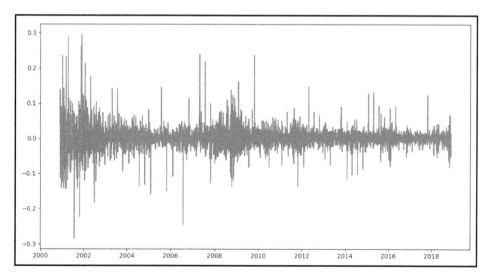

Analyzing the previous graph, we can see that the returns are normally distributed and have a stable mean.

Data scaling

By analyzing the `describe()` functions results, as shown in the *Exploratory analysis* section, we can see that the variables have different ranges.

As discussed in `Chapter 2`, *Modeling the Real Estate Market Using Regression Analysis*, when the predictors have different ranges, the impact on response variables by the feature having a greater numeric range could be more than the one having a less numeric range. This could, in turn, impact the prediction's accuracy.

Our goal is to improve predictive accuracy and not allow a particular feature to impact the prediction due to a large numeric value range. Thus, we may need to scale values under different features so that they fall under a common range. Through this statistical procedure, it is possible to compare identical variables belonging to different distributions and also different variables or variables expressed in different units.

 Remember, it is a good practice to rescale the data before training an LSTM algorithm. With rescaling, data units are eliminated, allowing you to compare data from different locations easily.

In this case, we will use the min-max method (usually called feature scaling) to get all the scaled data in the range [0, 1]. The formula to achieve this is as follows:

$$x_{scaled} = \frac{x - x_{min}}{x_{max} - x_{min}}$$

To perform feature scaling, we can use the preprocessing package that's available in the `sklearn library`. The `sklearn.preprocessing` package provides several common utility functions and transformer classes to modify the features available in a representation that best suits our needs. As always, we start by importing the package:

```
from sklearn.preprocessing import MinMaxScaler
```

To scale features between a given minimum and maximum value, in our case between 0 and 1, that the maximum absolute value of each feature is scaled to unit size, the `MinMaxScaler()` function can be used. Let's start by defining the scaler:

```
scaler = MinMaxScaler()
```

Now, we can scale the features:

```
DataScaled = scaler.fit_transform(Data)
```

The `fit_transform()` function is used to fit to the data and then transform it. A `numpy` array of shape is returned. This function is particularly useful as it stores the transformation parameters being used. These parameters will be useful when, after having made the forecasts, we have to report the data in the initial form (before normalization) to compare it with actual data.

Data splitting

Now, let's split the data for the training and the test model. Training and testing the model forms the basis for further usage of the model for prediction in predictive analytics. Given a dataset of 4,529 rows of data, we split it into a convenient ratio (say 70:30), and allocate 3,170 rows for training and 1,359 rows for testing.

In general, in the algorithms based on artificial neural networks, the splitting is done by selecting rows randomly to reduce bias. With time series data, the sequence of values is important, so this procedure is not practicable.

A simple method that we can use is to divide the ordered dataset into train and test. As we anticipated, the following code calculates the division point index and separates the data in the training datasets, with 70% of the observations for us to use to train our model; this leaves the remaining 30% to test the model:

```
TrainLen = int(len(DataScaled) * 0.70)
TestLen = len(DataScaled) - TrainLen
TrainData = DataScaled[0:TrainLen,:]
TestData = DataScaled[TrainLen:len(DataScaled),:]
```

The first two lines of code set the length of the two groups of data. The two lines that follow split the dataset into two parts: from row 1 to row `TrainLen` −1 for the train set, and from the `TrainLen` row to the last row for the test set. To confirm the correct split of data, we can print the length of the two datasets:

```
print(len(TrainData), len(TestData))
```

This gives the following results:

```
3170 1359
```

As we anticipated, the operation divided the dataset into `3170` rows (train set) and `1359` rows (test set).

Keras LSTM model

Our aim is to use the data in this dataset to predict the Amazon stock price on the data available in the .csv file. We need input and output to train and test our network.

It is clear that the input is represented by the data that's present in the dataset. Therefore, we must construct our output; we will do so by supposing we want to predict the Amazon stock price at time *t + 1* with respect to the value stored at time *t*. Therefore, we will have the following:

$$Input = data(t)$$
$$Output = data(t+1)$$

In Chapter 6, *Movie Reviews Sentiment Analysis Using Recurrent Neural Networks*, we said that a recurrent network has memory, and this is maintained by fixing the so-called **time step**. The time step is all about how many steps back in time backpropagation uses when calculating gradients for weight updates during training. In this way, we set TimeStep = 1. Then, we define a function that gives a dataset and a time step, which then returns the input and output data:

```
def DatasetCreation(dataset, TimeStep=1):
    DataX, DataY = [], []
    for i in range(len(dataset)- TimeStep -1):
        a = dataset[i:(i+ TimeStep), 0]
        DataX.append(a)
        DataY.append(dataset[i + TimeStep, 0])
    return np.array(DataX), np.array(DataY)
```

In this function, *dataX =Input= data(t)* is the input variable and *DataY=output= data(t + 1)* is the predicted value at the next time period. Let's use this function to set the train and test datasets that we will use in the next phase (network modeling):

```
TimeStep = 1
TrainX, TrainY = DatasetCreation(TrainData, TimeStep)
TestX, TestY = DatasetCreation(TestData, TimeStep)
```

By doing this, we have created all the data that's needed for the network's training and testing. This function converts an array of values into a dataset matrix.

Now, we have to prepare the two input datasets (TrainX and TestX) in the form required by the machine learning algorithm we intend to use (LSTM). To do this, it is necessary to deepen this concept.

In a classic feedforward network, like those already analyzed in the previous chapters, the input contains the values assumed by the variables for each observation made. This means that the input takes the following shape:

(number of observations, number of features)

In an LSTM/RNN network, the input for each LSTM layer must contain the following information:

- **Observations**: Number of observations collected
- **Time steps**: A time step is an observation point in the sample
- **Features**: One feature for each step

Therefore, it is necessary to add a temporal dimension to those foreseen for a classical network. Thus, the input shape becomes as follows:

(number of observations, number of time steps, number of features per steps)

In this way, the input for each LSTM layer becomes three-dimensional. To transform the input datasets in 3-D form, we will use the np.reshape() function, as follows:

```
TrainX = np.reshape(TrainX, (TrainX.shape[0], 1, TrainX.shape[1]))
TestX = np.reshape(TestX, (TestX.shape[0], 1, TestX.shape[1]))
```

The np.reshape() function gives a new shape to an array without changing its data. The function parameters that are used are as follows:

- TrainX, TestX: Array to be reshaped
- (TrainX.shape[0], 1, 1), (TestX.shape[0], 1, 1): New shape

The new shape should be compatible with the original shape. In our case, the new shape is *(3171,1,1)* for TrainX and *(1360,1,1)* for TestX. Now that the data is in the right format, it's time to create the model. Let's start by importing the libraries:

```
from keras.models import Sequential
from keras.layers import LSTM
from keras.layers import Dense
```

We will use a sequential model, that is, a linear stack of layers. To create a sequential model, we have to pass a list of layer instances to the constructor. We can also simply add layers via the add() method:

```
model = Sequential()
```

The `Sequential` class is used to define a linear stack of network layers that make up a model. Let's add an LSTM layer:

```
model.add(LSTM(256, input_shape=(1, TimeStep)))
```

As we saw in the long short-term memory in the *Keras* section, to add an LSTM layer, simply use the LSTM class. The following parameters are passed:

- `256`: The units, that is, the positive integer and dimensionality of the output space
- `input_shape=(1, TimeStep)`: The shape of the 3-D input tensor

In the following line, we will add a dense layer that implements the default sigmoid activation function:

```
model.add(Dense(1, activation='sigmoid'))
```

Before training a model, you need to configure the learning process, which is done via the `compile()` method:

```
model.compile(loss='mean_squared_error',
optimizer='adam',metrics=['accuracy'])
```

Three arguments are passed:

- **Adam optimizer**: An algorithm for first-order, gradient-based optimization of stochastic objective functions, based on adaptive estimates of lower order moments.
- **Mean squared error (MSE) loss function**: MSE measures the average of the squares of the errors—that is, the average squared difference between the estimated values and what is estimated. MSE is a measure of the quality of an estimator—it is always nonnegative, and has values close to zero.
- **Better accuracy metric**: A metric is a function that is used to evaluate the performance of your model during training and testing.

To train the model, the `fit()` method is used, as follows:

```
model.fit(TrainX, TrainY, epochs=100, batch_size=1, verbose=1)
```

Five arguments are passed:

- `TrainX`: Array of input training data.
- `TrainY`: Array of target (label) data.

- epochs=100: Number of epochs to train the model. An epoch is an iteration over the entire *x* and *y* data provided.
- batch_size=1: Number of samples per gradient update.
- verbose=1: An integer. 0, 1, or 2. Verbosity mode. 0 = silent, 1 = progress bar, 2 = one line per epoch.

To print a summary of the model, simply type the following:

```
model.summary()
```

The following screenshots shows the results:

```
Layer (type)                     Output Shape        Param #
=================================================================
lstm_9 (LSTM)                    (None, 256)          264192
_____
dense_10 (Dense)                 (None, 1)            257
=================================================================
Total params: 264,449
Trainable params: 264,449
Non-trainable params: 0
```

To evaluate the performance of the model we have just adapted, we use the evaluate() function, as follows:

```
score = model.evaluate(TrainX, TrainY, verbose=0)
print('Keras Model Loss = ',score[0])
print('Keras Model Accuracy = ',score[1])
```

This function returns the loss value and metrics values for the model in test mode. Computation is done in batches. The following results are returned:

```
Keras Model Loss = 2.4628453362992094e-06
Keras Model Accuracy = 0.0003156565656565657
```

The model is now ready for use. We can therefore use it to execute our predictions:

```
TrainPred = model.predict(TrainX)
TestPred = model.predict(TestX)
```

The predict() function has been used, which generates output predictions for the input samples. Computation is done in batches. A numPy array of predictions is returned. Previously, when data scaling was performed, we used the fit_transform() function.

As we said previously, this function is particularly useful as it stores the transformation parameters being used: these parameters are useful when, after having made the forecasts, we have to report the data in the initial form (before normalization) to compare it to the actual data. In fact, now, the predictions must be reported in original form so that they can be compared with the actual values:

```
TrainPred = scaler.inverse_transform(TrainPred)
TrainY = scaler.inverse_transform([TrainY])
TestPred = scaler.inverse_transform(TestPred)
TestY = scaler.inverse_transform([TestY])
```

This code block is used exclusively to cancel the effect of normalization and to restore the initial form to the dataset. We have used the `inverse_transform()` function of the `sklearn.preprocessing` library. This function scales back the data to the original representation. Only the data used to scale along the features axis is passed.

To verify the correct prediction of data, we can now visualize the results by drawing an appropriate graph. To display the time series correctly, a prediction shift is required. This operation must be carried out both on the train set and the test set:

```
TrainPredictPlot = np.empty_like(DataScaled)
TrainPredictPlot[:, :] = np.nan
TrainPredictPlot[1:len(TrainPred)+1, :] = TrainPred
```

As we stated previously, the same operation must then be performed on the test set:

```
TestPredictPlot = np.empty_like(DataScaled)
TestPredictPlot[:, :] = np.nan
TestPredictPlot[len(TrainPred)+(1*2)+1:len(DataScaled)-1, :] = TestPred
```

Finally, we have to plot the actual data and the predictions:

```
plt.plot(scaler.inverse_transform(DataScaled))
plt.plot(TrainPredictPlot)
plt.plot(TestPredictPlot)
plt.show()
```

The following screenshot shows the actual data and the predictions:

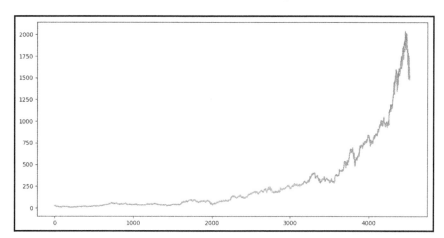

From the analysis of the previous graph, we can see that what is reported by the model accuracy is confirmed by the graph. In fact, we can see that the model has done an excellent job of fitting both the training and test datasets.

Summary

In this chapter, we explored the basic concepts of forecasting techniques. Forecast horizon and several forecast methods were analyzed, all in relation to time series data. A time series constitutes a sequence of observations on a phenomenon. In a time series, we can identify several components—trend, seasonality, cycle, and residual. We learned how to remove seasonality from a time series with a practical example.

Then, the models most widely used to represent time series were addressed—AR, MA, ARMA, and ARIMA. For each model, the basic concepts were analyzed and then a mathematical formulation of the model was provided.

Finally, a Keras LSTM model for time series analysis was proposed. Using a practical example, we saw how we can deal with a time series regression problem with a recurrent neural network model of the LSTM type.

In the next chapter, we will learn about the basic concepts of image recognition and how optical character recognition works. We will also understand the differences between pattern matching and gradient matching and autoencoder basics, and learn how to implement the autoencoder model in Keras.

8
Reconstruction of Handwritten Digit Images Using Autoencoders

The term **handwriting recognition (HWR)** refers to the ability of a computer to receive and interpret as text intelligible handwritten input from sources such as paper documents, photographs, and touchscreens. Written text can be detected on a piece of paper with optical scanning (**optical character recognition (OCR)**) or intelligent word recognition.

An autoencoder is a neural network, whose purpose is to code its input into small dimensions, and the result obtained helps to reconstruct the input itself. Autoencoders are made up of the union of the following two subnets: encoder and decoder. The encoder and the decoder will be differentiable with respect to the distance function, so the parameters of the encoding/decoding functions can be optimized to minimize the loss of reconstruction, using the gradient stochastic. In this chapter, an autoencoder is used to reconstruct handwritten digit images.

The following topics will be covered:

- Basic concepts of image recognition
- Optical character recognition
- Generative neural networks
- The Keras autoencoders model
- Implementing autoencoder Keras layers to reconstruct handwritten digit images

In this chapter, we will learn how image recognition models are structured, learn how optical character recognition works, and understand the essential notions of generative neural networks. We will also understand autoencoder basics, and learn how to implement the autoencoder model.

Basic concepts of image recognition

Identifying and correctly cataloging objects within images is not a simple task. Humans and animals have always done this automatically, obtaining excellent results. The automatic recognition algorithms try to extend this feature to machines. These algorithms have made great strides in recent years, allowing the automatic recognition of many objects and returning acceptable errors.

Image digitization

The analog representation of an information is based on a continuous set of values. The digital representation is based on a discrete set of values. Photographic image (analogue) is composed of millions of very small and spatially irregular colored pigments. A digital image is composed of pixels arranged on a regular square grid: The pixel is generally square but can also take different shapes. The digitization process determines the transition from a continuous set of (analog) values to a discrete set of (digital) values.

An analogue image is comparable to a function of two variables, $f(x, y)$ in which f is the brightness of the image at the position of real coordinates (x, y). The brightness, in general, will have real or integer values: the second case is the result of a sampling process that converts a continuous range of values (for example, between 0 and 100% brightness) in a finite number of levels. In reality, the possibility that the range of values is continuous is an approximation.

A digital image defined in a discrete two-dimensional space is derived from an analogical image, $f(x, y)$, defined in a continuous space through a sampling process (digitization). In the digitization process, the image $f(x, y)$, defined in the continuous, is divided in to N rows and M columns. The intersection of a row and a column is named **pixels**. The value assigned to the whole coordinates (m, n) with $m = 0,1,2, ..., M$ and $n = 0,1,2, ..., N$ is a physical signal revealed by a sensor: this signal is a function of many variables including, for example, time (t).

The brightness of the 2-D signal in a given position is therefore represented with an integer value, chosen among L different gray levels. Parameters as a number of columns (width), rows (height), and gray levels (depth), often take standard values for digital images. Width and height are often of the 2 K form, with $K \in \{8, 9, 10\}$; this is motivated by the structure of the digital circuits of the computer, or by the use of certain algorithms such as Fast Fourier Transform (**FFT**), which preferentially require that the dimensions of the image on which they work are powers of 2. The number of distinct gray **levels** (**L**) is normally a power of 2, that is, $L = 2 B$ where B is the number of bits in the binary representation of the brightness levels. Values commonly used for image depth (grayscale) are: 2, 64, 256, 65536. When $B > 1$, we talk about a gray-level image; when $B = 1$ the image is binary. In a binary image, there are only two levels of gray referred to as black and white, or 0 and 1.

FFT is an algorithm optimized to calculate the discrete Fourier transform (DFT) and its inverse. The FFT is used in a wide variety of applications, from the processing of digital signals to the solution of differential equations to partial derivatives to algorithms for multiplying large integers thanks to the low computational cost.

In Chapter 5, *Fashion Article Recognition Using Convolutional Neural Networks*, we have seen a practical example of digitizing a binary image. In the coding of an image, it is divided into a grid of small squares, each of which represents a pixel. At this point, to encode the color images, it will be enough to identify for each square a certain number of shades and different color gradations. Then, we code each one by means of an appropriate sequence of bits. Here is a simple binary image encoding:

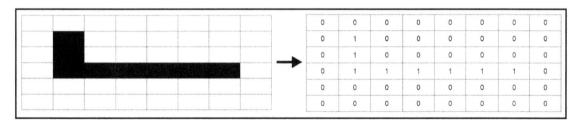

The **two-dimensional** (**2-D**) digital image is therefore a signal consisting of square samples (pixels, picture elements) uniformly organized on a rectangular 2-D grid (a mosaic matrix). The number of cells in the grid defines the resolution of the image.

For reasons of mass storage space and transfer rates via data networks, files containing images are generally compressed with lossy or lossless methodologies. Lossless methods, although less effective, are naturally more suitable for medical diagnostic images, as they do not result in a loss of image resolution.

While lossless compression allows us to reconstruct the original information contained in the file, lossy compression modifies the information irreversibly to the advantage of a greater compression ratio. In loss compression, the rebuilt image decompressing the file deceives the eye, but contains significant differences. Usually, these differences are not perceptible, because the part of information lost is still the one that the user would not have noticed. It has been established that the eye cannot distinguish two black and white images that have the first $2^6 = 64$ gray levels and the second $2^8 = 256$ gray levels.

In the following figure, a beautiful color image of the Colosseum, also known as the **Flavian Amphitheatre**, an oval amphitheater in the center of the city of Rome, Italy, has been converted into grayscale. The first image (on the left) has a depth of 64 while the second (on the right) has a depth of 256. No significant variations are appreciated, except in the part relative to the sky (background):

Another type of difference that cannot be found is the brightness and color of a pixel; it has been shown that the human eye is much more sensitive to changes in brightness than in hue, so it is possible to eliminate some nuances from an image without the eye detecting it.

Image recognition

The operations of classification and indexing of the images are based on the automatic analysis of the image content, constituting the main application field of the imaging analysis. The objective of an automatic image recognition system consists in the description, through mathematical models and computer implementations, of the content of an image, trying, as far as possible, to respect the principles of the human visual system. To this end, the information contained in an image is represented according to three levels of abstraction, following a bottom-up approach:

- **The first level** includes the representation of the primitive characteristics, consisting of the color, the plot and the elementary geometric shapes.

- **The second level** proposes to provide a more detailed description of the elements mentioned, providing the representation of more complex objects through their aggregation and their spatial arrangements (logical characteristics).

- **The third level**, finally, includes the description of the abstract characteristics, such as the significance of the represented scenes and the sensations induced in an observer.

The development of a system of automatic recognition of the images includes several areas of interest, each of them connected with the main problems of image processing and information retrieval. However, we can identify some key points:

- Identification of the most suitable modalities for the description of the image content. For some simple applications, analysis of color distribution alone may be sufficient, while more complex applications may require the joint use of multiple descriptors.

- Choice of methods of extraction of the characteristics previously identified.

- Determination of the most appropriate methods for the compact storage of large collections of images and the characteristics extracted from them. In this context, the literature is very broad, and includes various solutions, typically in a tree, for indexing multidimensional spaces and efficient access to large databases.

- Search for comparison methods modeling judgment metrics commonly used by man. This is a very important aspect for the purpose of comprehensibility and usability of the results obtained, as it allows us to adopt in the system perceptual analysis techniques, or similar to those that would be provided by a human user.

- Development of user-friendly interfaces for the interaction between man and machine, in such a way as to make the use of the system as simple and intuitive as possible, even by an inexperienced user.

These features will be highlighted in the practical application that we will address later.

Optical character recognition

We have always been particularly sensitive to the problem of the automatic recognition of writing in order to achieve a simpler interaction between humans and machines. Especially in the last few years, this problem has found interesting developments and more and more efficient solutions thanks to a very strong economic interest and an ever-greater capacity to process the data of modern computers. In particular, some countries, such as Japan, and Asian countries in general, are investing heavily in terms of research and financial resources, making state-of-the-art OCR.

It is easy to understand the interest of these countries in this field of research. In fact, we try to create devices able to interpret the ideograms characteristic of those cultures to allow greater comfort in the interaction with the machines. Since there are currently no input devices, such as keyboards, that can represent thousands of characters, we try to acquire this information directly from the script via a digitized scan. However, even in the West, great importance has been given to research into the optical recognition of writing. There are many applications that certainly benefit from an automatic reading; just think, for example, of the automatic interpretation of preprinted models or the recognition of addresses and codes of postal initiation on envelopes.

Approaches to the problem

The approaches to the problem are basically of two types: the approach based on pattern matching or on the comparison of the model, and the one based on structural analysis. Often, these two techniques are used in combination, managing to obtain remarkable results in terms of recognition and speed.

The first patents obtained for OCR date back to the 1930s and were registered in Germany by Tausheck (1929—reading machine shown in the following diagram), and in the United States thanks to Hendel (1933). In the following diagram is shown a Tausheck reading-machine scheme:

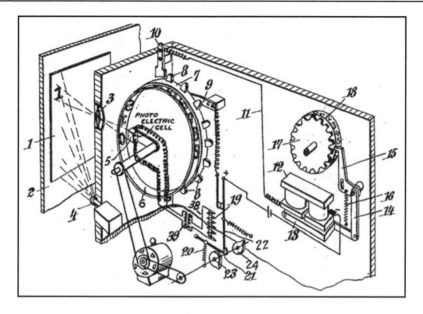

The basic idea is the same and is very simple. Both made use of a simple machine based on a mask overlay approach (template/mask matching). The device used, of course, mirrored the technologies of the time, and was based on an optomechanical approach. A light, which passed through a mechanical mask, was captured by a sensor and then acquired. The recognition of a given character was linked to the greater or lesser correspondence between the sample and the prototype based on the physical overlap of the two elements. In fact, if the light could not reach the sensor, there was a perfect overlap and therefore recognition of the character. This approach is based on the Euclidean axiom of the overlap of forms.

This methodology, certainly valid, however, has a serious gap in terms of generalization. A small variation of the sample symbol, compared to the prototype, may correspond to a failure to recognize the character. This observation also applies if the sample character is slightly smaller or larger than the prototype, or is slightly rotated compared to the prototype. The following diagram shows how handwritten digits (0-9) change during rotation:

These simple alterations lead to errors in recognition. Considerations of this kind show that an approach based only on overlapping does not lead to good results in terms of recognition, even if such a method has the great advantage of being simple, intuitive, and easily applicable both at an algorithmic level and at a mechanical level. From the beginning, therefore, the problem was strongly felt to find a method of comparison between the sample and the prototype that was invariant with respect to scaling and rotation.

Another important consideration must be made on the term of comparison between the sample and prototype. In the overlap-based approach, the characteristic traits and the shape of the two symbols are compared, but this is only one way to proceed. In fact, we could compare some other characteristics (features) that can also be numerical values extracted from appropriate measurements made on the symbols. For example, the moments of inertia of the symbols can be calculated with respect to the orthogonal Cartesian axes or the mass or position of the center of gravity, and so on. Similar symbols will have measurements similar or otherwise included in a certain proximity range.

If the characteristics to be quantified will be n, we can represent each symbol as a point in an n-dimensional hyperspace. In recent years, considerable progress has been made in the state of OCR, but the basic idea of the machines of Tausheck and Hendel continues to be valid. This intuition is based on the principle of overlapping forms, and has given life to a whole series of methods that go by the name of the **template-matching method**, which together with the structural methods constitute the two strands of development of calligraphic recognition software.

Generative neural networks

A Generative neural network aims to generate all the values of a phenomenon, both those that can be observed (input) and those that can be calculated from the ones observed (target). We try to understand how such a model can succeed in this goal by proposing a first distinction between generative and discriminative models.

Neural networks can be used as generative models: algorithms able to replicate the distribution of data in input to then be able to generate new values starting from that distribution. Usually, an image dataset is analyzed, and we try to learn the distribution associated with the pixels of the images to produce shapes similar to the original ones.

Often, in machine learning, we need to predict the value of a target vector y given the value of an input x vector. From a probabilistic perspective, the goal is to find the conditional probability distribution, $p(y|x)$.

The conditional probability of an event y with respect to an event x is the probability that y occurs, knowing that x is verified. This probability, indicated by $p(y|x)$, expresses a correction of expectations for y, dictated by the observation of x.

The most common approach to this problem is to represent the conditional distribution using a parametric model, and then determine the parameters using a training set consisting of pairs, (x_n, y_n), that contain both the values of the input variables and the relative vectors of corresponding outputs. The resulting conditional distribution can be used to make predictions of the target, (y) for new input values, (x). This is known as a discriminatory approach, since the conditional distribution discriminates directly between the different values of y.

As an alternative to this approach, we can look for the joint probability distribution, $p(x \cap y)$, and then use this joint distribution to evaluate the conditional probability $p(y|x)$ in order to make predictions of y for new values of x. This is known as the **generative** approach, because by sampling from the joint distribution, it is possible to generate synthetic examples of the vector of characteristics x.

The joint probability distribution $p(x, y)$ is a probability distribution that gives the probability that each of the x, y vectors falls in any particular range or discrete set of values specified for that variable.

A generative approach, regardless of the type of data and the theoretical model used, is divided into two basic steps:

1. The first step involves the construction of the generative model. The input data is processed with the aim of deducing their distribution. To do this, input data can simply be reorganized into a different structure, or it can represent new information extracted from input data from specific algorithms. The result of the construction of the generative model is the presentation of data according to the distribution to which it has been approximated.

2. Once the generative model has been built on the input data, this allows sampling, which leads to the formation of new data that shares the same distribution with the input data.

The construction of a generative model allows highlighting features and properties implicitly present in the initial data. The individual approaches are then distinguished by the type of processing performed on the data to explain these characteristics, and consequently for the type of variables on which an approximate data distribution is obtained.

Why are AI researchers so excited about generative models? Let's take a simple example: suppose we provide the system with a series of images of cats. Suppose then, that after seeing these images, the computer is able to generate new photos of cats in a completely independent manner. If the computer were able to do it and the images that were produced had the right number of legs, tails, ears, and so on, it would be easy to prove that the computer knows which parts make up the cat, even if no one has ever explained cat anatomy to it. So, in a sense, a good generative model is proof of the basic knowledge of concepts by computers.

This is why researchers are so enthusiastic about building generative models. These models seem to be a way to train computers to understand concepts without the need for researchers to teach them *a priori* concepts.

The restricted Boltzmann machine

A Boltzmann machine is a probabilistic graphic model that can be interpreted as a stochastic neural network. Boltzmann machines were first introduced in 1985 by Geoffrey Hinton and Terry Sejnowski. It being stochastic is due to the behavior of the neurons; within them, in the activation function, they will have a probabilistic value that will influence the activation of the neuron.

In practice, a Boltzmann machine is a model (including a certain number of parameters) that, when applied to a data distribution, is able to provide a representation. This model can be used to extract important aspects of an unknown distribution (target distribution) starting only from a sample of the latter. The data samples referred to by a Boltzmann machine are also called **training data**. The following diagram shows a Boltzmann machine's architecture:

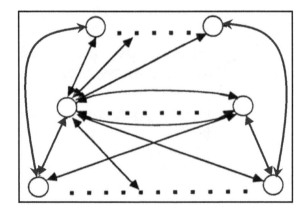

Training a Boltzmann machine means adapting its parameters so that the probability distribution represented by it interpolates the training data as best as possible. The training of a Boltzmann machine is rather demanding work from a computational point of view.

However, this problem can be made easier by imposing restrictions on the topology of the network on which you are working; this defines **restricted Boltzmann machines (RBM)**.

In Boltzmann machines, there are two types of units:

- **Visible units** (or neurons since, as we said, a Boltzmann machine can be interpreted as a neural network).

- **Hidden units** (or neurons).

Even in RBMs, there are both of these types of units and we can imagine them as arranged on two levels:

- **Visible units** are the components of an observation (for example, if our data consists of images, we can associate a visible unit with each pixel).

- **Hidden units** instead give us a model of the dependencies that exist between the components of our observation (for example, the dependency relationships that exist between the pixels of an image).

Hidden units can therefore be seen as detectors of data characteristics. In the RBM graph, every neuron is connected to all the neurons of the other level, while there are no connections between neurons of the same level; it is precisely this restriction that gives the RBM its name, as shown in the following diagram:

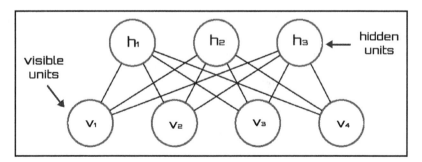

After successful training, an RBM provides a very good representation of the distribution that underlies training data. It is a generative model that allows sampling new data starting from the learned distribution; for example, new image structures can be generated starting from studied images. Having a generative model makes useful applications possible. For example, you can think of integrating some **visible units** corresponding to a partial observation (that is, you fix the values of the observed variables and consider them constant) and then produce the remaining **visible units** to complete the observation; in the image analysis example, this can be useful for an image completion task.

As generative models, RBMs can also be used as classifiers. Consider an application of this type:

- An RBM is trained to learn the joint probability distribution of the input data (explanatory variables) and the corresponding labels (response/output variables), both represented in the graph of the network, from the visible units of the RBM.

- Subsequently, a new input pattern, this time without labels, can be linked to the visible variables. The corresponding labels can be predicted by sampling directly from the Boltzmann machine.

The Boltzmann machine is able to complete partial patterns of data on visible units. If we divide the visible units into units of input and output, given the input pattern, the Boltzmann machine completes it by producing the outputs (classification). Otherwise, it works as associative memory, returning the most similar pattern among those learned to the (partial) data.

Autoencoders

An autoencoder is a neural network whose purpose is to code its input into small dimensions and the result obtained, to be able to reconstruct the input itself. Autoencoders are made up of the union of the following two subnets:

- An **encoder**, which calculates the function:

$$z = \phi(x)$$

Given an input x, the encoder encodes it in a variable z, also called a latent variable. z usually has much smaller dimensions than x.

- An **decoder**, which calculates the following function:

$$x' = \psi(z)$$

Since z is the code of x produced by the encoder, the decoder must decode it so that x' is similar to x. The training of autoencoders is intended to minimize the mean squared error between the input and the result.

Mean squared error (**MSE**) is the average squared difference between the outputs and targets. Lower values are indicative of better results. Zero means there is no error.

For n observations, MSE is given by the following formula:

$$MSE = \sum_{i=0}^{n}(x_i - x_i')^2$$

Finally, we can summarize that the encoder encodes the input in a compressed representation and the decoder returns from it a reconstruction of the input, as shown in the following diagram (St Mark's Campanile – Venice (Italy)):

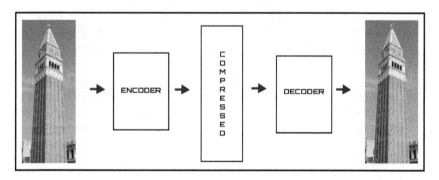

Let's define the following terms:

- **W**: input → hidden weights

- **V**: hidden → output weights

The previous formulas become the following:

$$z = \phi(W^* x)$$

And, they also become the following:

$$x' = \psi(V^*W1^* x)$$

Finally, the training of autoencoders is intended to minimize the following quantity:

$$\sum_{i=0}^{n}(x_i - V * W * x_i)^2$$

The purpose of autoencoders (reconstruct the input itself) is not simply to perform a sort of compression of the input or to look for an approximation of the identity function. There are techniques that allow, starting from a hidden layer of reduced dimensions, the direction of the model to give greater importance to some data properties, thus giving rise to different representations based on the same data.

Variational autoencoders

Variational autoencoders (VAEs) are inspired by the concept of autoencoders: a model consisting of two neural networks called encoders and decoders. As we have seen, the encoder network tries to code its input in a compressed form, while the network decoder tries to reconstruct the initial input, starting from the code returned by the encoder.

However, the functioning of the VAE is very different than that of simple autoencoders. VAEs allow not only coding/decoding of input but also the generation of new data. To do this, they treat both the code z and the reconstruction/generation x' as if they belonged to a certain probability distribution. In particular, the VAEs are the result of the combination of deep learning and Bayesian inference, in the sense that they consist of a neural network trained with the backpropagation algorithm modified with a technique called **reparameterization**.

While deep learning has proven to be very effective in the approximation of complex functions, the Bayesian statistics allow managing the uncertainty derived from a random generation in the form of probabilities.

The VAE uses the same structure to generate new images, similar to those belonging to the training set. In this case, the encoder does not directly produce a code for a given input but calculates the mean and variance of a normal distribution. A value is taken from this distribution and it is decoded by the decoder. The training consists of modifying the encoder and decoder parameters so that the result of the decoded that is so carried out is as similar as possible to the starting image. At the end of the training, we start from the normal distribution with mean and variance produced by the encoder; the decoder will be able to produce images similar to those belonging to the training set.

Let's define the following terms:

- **X**: Input data vector

- **z**: Latent variable

- **P(X)**: Probability distribution of the data

- **P(z)**: Probability distribution of the latent variable

- **P(X|z)**: Posterior probability, that is, the distribution of generating data given the latent variable

The posterior probability $P(X|z)$ is the probability of the condition X given the evidence z.

Our goal is to generate data according to the characteristics contained in the latent variable, so we want to find $P(X)$. For this purpose, we can use the law of total probability according to the following formula:

$$P(X) = \int P(X|z)P(z)dz$$

To understand how we arrived at this formulation, we reason by step. Our first task in defining the model is to infer good values of the latent variables starting from the observed data, or to calculate the posterior $p(z|X)$. To do this, we can use the Bayes theorem:

$$P(z|X) = \frac{P(X|z)P(z)}{P(X)}$$

In the previous formula, the $P(X)$ term appears. In the context of Bayesian statistics, it may also be referred to as the evidence or model evidence. The evidence can be calculated by marginalizing out the latent variables. This brings us to the starting formula:

$$P(X) = \int P(X|z)P(z)dz$$

The computational estimate of this integral requires an exponential time as it must be evaluated on all the configurations of latent variables. To reduce the computational cost, we are forced to approximate the estimate of the posterior probability.

In VAE, as the name suggests, we deduce $p(z \mid X)$ using a method called variational inference (VI). VI is one of the most used methods in Bayesian inference. This technique considers inference as an optimization problem. In doing this, we use a simpler distribution that is easy to evaluate (for example, Gaussian) and minimize the difference between these two distributions using the Kullback-Leibler divergence metric.

The Kullback-Leibler divergence metric is a nonsymmetric measure of the difference between two probability distributions, P and Q. Specially, the Kullback-Leibler divergence of Q from P, denoted by DKL $(P \mid\mid Q)$, is the measurement of the information lost when Q is used to approximate P.

For discrete probability distributions P and Q, the Kullback-Leibler divergence from Q to P is defined as follows:

$$D_{KL}(P||Q) = -\sum_i P(i)log\frac{Q(i)}{P(i)}$$

Analyzing the formula makes it evident that the divergence of Kullback-Leibler is the expectation of the logarithmic difference between the probabilities P and Q, where the expectation is taken using the probability P.

The generative adversarial network

The **generative adversarial network (GAN)** is a generative model consisting of two networks that are jointly trained, called generator and discriminator. The dynamics between these two networks are like those between a forger and an investigator. The forger tries to produce faithful imitations of authentic works of art, while the investigator tries to distinguish the fakes from the originals.

In this analogy, the forger represents the generator and the investigator represents the discriminator. The generator accepts input values belonging to a fixed distribution and tries to produce images similar to those of the dataset. The discriminator tries to distinguish the data created by the generator from those belonging to the dataset. These two networks are jointly coached:

- The **discriminator** tries to return output = 1 if the input belongs to the dataset and returns 0 if its input was generated by the generator.

- The **generator** instead tries to maximize the possibility that the discriminator will make mistakes.

The generator acquires a random input noise and tries to create a sample of data, while the discriminator takes input from either real-world examples or the generator, as shown in the following diagram:

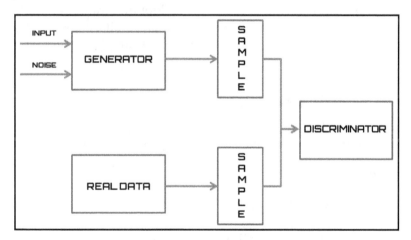

For simplicity, the two opposing networks are of the multilayer perceptron type; however, the same structure can be modeled with deep networks. For example, to generate new images, instead of sampling data from a complex distribution, the approach used in these networks is to start from values belonging to a simple distribution or from random values.

Subsequently, they are mapped through a second distribution that will be learned during the training.

In such a system, training leads to constant competition between generator and discriminator. Under these conditions, the optimization process can be carried out independently on both sides. Naming *G(z)* the generator and *D(x)* the discriminator, the training of the model aims to maximize the probability of the discriminator to assign 1 to values coming from the training set, instead of 0 to those produced by the generator. On the other hand, we want to teach the generator to minimize the following quantity:

$$log(1 - D(G(z)))$$

The training is then performed by applying the gradient descent technique to the following expression:

$$\min_{G} \max_{D} V(D, G) = E_{x \sim p_{data}(x)}[log D(x)] + E_{z \sim p_z(z)}[log(1 - D(G(z)))]$$

This method originates from game theory, in particular from the method called the **two-player minimax game**. The algorithms of this type adopt the strategy of minimizing the maximum possible loss resulting from the choice of a player. It can happen that, in the training process, the discriminator is not able to classify examples generated by real ones.

The adversarial autoencoder

The **adversarial autoencoder** (**AAE**) is a generative model produced by the union of VAE and GAN. To explain the model, we start by defining the following terms:

- **x**: Autoencoder input

- **z**: Code produced from x

- **p(z)**: The distribution we want to impose

- **q(z|x)**: Distribution learned from the encoder

- **p(x|z)**: Distribution learned from the decoder

- **pdata**: Distribution of the data

- **p(x)**: Distribution of the model

We consider the function $q(z|x)$ as a posterior distribution of $q(z)$, which is defined as follows:

$$q(z) = \int q(z|x)p_{data}(x)dx$$

We try to impose the equality $q(z)=p(z)$ on the model. The difference with a VAE is due to the fact that what drives $q(z)$ towards $p(z)$ is an adversarial network. The encoder of the VAE is considered the generator of a GAN for which a discriminator can be used. This tries to distinguish data belonging to $q(z)$ from that coming from $p(z)$. The following diagram shows an AAE architecture:

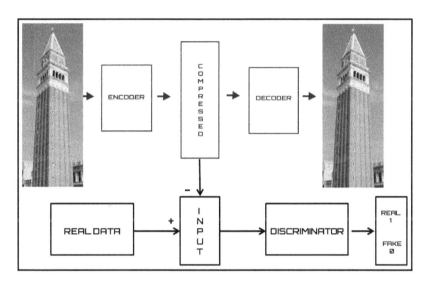

The trainings of the adversarial network and of the autoencoder take place jointly, using stochastic gradient descent. Finally, let's summarize the main differences between all types of autoencoders. As we anticipated in the Autoencoders section, autoencoders automatically learn a compressed representation of input, first compressing the input (encoder) and then decompressing it (decoder) to match the original input. Learning is facilitated by using the distance function that quantifies the loss of information that occurs from lossy compression. So learning in an autoencoder is a form of unsupervised learning as there is no labeled data.

Variational autoencoders, instead of simply learning a function that represents data as autoencoders do, they learn the parameters of a probability distribution that represents the data. Since it learns to model data, we can sample from the distribution and generate new samples of input data. It is therefore a generative model that is formalized in the form of GAN.

The Keras autoencoders model

As we said in the *Autoencoders* section, an autoencoder is a neural network whose purpose is to code its input into small dimensions and the result obtained to be able to reconstruct the input itself. Autoencoders are made up of the union of the following two subnets: encoder and decoder. To these functions is added another; it's a loss function calculated as the distance between the amount of information loss between the compressed representation of the data and the decompressed representation.

The encoder and the decoder will be differentiable with respect to the distance function, so the parameters of the encoding/decoding functions can be optimized to minimize the loss of reconstruction, using the gradient stochastic.

As we saw in `Chapter 1`, *Getting Started with Keras*, there are two types of models available in Keras:

- Sequential model

- Keras functional API

In this case, we will adopt the Keras functional API model. The Keras functional API is the way to go for defining complex models, such as multioutput models, directed acyclic graphs, or models with shared layers.

To build an autoencoder model in Keras, let's follow four simple steps:

1. Define the input:
   InputModel = Input(shape=(784,))

2. Add the encoded layer:
   EncodedLayer = Dense(32, activation='relu')(InputModel)

3. Add the decoded layer:
   DecodedLayer = Dense(784, activation='sigmoid')(EncodedLayer)

4. Instantiate a model as follows:

   AutoencoderModel = Model(InputModel, DecodedLayer)

In the following section, we will deepen each step by solving a practical case.

Implementing autoencoder Keras layers to reconstruct handwritten digit images

Handwriting recognition (HWR) is a very commonly used procedure in modern technology. The image of the written text can be detected offline from a piece of paper by optical scanning (**optical character recognition (OCR)**) or intelligent word recognition.

Technically, recognition of handwriting is the ability of a computer to receive and interpret a handwritten intelligible input from sources such as paper documents, photos, touchscreens, and other devices.

HWR is performed through various techniques that generally require OCR. However, a complete script recognition system also manages formatting, carries out correct character segmentation, and finds the most plausible words.

The MNIST dataset

The **Modified National Institute of Standards and Technology (MNIST)** is a large database of handwritten digits. It has a set of 70,000 examples of data. It is a subset of NIST's larger dataset. The digits are of 28x28 pixel resolution and are stored in a matrix of 70,000 rows and 785 columns; 784 columns form each pixel value from the 28x28 matrix, and one value is the actual digit. The digits have been size-normalized and centered in a fixed-size image.

The digit images in the MNIST set were originally selected and experimented with by Chris Burges and Corinna Cortes using boundingbox normalization and centering. Yann LeCun's version uses centering by center of mass within a larger window. The data is available on Yann LeCun's website at `http://yann.lecun.com/exdb/mnist/`.

The following diagram shows a sample of images of 0-8 from the MNIST dataset:

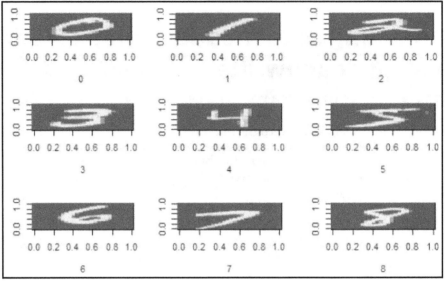

This dataset is already available in the Keras library (`keras.datasets`), and contains 60,000 28x28 grayscale images of the 10 digits, along with a test set of 10,000 images. Let's start importing the library:

```
from keras.datasets import mnist
```

To import the `mnist` dataset, the following code must be used:

```
(XTrain, YTrain), (XTest, YTest) = mnist.load_data()
```

The following tuples are returned:

- `XTrain`, `XTest`: A uint8 array of grayscale image data with the (`num_samples`, 28, 28) shape

- `YTrain`, `YTest`: A uint8 array of digit labels (integers in the range 0-9) with the (`num_samples`) shape

The following information is returned:

```
Downloading data from https://s3.amazonaws.com/img-datasets/mnist.npz
11493376/11490434 [==============================] - 17s 1us/step
```

Now, let's check the contents of the four objects we imported. First, we get the type of such objects. To do this, we will use the built-in function, `type()`, as follows:

```
print('XTrain class = ',type(XTrain))
print('YTrain class = ',type(YTrain))
print('XTest shape = ',type(XTest))
print('YTest shape = ',type(YTest))
```

Regarding the `type()` function: if a single argument (object) is passed, the type of the given object is returned. If three arguments (name, bases, and dict) are passed, a new type object is returned. The following results are obtained:

```
XTrain class = <class 'numpy.ndarray'>
YTrain class = <class 'numpy.ndarray'>
XTest shape = <class 'numpy.ndarray'>
YTest shape = <class 'numpy.ndarray'>
```

So, four `numpy.ndarray` objects are returned. An array object represents a multidimensional, homogeneous array of fixed-size items. An associated data-type object describes the format of each element in the array (its byte-order, how many bytes it occupies in memory, whether it is an integer, a floating point number, or something else, and so on). Now, we extract the number of elements contained in each array:

```
print('XTrain shape = ',XTrain.shape)
print('XTest shape = ',XTest.shape)
print('YTrain shape = ',YTrain.shape)
print('YTest shape = ',YTest.shape)
```

The shape attribute for `numpy` arrays returns the dimensions of the array. The following results are obtained:

```
XTrain shape = (60000, 28, 28)
XTest shape = (10000, 28, 28)
YTrain shape = (60000,)
YTest shape = (10000,)
```

As we anticipated, the 70,000 items in the database were divided into 60,000 items for training and 10,000 items for testing. We have previously said that the data output is represented by integers in the range 0-9. We are looking for confirmation of this assumption:

```
print('YTrain values = ',np.unique(YTrain))
print('YTest values = ',np.unique(YTest))
```

To extract the output values, the numpy.unique() function was used, which find the unique elements of an array. This function returns the sorted unique elements of an array. There are three optional outputs in addition to the unique elements: the indices of the input array that give the unique values, the indices of the unique array that reconstruct the input array, and the number of times each unique value comes up in the input array. The following results are returned:

```
YTrain values = [0 1 2 3 4 5 6 7 8 9]
YTest values = [0 1 2 3 4 5 6 7 8 9]
```

It may be useful to analyze the distribution of the two values in the available arrays. To start, we count the number of occurrences:

```
unique, counts = np.unique(YTrain, return_counts=True)
print('YTrain distribution = ',dict(zip(unique, counts)))
unique, counts = np.unique(YTest, return_counts=True)
print('YTest distribution = ',dict(zip(unique, counts)))
```

The numpy.unique function was once again applied: in this case, the return_counts attribute was added, which if set to True also returns the number of times the unique item appears. Then, the dict() function was applied, which creates a new dictionary, while the zip() function makes an iterator that aggregates elements from each of the iterables, and returns an iterator of tuples, where the i-th tuple contains the i-th element from each of the argument sequences or iterables. The iterator stops when the shortest input iterable is exhausted. The following results are shown:

```
YTrain distribution = {0: 5923, 1: 6742, 2: 5958, 3: 6131, 4: 5842, 5:
5421, 6: 5918, 7: 6265, 8: 5851, 9: 5949}
YTest distribution = {0: 980, 1: 1135, 2: 1032, 3: 1010, 4: 982, 5: 892, 6:
958, 7: 1028, 8: 974, 9: 1009}
```

We can also see it in a graph:

```
import matplotlib.pyplot as plt
plt.figure(1)
plt.subplot(121)
plt.hist(YTrain, alpha=0.8, ec='black')
plt.xlabel("Classes")
plt.ylabel("Number of occurrences")
plt.title("YTrain data")

plt.subplot(122)
plt.hist(YTest, alpha=0.8, ec='black')
plt.xlabel("Classes")
plt.ylabel("Number of occurrences")
plt.title("YTest data")
plt.show()
```

To visualize the number of occurrences of the two classes, the `histogram` has been adopted. A histogram is a graphical representation of a numerical distribution, showing the shape of a distribution. It consists of adjacent rectangles (`bins`), whose bases are aligned on an axis oriented and equipped with a unit of measure (the axis assumes the unit of measure of the character and can be safely understood as the X-axis). The adjacency of the rectangles reflects the continuity of the character. Each rectangle has a base length equal to the width of the corresponding class; the height is calculated as a frequency density, so it is equal to the ratio between the frequencies (absolute) associated with the class and the amplitude of the class. To plot a histogram in Python, use the `hyst()` function of the matplotlib library. This function plots a histogram. Compute and draw the histogram of specific data. The return value is a tuple (n, bins, patches) or ([n_0, n_1, ...], bins, [patches$_0$, patches$_1$,...]) if the input contains multiple data. Multiple data can be provided as a list of datasets of potentially different length ([x_0, x_1, ...]), or as a 2-D ndarray in which each column is a dataset.

To compare the results obtained on both output datasets (YTrain, YTest), two histograms were traced and displayed side by side, as shown in the following figure:

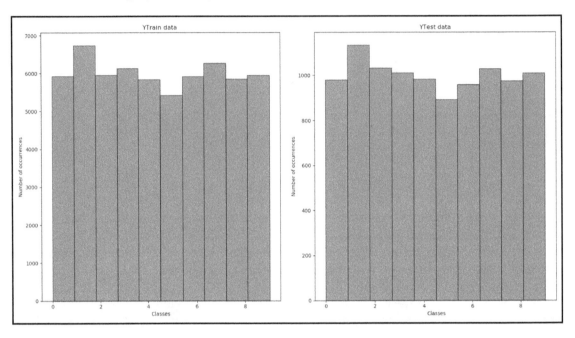

From the analysis of the previous figure, we can see that in both datasets the 10 digits are represented in the same proportions. In fact, the bars seem to have the same dimensions even if the vertical axis has different ranges.

Min–max normalization

Now, we have to normalize all values between 0 and 1. The MNIST images are stored in pixel format, where each pixel (totally 28x28) is stored as an 8-bit integer, giving a range of possible values from 0 to 255. Typically, 0 is taken to be black, and 255 is taken to be white.

The values in between make up the different shades of gray. Now, to normalize all values between 0 and 1, simply divide each value by 255. So, the pixel containing the value 255 will become 1, and the one containing 0 will remain as such; in between lie all the other values:

```
XTrain = XTrain.astype('float32') / 255
XTest = XTest.astype('float32') / 255
```

By using the `astype()` function, we have converted the input data in float32 (singleprecision float: sign bit, 8-bits exponent, 23-bits mantissa). As we said, each sample image consists of a 28x28 matrix. To reduce the dimensionality, we will flatten the 28x28 images into vectors of size 784:

```
XTrain = XTrain.reshape((len(XTrain), np.prod(XTrain.shape[1:])))
XTest = XTest.reshape((len(XTest), np.prod(XTest.shape[1:])))
```

The `reshape()` function gives a new shape to an array without changing its data. The new shape should be compatible with the original shape. The first dimension of the new shape is the number of observations returned from the `len()` function, (len(XTrain), and len(XTest)) functions. The second dimension represents the product of the last two dimensions of the starting data (*28x28 = 784*). To understand this transformation better, we print the shape of the starting dataset first and then the shape of the transformed dataset:

```
print (XTrain.shape)
print (Xtest.shape)
```

The following are the results before and after the dataset reshape:

```
(60000, 784)
(10000, 784)
```

We have confirmed that these are two tensors that have the number of observations as their first dimension, and as a second dimension, `784`.

Keras model architecture

Now, we will build the model using the Keras functional API. Let's start importing the libraries:

```
from keras.layers import Input
from keras.layers import Dense
from keras.models import Model
```

This code imports the following functions:

- `Input`: Used to instantiate a Keras tensor. A Keras tensor is a tensor object from the underlying backend (Theano, TensorFlow, or CNTK). We augment it with certain attributes that allow us to build a Keras model just by knowing the input and output of the model.

- `Dense`: Used to instantiate a regular densely connected NN layer.

- `Model`: Used to define the model. The model is the thing that you can summarize, fit, evaluate, and use to make predictions. Keras provides a `Model` class that you can use to create a model from your created layers. It only requires that you specify the input and output layers.

So, to start we have to define the input:

```
InputModel = Input(shape=(784,))
```

This returns a tensor that represents our input placeholder. Later, we will use this placeholder to define a model. At this point, we can add layers to the architecture of our model:

```
EncodedLayer = Dense(32, activation='relu')(InputModel)
```

The `Dense` class is used to define a fully connected layer. We have specified the number of neurons in the layer as the first argument (32), the activation function using the activation argument (`relu`), and finally the input tensor (`InputModel`) of the layer.

Remember that given an *x* input, the encoder encodes it in a *z* variable, also called a latent variable. The *z* variable usually has much smaller dimensions than *x*; in our case, we have passed from 784 to 32 with a compression factor of 24.5.

Now, let's add the decoding layer:

```
DecodedLayer = Dense(784, activation='sigmoid')(EncodedLayer)
```

This layer is the lossy reconstruction of the input. For another time, we have used the `Dense` class with `784` neurons (dimensionality of the output space), the `sigmoid activation function`, and `EncodedLayer` output as input. Now, we have to instantiate a model, as follows:

```
AutoencoderModel = Model(InputModel, DecodedLayer)
```

This model will include all layers required in the computation of `DecodedLayer` (output) given `InputModel` (input). In the following list are some useful attributes of the `Model` class:

- `model.layers`: A flattened list of layers comprising the model graph

- `model.inputs`: The list of input tensors

- `model.outputs`: The list of output tensors

To print a summary of the autoencoder model, simply type the following:

```
AutoencoderModel.summary()
```

In the following figure are shown the results:

```
Layer (type)                 Output Shape              Param #
=================================================================
input_1 (InputLayer)         (None, 784)               0

dense_1 (Dense)              (None, 32)                25120

dense_2 (Dense)              (None, 784)               25872
=================================================================
Total params: 50,992
Trainable params: 50,992
Non-trainable params: 0
```

Exploring model results

So, we have to configure the model for training. To do this, we will use the compile method, as follows:

```
AutoencoderModel.compile(optimizer='adadelta', loss='binary_crossentropy')
```

This method configures the model for training. Only two arguments are used:

- `optimizer`: String (name of optimizer) or optimizer instance.

- `loss`: String (name of objective function) or objective function. If the model has multiple outputs, you can use a different loss on each output by passing a dictionary or a list of losses. The loss value that will be minimized by the model will then be the sum of all individual losses.

We have used `adadelta optimizer`. This method dynamically adapts over time, using only first-order information, and has minimal computational overhead beyond vanilla stochastic gradient descent. The method requires no manual tuning of the learning rate and appears robust to noisy gradient information, different model architecture choices, various data modalities, and selections of hyperparameters.

Furthermore, we have used `binary_crossentropy` as a loss function. The loss functions are computationally feasible functions representing the price paid for inaccuracy of predictions in classification problems.

At this point, we can train the model:

```
history = AutoencoderModel.fit(XTrain, YTrain,
            batch_size=256,
            epochs=100,
            shuffle=True,
            validation_data=(XTest, YTest))
```

The `fit()` method trains the model for a fixed number of epochs (iterations on a dataset).

Here, the arguments passed are explained to understand their meaning better:

- `XTrain`: A NumPy array of training data (if the model has a single input), or list of NumPy arrays (if the model has multiple inputs). If the input layers in the model are named, you can also pass a dictionary mapping input names to NumPy arrays. The *x* can be none (default) if feeding from framework-native tensors (for example, TensorFlow data tensors).

- `XTrain`: A NumPy array of target (label) data if the model has a single output, or a list of NumPy arrays if the model has multiple outputs. If the output layers in the model are named, you can also pass a dictionary mapping output names to NumPy arrays. The *y* can be none (default) if feeding from framework-native tensors (for example, TensorFlow data tensors).

- `batch_size`: Integer or none. This is the number of samples per gradient update. If unspecified, `batch_size` will default to 32.

- `epochs`: An integer. This is the number of epochs to train the model. An epoch is an iteration over the entire *x* and *y* data provided. Note that in conjunction with `initial_epoch`, epochs is to be understood as the final number of epochs. The model is not trained for a number of iterations given by epochs, but merely until the epoch of index epochs is reached.

- `shuffle`: A Boolean to decide whether to shuffle the training data before each epoch or `str` (for batch). A batch is a special option for dealing with the limitations of HDF5 data; it shuffles in batch-sized chunks. It has no effect when `steps_per_epoch` is anything other than none.

- `validation_data`: A tuple (`x_val` and `y_val`) or tuple (`x_val`, `y_val`, and `val_sample_weights`) on which to evaluate the loss and any model metrics at the end of each epoch. The model will not be trained on this data. `validation_data` will override `validation_split`.

A `history` object is returned. Its `history.history` attribute is a record of training loss values and metrics values at successive epochs, as well as validation loss values and validation metrics values. When the `fit()` function is performed, the loss and the accuracy at the end of each training epoch are displayed, as shown in the following figure:

```
Epoch 90/100
60000/60000 [==============================] - 4s 62us/step - loss: 0.0985 - val_loss: 0.0969
Epoch 91/100
60000/60000 [==============================] - 4s 65us/step - loss: 0.0984 - val_loss: 0.0968
Epoch 92/100
60000/60000 [==============================] - 4s 66us/step - loss: 0.0984 - val_loss: 0.0968
Epoch 93/100
60000/60000 [==============================] - 4s 64us/step - loss: 0.0983 - val_loss: 0.0967
Epoch 94/100
60000/60000 [==============================] - 4s 63us/step - loss: 0.0983 - val_loss: 0.0967
Epoch 95/100
60000/60000 [==============================] - 4s 61us/step - loss: 0.0982 - val_loss: 0.0967
Epoch 96/100
60000/60000 [==============================] - 4s 61us/step - loss: 0.0982 - val_loss: 0.0967
Epoch 97/100
60000/60000 [==============================] - 4s 61us/step - loss: 0.0982 - val_loss: 0.0966
Epoch 98/100
60000/60000 [==============================] - 4s 63us/step - loss: 0.0981 - val_loss: 0.0966
Epoch 99/100
60000/60000 [==============================] - 4s 62us/step - loss: 0.0981 - val_loss: 0.0965
Epoch 100/100
60000/60000 [==============================] - 4s 62us/step - loss: 0.0981 - val_loss: 0.0965
```

Our model is now ready, so we can use it to rebuild the handwritten digits automatically. To do this, we will use the `predict()` method:

```
DecodedDigits = AutoencoderModel.predict(XTest)
```

This method generates output predictions for the input samples (`XTest`). To get an idea of how the loss function varies during the epochs, it can be useful to create a plot of loss on the training and validation datasets over training epochs. To do this, we will use the matplotlib library, as follows:

```
plt.plot(history.history['loss'])
plt.plot(history.history['val_loss'])
plt.title('Autoencoder Model loss')
plt.ylabel('loss')
plt.xlabel('epoch')
plt.legend(['Train', 'Test'], loc='upper left')
plt.show()
```

A plot of loss on the training and validation datasets over training epochs is shown in the following diagram:

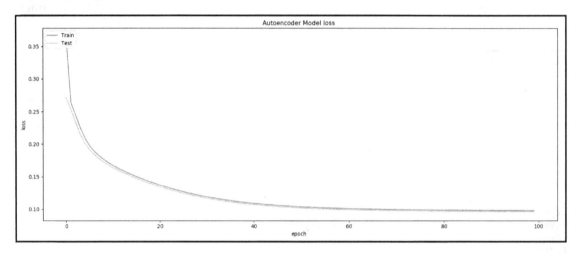

We have therefore finished; the model has been trained and later used to make predictions. So, we can just print to the screen the starting handwritten digits and those reconstructed from our model. Of course, we will do it only for some of the 60,000 digits contained in the dataset; in fact, we will limit ourselves to displaying the first five. We will also use the matplotlib library in this case:

```
n=5
plt.figure(figsize=(20, 4))
for i in range(n):
    ax = plt.subplot(2, n, i + 1)
    plt.imshow(XTest[i+10].reshape(28, 28))
    plt.gray()
    ax.get_xaxis().set_visible(False)
    ax.get_yaxis().set_visible(False)
    ax = plt.subplot(2, n, i + 1 + n)
    plt.imshow(DecodedDigits[i+10].reshape(28, 28))
    plt.gray()
    ax.get_xaxis().set_visible(False)
    ax.get_yaxis().set_visible(False)
plt.show()
```

The results are shown in the following figure:

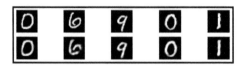

As you can see in the preceding figure, the result is very close to the original, meaning that the model works well.

Summary

In this chapter, we learned how to solve a handwritten digit-recognition problem. Starting from the basics of the OCR and computer vision concepts, we learned how to elaborate simple images.

We analyzed different types of generative models. A Boltzmann machine is a probabilistic graphic model that can be interpreted as a stochastic neural network. In practice, a Boltzmann machine is a model (including a certain number of parameters) that, when applied to a data distribution, is able to provide a representation. This model can be used to extract important aspects of an unknown distribution (target distribution) starting only from a sample of the latter.

Finally, an autoencoder was used for handwritten digit recognition. An autoencoder is a neural network whose purpose is to code its input into small dimensions, and the result obtained, to be able to reconstruct the input itself. The purpose of autoencoders is not simply to perform a sort of compression of the input or look for an approximation of the identity function; there are also techniques that allow us to direct the model (starting from a hidden layer of reduced dimensions) to give greater importance to some data properties.

In the next chapter, we will learn the basics of robot control theory, discover available environments to simulate robot mobility, understand reinforcement learning and Deep Q Network basics, and learn how to control robot movement.

9
Robot Control System Using Deep Reinforcement Learning

Robots are now an integral part of our living environments. In the industrial field, they represent a valid aid by replacing workers in heavy duty tasks. The task of a robot control system is to execute a planned sequence of movements and to identify an alternative path in the presence of obstacles. Neural networks are exceptionally effective at getting good characteristics highly structured data. We could, then, represent our Q function with a neural network, which takes the status and action as input and outputs for the corresponding Q value. Deep reinforcement learning methods use deep neural networks to approximate any of the following reinforcement learning components: value function, policy, and model. In this chapter, you will learn how to use deep reinforcement learning methods to control robot movements in a specific environment.

In this chapter, we will cover the following topics:

- Robot control overview
- Environment to control robot mobility
- Reinforcement learning basics
- Keras **Deep Q Network (DQN)**
- DQN to control a robot's mobility

In this chapter, we will learn about the basics of robot control theory and discover available environments to simulate robot mobility. Then, we will understand reinforcement learning basics and and the different techniques available: Dynamic Programming, Monte Carlo methods,Temporal difference learning, and DQN. Finally we will learn how to control a robot's movement using DQN.

Robot control overview

A robot is a machine that performs certain actions based on the commands that are provided, either on the basis of direct human supervision, or independently based on general guidelines, using **Artificial Intelligence (AI)** processes. These tasks should typically be performed to replace or assist humans, such as in the fields of manufacturing, construction, or the handling of heavy and dangerous materials, in prohibitive or incompatible environments with the human condition, or simply to free a person from commitments. The following image shows a **remotely operated underwater vehicle (ROV)**:

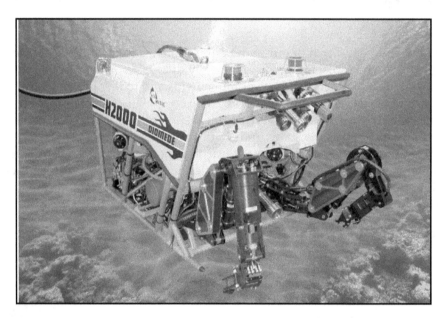

A robot should be equipped with guided connections, thus using feedback between perceptions and actions, and should not be guided by direct human control. Actions can be performed with electromagnetic motors or actuators that move a limb, open and close a gripper, or move the robot. Step-by-step control and feedback are provided by a program that runs from an external or internal robot computer, or from a microcontroller. Based on the following definition, the robot concept can include almost all automated devices:

> *"Robotics is a science that studies the behavior of intelligent beings and tries to develop methods that allow a machine, called a robot, equipped with appropriate devices to perceive the surrounding environment and interact with it (sensors and actuators), to perform specific tasks."*

This represents the solution to various problems for humans, who can get rid of tasks that are too boring, time-consuming, dangerous, tiring, simple, or precise. This discipline stems from man's desire to create artificial and autonomous devices with AI.

Robotics is not only important so that we can learn how to build and use robots, but also to learn about a method of reasoning and experimentation; in fact, it incorporates many interdisciplinary studies, such as mechanics, electronics, information technology, sensors, AI, and mathematics.

In 1979, the American Institute of Robots gave a definition of a robot as a programmable and multifunctional tool that's designed to move materials, components, or tools through various programmed movements.

Twenty years later, this definition could be considered incomplete, given that nowadays a robot is seen as an instrument that's used in science and in industry to take the place of a human being. It could, or could not, resemble a human being and perform, or not perform, that person's duties.

In science fiction, the concern that robots can compete with people, rebel, or even exterminate is a very common topic. Remember that the term comes from a Czech word, *Robota*, meaning forced labor; the word robot was first used to denote a fictional humanoid in a 1920 play, R.U.R., by Karel Čapek, a Czech writer, but it was Karel's brother Josef Čapek who was the word's true inventor.

 For a more detailed description of the history of the robots you can consult the relative entry in the free wikipedia encyclopedia available at the following link: https://en.wikipedia.org/wiki/History_of_robots

Three laws of robotics

In the *I, Robot series of stories*, Isaac Asimov enunciated the three laws of robotics in an attempt to control competition between robots and human beings:

- A robot may not injure a human being or, through inaction, allow a human being to come to harm
- A robot must obey any orders given to it by human beings, except where such orders would conflict with the first law
- A robot must protect its own existence as long as such protection does not conflict with the first or second law

The features of a robot can be summarized as follows:

- **Programmability**: Processing capacity that the designer can combine as they wish
- **Mobility**: Possibility to interact physically with the environment
- **Flexibility**: Ability to exhibit behavior suited to the situation
- **Autonomy**: Possibility of performing your own duties without interference or conditioning by other members

Thanks to the two essential elements available in every robotic device, that is, a **sensor** and an **actuator**, these features are possible. A sensor is a device that transforms a physical quantity that you want to measure into a signal of a different nature (typically electric) that can be more easily measured or memorized. An actuator is a device that converts energy from one form to another so that it acts in the physical environment instead of a person. That is, it is any device used to operate mechanical members or to intervene on hydraulic circuits following commands that are sent to it by means of an electronic control system.

Short robotics timeline

The construction of automated devices dates back to ancient times, in fact between 400-350 BC. The Greek Architect of Taranto built a flying dove that was set in motion by a jet of steam. In 1200 B.C., the first rudimentary automata was being built: Roger Bacon creates a talking head.

This means that the idea of constructing an artificial individual, endowed with movement and autonomy in their actions, is not therefore of the last few centuries, nor a consequence of the development of information technology and of robotics. The following image is of the dredge of Leonardo da Vinci, exhibited at the L. Da Vinci National Museum of Science and Technology in Milan:

To describe the level of advancement of a robot, the term generation robots can be used. This term was coined by Professor Hans Moravec, Principal Research Scientist at the Carnegie Mellon University Robotics Institute, for describing the near future evolution of robot technology.

First-generation robots

Robots that characterize the first generation, which began in 1970, are robotic arms. These are programmable machines that cannot control the actual execution modes and cannot interact with their external environment.

Robots of the first generation are low-tech devices; in fact, they do not operate under servo controls. They are very noisy because of the noise produced by the impact between the arm itself and the mechanical stops used to limit its movement. The use of these types of robots is mainly industrial. When they were invented, they were used for loading and unloading goods or to make simple movements with materials.

Second-generation robots

The assembly line, on the other hand, is part of the second generation of robots. It consists of programmable machines with the possibility of recognizing the external environment.

The technology that's used is of medium quality, and unlike the first generation, robotic arms are equipped with servo controls, and can be programmed for point-to-point displacements. The following image is an example of a factory automation with industrial robots:

These are controlled by regular programmable logic controllers or minicomputers and are also programmable. They have specific software that's dedicated to specific applications.

Thus, if the robot was intended to perform a certain task, such as loading a machine, it was very difficult to use it for another operation, such as welding. To do this, the control system had to be changed. This kind of machine has poor diagnostic capabilities and therefore it is up to the user to go back to the actual causes of a possible failure.

Third-generation robots

These are self-programmable machines that have the ability to interact with the external environment and the external operator in a complex way (vision, voice, and so on) and are able to self-instruct themselves for the execution of an assigned task. The third generation (late 1980s) has now evolved to the point of being able to perform highly sophisticated operations such as space inspections, adaptive arc welding, and assembly operations. The following image shows Sojourner, which is the Mars Pathfinder robotic Mars rover that landed on July 4, 1997:

The technology that's used is of a high standard, and programming can be done online using a prehensile keyboard or offline through a video display. Programming languages do not work at a low level like the second generation ones.

They can be interfaced with a Computer-aided design (CAD) database or with a host computer for data loading/unloading. They are also capable of sending messages to the operator to describe the nature and location of any failures. The simultaneous use of this kind of robot is to perform intelligent tasks.

Fourth-generation robots

Fourth-generation robots are considered the robots of the future. These robots are called androids or humanoids, or automata with human features that mimic human actions and functions. The movie Automata (directed by Gabe Ibanez, with Antonio Banderas as the main actor) is one such example we can infer here. In the movie, the study was divided into two: on the one hand, the scholars focused on the surprising humanoids, similar to dummies with silicon faces, makeup, and clothes. On the other hand, the so-called **bipeds** have developed, with human shapes but similar to cartoon robots, which are also equipped with the ability to learn and move using a wide range of movements.

They are no longer just industrial but also social robots, and are sometimes used to investigate the social interaction of humans.

Automatic control

Technically speaking, a robot can be seen as a particular type of automatic control, that is, an automaton that's physically located in an environment of which it can perceive certain characteristics through components called **sensors**, and on which it can perform actions with the aim of making changes to it. These actions are performed by so-called **actuators**.

All of this is interposed between measurements made by sensors. The commands given to the actuators can be defined as the control program or the controller of the robot.

This is the component in which the intelligence of the robot is encoded and, in a certain sense, it therefore constitutes a brain that must guide its actions in order to obtain the desired behavior. A controller can be implemented in various ways: usually, it is software that's running on one or more microcontrollers that's physically integrated into the system (onboard), but it can also be obtained through electronic circuits (analog or digital) that are directly wired into the hardware of the robot. The abstract nature of the software obviously makes it the most flexible solution as this entity is itself easily transferable from one storage medium to another: consequently, to change the controller, and with it the whole behavior assumed by the robot, it is sufficient to change the control software while the hardware remains unchanged, thus allowing us to make changes at virtually no cost.

The environment for controlling robot mobility

A typical feature of autonomous systems is mobility. A robot that performs the intended task needs to move physically within an environment, and must inevitably incorporate a certain autonomy that allows it to move safely, avoiding obstacles and not posing a threat to any nearby living beings.

Obviously, different levels of autonomy can be identified, from fully autonomous systems that never, or almost never, require human intervention, to remote controlled systems that can be more or less autonomous, depending on whether they rely solely on the commands given to them or whether some part of the operations is decided by the robot itself.

To create an automatic system to control the mobility of a robot, it is essential to have a suitable environment that allows us to simulate the system in a virtual environment. In this way, we will be able to develop the system by reducing costs considerably.

OpenAI Gym

OpenAI Gym is a library that helps us implement algorithms that are based on reinforcement learning. It includes a growing collection of benchmark issues that expose a common interface, and a website where people can share their results and compare algorithm performance.

OpenAI Gym focuses on the episodic setting of reinforced learning. In other words, the robotic agent's experience is divided into a series of episodes. The initial state of the agent is randomly sampled by a distribution, and the interaction proceeds until the environment reaches a terminal state. This procedure is repeated for each episode, with the aim of maximizing the total reward expectation per episode and achieving a high level of performance in the fewest possible episodes.

 Gym is a toolkit for developing and comparing reinforcement learning algorithms. It supports the ability to teach agents everything from walking to playing games such as Pong or Pinball. The library is available at https://gym.openai.com/.

OpenAI Gym includes a growing collection of environments that address the most common problems in reinforcement learning. OpenAI Gym is supported by a website where each user has the possibility to publish the results obtained on a certain environment to compare the performance of the different algorithms with the community. Furthermore, users are encouraged to also share the source code that allowed them to obtain the results that are loaded, with detailed instructions for easy replication of the results obtained from them.

OpenAI Gym also provides abstractions and interfaces for the creation of new environments, and is able to manage rendering, freeing the developer from worrying about it. Since the framework was created specifically for the study of reinforcement learning algorithms, the interfaces proposed for the interactions between environment and agent exactly match the elements required by the problem.

OpenAI Gym assumes that the environment is episodic in nature and that the agent interacts with it at each step by performing one of the possible actions. Interacting with the environment, the agent obtains information such as status, reward, and a flag indicating the eventual completion of the episode. This is used by the agent to determine when it is appropriate to reset the environment and start a new episode.

There are several environments available, and the most used are as follows:

- **Classic control and toy text**: Completes small-scale tasks, mostly from the reinforcement learning literature. They're here to get you started.
- **Algorithmic**: Performs computations such as adding multi-digit numbers and reversing sequences.
- **Atari**: Plays classic Atari games.
- **2D and 3D robots**: Controls a robot in simulation.

Later, we will use one of the previously mentioned environments to control the movements of a robot.

Reinforcement learning basics

Reinforcement learning aims to create algorithms that can learn and adapt to environmental changes. This programming technique is based on the concept of receiving external stimuli that depend on the actions chosen by the agent. A correct choice will involve a reward, while an incorrect choice will lead to a penalty. The goal of the system is to achieve the best possible result, of course.

These mechanisms derive from the basic concepts of **machine learning** (ML) (learning from experience), in an attempt to simulate human behavior. In fact, in our mind, we activate brain mechanisms that lead us to chase and repeat what, in us, produce feelings of gratification and well-being. Whenever we experience moments of pleasure (for example, food, sex, and love), substances are produced in our brains that work by reinforcing that same stimulus, thus emphasizing it.

Along with this mechanism of neurochemical reinforcement, an important role is represented by memory. In fact, memory collects the experience of the subject so that it's able to repeat it in the future. Evolution has endowed us with this mechanism to push us to repeat gratifying experiences in the direction of the best solutions.

This is why we so powerfully remember the most important experiences of our life: experiences, especially those that are powerfully rewarding, are ingrained in memory and condition our future explorations. Previously, we have seen that learning from experience can be simulated by a numerical algorithm in various ways, depending on the nature of the signal used for learning and the type of feedback adopted by the system.

The following diagram shows a flowchart that displays an agent's interaction with the environment in a reinforcement learning setting:

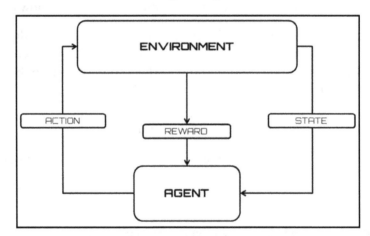

The following list shows the steps to follow to correctly apply a reinforcement learning algorithm:

1. Preparation of the agent.
2. Observation of the environment.
3. Selection of the optimal strategy.
4. Execution of actions.

5. Calculation of the corresponding reward (or penalty).

6. Development of updating strategies (if necessary).

7. Repetition of *step 2* through *step 5* iteratively until the agent learns the optimal strategies.

Reinforcement learning is based on a theory from psychology, which was elaborated on by following a series of experiments performed on animals. In particular, Edward Thorndike (American psychologist) noted that, if a cat is given a reward immediately after the execution of a behavior that's considered correct, then this increases the probability that this behavior will repeat itself. On the other hand, in the face of unwanted behavior, the application of a punishment decreases the probability of the repetition of an error.

On the basis of this theory, after defining a goal to be achieved, reinforcement learning tries to maximize the rewards received for the execution of the action or the set of actions that allows you to reach this designated goal.

Agent-environment interface

Reinforcement learning can be seen as a special case of the interaction problem, in terms of achieving a goal. The entity that must reach the goal is called an **agent**. The entity with which the agent must interact is called the **environment**, which corresponds to everything that is external to the agent.

So far, we are more focused on the term agent, but what does it represent? The agent (software) is a software entity that performs services on behalf of another program, usually automatically and invisibly. These pieces of software are also called **smart agents**.

What follows is a list of the most important features of an agent:

- It can choose between a continuous and a discrete set for an action on the environment.
- The action depends on the situation. The situation is summarized in the system state.
- The agent continuously monitors the environment (input) and continuously changes its status.
- The choice of the action is not trivial and requires a certain degree of intelligence.
- The agent has a smart memory.

The agent has a goal-directed behavior, but acts in an uncertain environment that is not known a *priori* or only partially known. An agent learns by interacting with the environment. Planning can be developed while learning about the environment through measurements made by the agent itself. This strategy is close to trial-and-error theory.

> *Trial-and-error is a fundamental method of problem solving. It is characterized by repeated, varied attempts that are continued until success, or until the agent stops trying.*

The agent-environment interaction is continuous: the agent chooses an action to be taken, and in response, the environment changes state, presenting a new situation to be faced.

In the particular case of reinforcement learning, the environment provides the agent with a reward. It is essential that the source of the reward is the environment to avoid the formation, within the agent, of a personal reinforcement mechanism that would compromise learning.

The value of the reward is proportional to the influence that the action has in reaching the objective, so it is positive or high in the case of a correct action, or negative or low for an incorrect action.

In the following list are some examples of real life in which there is an interaction between the agent and environment to solve a problem:

- A chess player, for each move, has information on the configurations of pieces that can be created, and on the possible countermoves of the opponent
- A little horse, in just a few hours, learns to get up and run
- A truly autonomous robot learns to move around a room to get out of it
- The parameters of a refinery (oil pressure, flow, and so on) are set in real time, so as to obtain the maximum yield or maximum quality

All of the examples that we've examined have the following characteristics in common:

- Interaction with the environment
- A specific goal that the agent wants to get
- Uncertainty or partial knowledge of the environment

From the analysis of these examples, it is possible to make the following observations:

- The agent learns from its own experience.
- The actions change the status (the situation) and the possibilities of choice change in the future (delayed reward).
- The effect of an action cannot be completely predicted.

- The agent has a global assessment of its behavior.
- It must exploit this information to improve its choices. Choices improve with experience.
- Problems can have a finite or infinite time horizon.

Essentially, the agent receives sensations from the environment through its sensors. Depending on its feelings, the agent decides on what actions to make in the environment. Based on the immediate result of its actions, the agent can be rewarded. If you want to use an automatic learning method, you need to give a formal description of the environment. It is not important to know exactly how the environment is made; what is interesting is to make general assumptions about the properties that the environment has.

Reinforcement learning algorithms

As we saw in the *Reinforcement learning basics* section, reinforcement learning is a programming technique that aims to develop algorithms that can learn and adapt to changes in the environment. This programming technique is based on the assumption of the agent being able to receive stimuli from the outside and to change its actions according to these stimuli. Therefore, a correct choice will result in a reward, while an incorrect choice will lead to a penalization of the system.

The goal of the system is to achieve the highest possible reward and consequently the best possible result. This result can be obtained through two approaches:

- The first approach involves evaluating the choices of the algorithm and then rewarding or punishing the algorithm based on the result. These techniques can also adapt to substantial changes in the environment. An example is image recognition programs that improve their performance with use. In this case, we can say that learning takes place continuously.
- In the second approach, a first phase is applied in which the algorithm is trained, and when the system is considered reliable, it is crystallized and no longer modifiable. This derives from the observation that constantly evaluating the actions of the algorithm can be a process that cannot be automated or that is very expensive.

These are only implementation choices, so it may happen that an algorithm includes the newly analyzed approaches. In the following sections we will analyze in detail the most common reinforcement learning algorithms.

Dynamic Programming

Dynamic Programming (DP) represents a set of algorithms that can be used to calculate an optimal policy, given a perfect model of the environment in the form of a **Markov Decision Process (MDP)**. The fundamental idea of DP, as well as reinforcement learning in general, is the use of state values and actions to look for good policies.

MDP is a discrete time stochastic control process. Stochastic processes are mathematical models that are used to study the evolution of phenomena following random or probabilistic laws. A stochastic process is called Markovian when, having chosen a certain instance, t, for observation, the evolution of the process, starting with t, depends only on t and does not depend in any way on the previous instances. Thus, a process is Markovian when, given the moment of observation, only this instance determines the future evolution of the process, while this evolution does not depend on the past.

The DP method approaches the resolution of MDP processes through the iteration of two processes called **policy evaluation** and **policy improvement**:

- The **policy evaluation** algorithm consists of applying an iterative method to the resolution of the Bellman equation. Since convergence is guaranteed to us only for k → ∞, we must be content with having good approximations by imposing a stopping condition.
- The **policy improvement** algorithm improves policy based on current values.

A policy defines the behavior of the learning agent at a given time. It maps both the detected states of the environment and the actions to be taken when they are in those states. This corresponds to what, in psychology, would be called as a *set of rules* or *associations of stimulus response*. The policy is the fundamental part of a reinforcing learning agent, in the sense that it alone is enough to determine behavior.

A Bellman equation, named after Richard E. Bellman, an American applied mathematician, is a necessary condition for the optimality associated with the DP method. It allows us to obtain the value of a decision problem at some point in time in terms of payoff from some initial choices and the value of the remaining decision problem resulting from those initial choices.

The iteration of these two processes (policy evaluation and policy improvement) is shown in the following diagram:

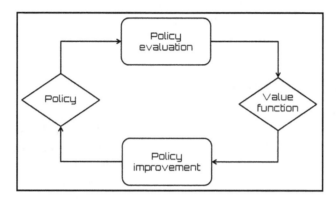

The policy evaluation block essentially computes the value function under the current policy. The policy improvement block improves policy based on current values of value function. A disadvantage of the policy iteration algorithm is that we have to evaluate the policy at every step. This involves an iterative process in which we do not know a priori the time of convergence, which will depend, among other things, on how the starting policy was chosen.

Monte Carlo methods

Monte Carlo (**MC**) methods for estimating the value function and discovering excellent policies do not require the presence of a model of the environment. They are able to learn through the use of the agent's experience alone or from samples of state sequences, actions, and rewards that are obtained from the interactions between the agent and the environment.

A value function represents how good a state is for an agent. It is equal to the total reward expected for an agent from the status s. The value function depends on the policy with which the agent selects the actions to be performed.

This experience can be acquired by the agent in line with the learning process or emulated by a previously populated dataset. The possibility of gaining experience during learning (online learning) is interesting because it allows them to obtain excellent behavior, even in the absence of a priori knowledge of the dynamics of the environment. Even learning through an already populated experience dataset can be interesting, because, if combined with online learning, it enables automatic policy improvement induced by others' experiences.

In general, MC methods rely on repeated random sampling to obtain numerical results. To do this, they use randomness to solve deterministic problems. In our case, we will use random sampling of states and action-state pairs, look at the rewards, and then review the policy in an iterative way. The iteration of the process will converge on optimal policy as we explore every possible action-state pair.

Temporal difference learning

Temporal difference (**TD**) learning algorithms are based on reducing the differences between estimates made by the agent at different times. TD algorithms try to predict a quantity that depends on the future values of a given signal. Its name derives from the differences used in predictions on successive time steps to guide the learning process. The prediction at any time is updated to bring it closer to the prediction of the same quantity at the next time step. In reinforcement learning, they are used to predict a measure of the total amount of reward expected in the future.

It is a combination of the ideas of the MC method and DP.

 MC methods allow for reinforcement learning problems to be solved based on the average of the results obtained. DP represents a set of algorithms that can be used to calculate an optimal policy when given a perfect model of the environment in the form of a MDP.

TD algorithms can learn directly from raw data, without a model of the dynamics of the environment (such as MC). This algorithm updates estimates based partly on previously learned estimates, without waiting for the final result (the bootstrap technique, such as DP).

It converges (using a fixed policy) if the time step is sufficiently small, or if it reduces over time.

The consecutive predictions are often related to each other; TD methods are based on this assumption. These methods try to minimize the error of consecutive time forecasts. To do this, calculate the value function update using the Bellman equation. As we've already mentioned, to improve the prediction, the bootstrap technique is used, thereby reducing the variance of the prediction in each update step.

The different types of algorithms based on time differences can be distinguished on the basis of the methodology of choosing an action that's been adopted. There are methods of time differences on-policy, in which the update is made on the basis of the results of actions determined by the selected policy and off-policy methods, in which various policies can be assessed through hypothetical actions – these are not actually undertaken. Unlike on-policy methods, the latter can separate the problem of exploration from that of control, learning tactics that are not necessarily applied during the learning phase.

The most used TD learning algorithms are as follows:

- SARSA
- Q-learning
- Deep Q-learning

In the following sections, we will analyze the main characteristics of the Deep Q-learning algorithm.

Keras DQNs

Q-learning is one of the most used reinforcement learning algorithms. This is due to its ability to compare the expected utility of available actions without requiring an environment model. Thanks to this technique, it is possible to find an optimal action for every given state in a finished MDP.

Q-learning

A general solution to the reinforcement learning problem is to estimate, thanks to the learning process, an evaluation function. This function must be able to evaluate, through the sum of the rewards, the optimality/utility or otherwise of a particular policy. In fact, Q-learning tries to maximize the value of the Q function (action-value function), which represents the maximum discounted future reward when we perform action a in the state s.

Q-learning, like SARSA, estimates the function value $q\ (s, a)$ incrementally, updating the value of the state-action pair at each step of the environment, following the logic of updating the general formula for estimating the values for the TD methods. Q-learning, unlike SARSA, has off-policy characteristics; that is, while the policy is improved according to the values estimated by $q\ (s, a)$, the value function updates the estimates by following a strictly greedy secondary policy: given a state, the chosen action is always the one that maximizes the value's max $q\ (s, a)$. However, the π policy has an important role in estimating values because, through it, the state-action pairs to be visited and updated are determined.

The following is some pseudocode for a Q-learning algorithm:

```
Initialize
    arbitrary action-value function
Repeat (for each episode)
    Initialize s
    choose a from s using policy from action-value function
    Repeat (for each step in episode)
        take action a
        observe r, s'
        update action-value function
        update s
```

Q-learning uses a table to store each state-action pair. At each step, the agent observes the current state of the environment and, using the π policy, selects and executes the action. By executing the action, the agent obtains the reward $Rt+1$ and the new state $St+1$. At this point, the agent is able to calculate $Q(St, at)$, thus updating the estimate.

Deep Q-learning

A Deep Q-learning network represents an evolution of the basic Q-learning method where the state-action is replaced by a neural network, with the aim of approximating the optimal value function.

Compared to the previous approaches, where it was used to structure the network in order to request both input and action and provide its expected return, Deep Q-learning revolutionizes the structure in order to request only the state of the environment and supply as many status-action values as there are actions that can be performed in the environment.

Keras-RL library

The `Keras-RL` library implements some state-of-the art deep reinforcement learning algorithms in Python and seamlessly integrates with the deep learning `keras` library.

 The Keras RL library was made by Matthias Plappert, a research scientist with an interest in machine learning and robotics, especially deep reinforcement learning. The Keras-RL project is available at `https://github.com/keras-rl/keras-rl`.

The following agents are available:

- **DQN**: Deep Q-learning network
- **DDPG**: Deep Deterministic Policy Gradient
- **NAF**: Normalized advantage functions (a continuous variant of the Q-learning algorithm)
- **CEM**: Cross-entropy method
- **SARSA**: State–action–reward–state–action algorithm

`keras-rl` works in the OpenAI Gym environment. This means that evaluating and playing around with different algorithms is easy. This does not limit the use of `keras-rl` libraries that can be adapted to all frameworks. You can use callbacks and metrics that are already available or define others based on your needs.

 The documentation that accompanies this library is available at `https://keras-rl.readthedocs.io/en/latest/`.

In the next section, we will show you how easy it is to use the library by solving a practical use case.

DQN to control a robot's mobility

Q-learning is one of the most used reinforcement learning algorithms. This is due to its ability to compare the expected utility of the available actions without requiring an environment model. Thanks to this technique, it is possible to find an optimal action for every given state in a finished **Markov Decision Process** (**MDP**).

A general solution to the reinforcement learning problem is to estimate, thanks to the learning process, an evaluation function. This function must be able to evaluate, through the sum of the rewards, the convenience or otherwise of a particular policy. In fact, Q-learning tries to maximize the value of the Q function (action-value function), which represents the maximum discounted future reward when we perform actions, *a*, in the state, *s*.

As we said in the *Deep Q-learning* section, DQN represents an evolution of the basic Q-learning method where the state-action is replaced by a neural network, with the aim of approximating the optimal value function. Let's explore the problem of controlling a robot by offering a solution based on the Deep Q-learning network.

OpenAI Gym installation and methods

The simulation environment will be Gym CartPole. To install OpenAI Gym, make sure that you have previously installed Python version 3.5+. Then, simply type the following command:

```
pip install gym
```

Now that we've done this, we will be able to insert the tools that have been made available by the library in a simple and immediate way.

The library also offers the possibility to directly clone the Gym's Git repository. This may be necessary if you want to change an environment or add other environments. To clone the Git repository, execute the following commands:

```
git clone https://github.com/openai/gym
cd gym
pip install -e .
```

Next, execute the following command:

```
pip install -e .[all]
```

In this way, we perform a full installation that contains all environments. This requires installing several more involved dependencies, including cmake and a recent pip version.

OpenAI Gym provides the `Env` class, which encapsulates the environment and its possible internal dynamics. The class has different methods and attributes to implement to create a new environment. The most important methods are called reset, step, and render.

The `reset()` method has the task of resetting the environment, initializing it to the initial state. Within the reset method, the definitions of the elements that make up the environment must be contained. In this case, this is the definition of the mechanical arm, and of the object to be grasped and its support.

The `step()` method has the task of moving the environment forward by one step. It requires the action to be performed as input and returns the new observation to the agent. Within this method, the management of the dynamics of the movements, the calculation of the status and of the reward, and the controls for completing the episode must be defined.

The third and last method is to render to which interior must be defined as the elements at each step must be represented. This method involves different types of rendering, such as human, `rgb_array`, or `ansi`. With the human type, the rendering is done on the screen or command-line interface and the method does not return anything; with the `rgb_array` type, invoking the method returns an n-dimensional array representing the RGB pixels of the screen; by choosing the third type, the return method returns a string containing a textual representation. To render, OpenAI Gym provides the viewer class, through which you can draw the elements of the environment as a set of polygons and circles.

Regarding the attributes of the environment, the `Env` class provides the definition of action space, observation space, and reward range. The action space attribute represents the action space, which is the set of possible actions that the agent can perform within the environment. Using the observation space attribute, the number of parameters that make up the state is defined and, for each of them, the range of values that can be assumed. The reward range attribute contains the minimum and maximum rewards that are obtainable in the environment. This is set to (-∞, + ∞) by default.

Using the `Env` class that's proposed by the framework as a basis for new environments, the common interface provided by the toolkit is adopted. In this way, the environments that are created can be integrated into the toolkit library and their dynamics can be learned from algorithms that have already been implemented by users of the OpenAI Gym community.

The CartPole system

The CartPole system is a classic problem of reinforcement learning. The system consists of a pole (which acts like an inverted pendulum) attached to a cart using a joint, as shown in the following diagram:

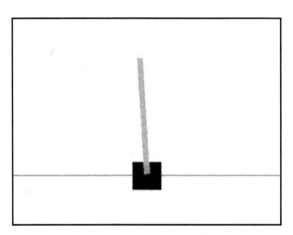

The system is controlled by applying a force of +1 or -1 to the cart. The force applied to the cart can be controlled, and the objective is to swing the pole upward and stabilize it. This must be done without the cart falling to the ground. At every step, the agent can choose to move the cart left or right, and it receives a reward of 1 for every time step that the pole is balanced. If the pole ever deviates by more than 15 degrees from upright, the procedure ends:

1. To run the CartPole example using the OpenAI Gym library, simply type the following code:

```
import gym
env = gym.make('CartPole-v0')
env.reset()
for i in range(1000):
    env.render()
    env.step(env.action_space.sample())
```

2. After introducing the environment, we move on to the practical use. To start, we will import the library:

```
import gym
```

3. This code imported the OpenAI Gym library, which will help us to define the environment, as follows:

```
ENV_NAME = 'CartPole-v0'
```

4. In this way, we have set the name of the environment, so let's get it:

```
env = gym.make(ENV_NAME)
```

The make method creates the environment that our agent will run in. An environment is a problem with a minimal interface that an agent can interact with. We initialize the newly set environment by resetting it using the reset() method:

```
env.reset()
```

An initial observation is returned: this value represents our initial state. At this point, we will use a for loop to run an instance of the CartPole-v0 environment for 1000 time steps, rendering the environment at each step:

```
for i in range(1000):
    env.render()
    env.step(env.action_space.sample())
```

Calling the render() method will visually display the current state, while subsequent calls to env.step() will allow us to interact with the environment, returning the new states in response to the actions with which we call it.

In this way, we have adopted random actions at each step. At this point, it is certainly useful to know what actions we are doing on the environment to decide future actions. The step() method returns exactly this. In effect, this method returns the following four values:

- observation: An environment-specific object representing your observation of the environment.
- reward: The amount of reward achieved by the previous action. The scale varies between environments, but the goal is always to increase your total reward.
- done: This determines whether it's time to reset the environment again. Most (but not all) tasks are divided into well-defined episodes, and done being True indicates that the episode has terminated.
- info: This shows you diagnostic information that's useful for debugging. It can sometimes be useful for learning.

A window will be displayed that contains our system. This is not stable and will soon move out of the screen. This is because the cart is pushed randomly, without taking into account the position of the pole.

To solve this problem, that is, to balance the pole, it is therefore necessary to set the push in the opposite direction to the inclination of the pole. Therefore, we have to set only two actions, -1 or +1, pushing the cart to the left or the right. But in order to do so, we need to know the data deriving from the observation of the environment at all times. As we have already said, these pieces of data are returned by the step() method. In particular, they are contained in the observation object.

This object contains the following parameters:

- Cart position
- Cart velocity
- Pole angle
- Pole velocity at tip

These four values become the input of our problem. As we have also anticipated, the system is balanced by applying a push to the cart. There are two possible options:

- Push the cart to the left (0)
- Push the cart to the right (1)

It is clear that this is a binary classification problem: four inputs and a single binary output.

First, let's consider how we can extract the values to be used as input. To extract these parameters, we just have to change the preceding proposed code:

```
env = gym.make('CartPole-v0')
observation = env.reset()
for i in range(1000):
    env.render()
    print(observation)
    observation, reward, done, info = env.step(env.action_space.sample())
```

By running the preceding code, we can see that the values contained in the observation object are now printed on the screen. All of this will be useful soon. Using the values that are returned from the environment observations, the agent has to decide on one of two possible actions: to move the cart left or right.

Q-learning solution

Now we have to face the most demanding phase: training of our system. In the *Q-learning* section, we said that the Gym library is focused on the episodic setting of reinforcement learning. The agent's experience is divided into a series of episodes. The initial state of the agent is randomly sampled by a distribution, and the interaction proceeds until the environment reaches a terminal state. This procedure is repeated for each episode, with the aim of maximizing the total reward expectation per episode and achieving a high level of performance in the fewest possible episodes.

In the learning phase, we must estimate an evaluation function. This function must be able to evaluate, through the sum of the rewards, the convenience or otherwise of a particular policy. In other words, we must approximate the evaluation function. How can we do this?

One solution is to use an artificial neural network as a function approximator. Recall that the training of a neural network aims to identify the weights of the connections between neurons. In this case, we will choose random values with weights for each episode. At the end, we will choose the combination of weights that has collected the maximum reward.

The state of the system at a given moment is returned to us by the observation object. To choose an action from the actual state, we can use a linear combination of the weights and the observation. This is one of the most important special cases of function approximation, in which the approximate function is a linear function of the weight vector, w. For every state, s, there is a real-valued vector, $x(s)$, with the same number of components as w. Linear methods approximate the state-value function by the inner product between w and $x(s)$.

In this way, we have specified the methodology that we intend to adopt for the solution of the problem. Now, to make the whole training phase easily understandable, we report the whole code block and then comment on it in detail on a line-by-line basis:

```
import gym
import numpy as np
env = gym.make('CartPole-v0')
np.random.seed(1)
env.seed(1)
HighReward = 0
BestWeights = None
for i in range(200):
    observation = env.reset()
    Weights = np.random.uniform(-1,1,4)
    SumReward = 0
    for j in range(1000):
        env.render()
        action = 0 if np.matmul(Weights,observation) < 0 else 1
        observation, reward, done, info = env.step(action)
```

```
        SumReward += reward
        print( i, j, Weights, observation, action, SumReward,BestWeights)
    if SumReward > HighReward:
        HighReward = SumReward
        BestWeights = Weights
```

The following part of the code deals with importing the libraries:

```
import gym
import numpy as np
```

Then, we move on to creating the environment by calling the make() method:

```
env = gym.make('CartPole-v0')
```

This method creates the environment that our agent will run in. To make the experiment reproducible, in the sense that it provides the same results with each reproduction, it is necessary to set the seed. To set the seed value, the NumPy library's random.seed() function is used:

```
np.random.seed(1)
```

The seed() function sets the seed of the random number generator, which is useful for creating simulations or random objects that can be reproduced. You have to use this function every time you want to get a reproducible random result. .seed must also be set for the environment:

```
env.seed(1)
```

Now let's initialize the parameters we will use:

```
HighReward = 0
BestWeights = None
```

The HighReward variable will contain the maximum reward that's obtained, up to the current episode; this value will be used as a comparison value. The BestWeights variable will contain the sequence of weights that has registered the maximum reward. We can now implement the best weight sequence search through an iterative procedure for episodes:

```
for i in range(200):
```

We decide to execute the procedure 200 times, so we initialize the system using the reset() method:

```
observation = env.reset()
```

In each episode, we use a sequence of weights, equal in number to the observations of the environment, which, as we stated previously, is four (cart position, cart velocity, pole angle, and pole velocity at tip):

```
Weights = np.random.uniform(-1,1,4)
```

To fix the weights, we have used the `np.random.uniform()` function. This function draws samples from a uniform distribution. The samples are uniformly distributed over the half-open interval (low and high). It includes low but excludes high.

In other words, any value within the given interval is equally likely to be drawn by a uniform distribution. Three parameters have been passed: the lower boundary of the output interval, its upper boundary, and the output shape. In our case, we requested four random values in the interval (-1, 1). After doing this, we need to initialize the sum of the rewards:

```
SumReward = 0
```

At this point, we implement another iterative cycle to determine the maximum reward we can get with these weights:

```
for j in range(1000):
```

Calling the `render()` method will visually display the current state:

```
env.render()
```

Now, we have to decide on the `action`:

```
action = 0 if np.matmul(Weights,observation) < 0 else 1
```

As we stated previously, to decide on the action we have used a linear combination of two vectors: weights and observation. To perform a linear combination, we have used the `np.matmul()` function; it implements a matrix product of two arrays. So, if this product is <0, the action is 0 (move left); otherwise, the action is 1 (move right).

It should be noted that a negative product means that the pole is tilted to the left, so in order to balance this trend, it is necessary to push the cart toward the left. A positive product means that the pole is tilted to the right, so in order to balance this trend, it is necessary to push the cart toward the right.

Now, we will use the `step()` method to return the new states in response to the actions with which we call it. Obviously, the action we pass to the method is the one we have just decided:

```
observation, reward, done, info = env.step(action)
```

As we stated previously, this method returns the following four values:

- `observation`: An environment-specific object representing your observation of the environment.
- `reward`: The amount of reward achieved by the previous action. The scale varies between environments, but the goal is always to increase your total reward. It is of the float type.
- `done`: This states whether it's time to reset the environment. Most (but not all) tasks are divided into well-defined episodes, and `done` being True indicates that the episode has terminated. It is of the Boolean type.
- `info`: This is diagnostic information that's useful for debugging. It can sometimes be useful for learning. It is of the dict type.

We can then update the sum of the rewards with the reward we've just obtained. Remember: for every time step where we keep the pole straight, we get +1 reward:

```
SumReward += reward
```

We just have to print the values obtained in this step:

```
print( i, j, Weights, observation, action, SumReward, BestWeights)
```

At the end of the current iteration, we can make a comparison to check whether the total reward obtained is the highest one obtained so far:

```
if SumReward > HighReward:
```

If it is the highest reward obtained so far, update the `HighReward` parameter with the following value:

```
HighReward = SumReward
```

Once this is done, fix the sequence of `Weights` of the current step as the best one:

```
BestWeights = Weights
```

With this instruction, the training phase ends, which will give us the sequence of weights that best approximates the evaluation function. We can now test the system.

When the training phase is achieved, in practice it means that we have found the sequence of weights that best approximates this function, that is, the one that has returned the best reward achievable. Now, we have to test the system with these values to check whether the pole is able to stand for at least 100 time steps.

Now, since we are already done with the training phase, to make the whole testing phase easily understandable, we will report the whole code block and then comment on it in detail on a line-by-line basis:

```
observation = env.reset()
for j in range(100):
    env.render()
    action = 0 if np.matmul(BestWeights,observation) < 0 else 1
    observation, reward, done, info = env.step(action)
    print( j, action)
```

First, we have to initialize the system once again by using the `reset()` method:

```
observation = env.reset()
```

Then, we have to run an iterative cycle to apply the results that are obtained in the training phase:

```
for j in range(100):
```

For each step, we will call the `render()` method to visually display the current state:

```
env.render()
```

Now, we have to decide on the action to perform on the system based on the best weights obtained in the training phase and on the observations of the current state:

```
action = 0 if np.matmul(BestWeights,observation) < 0 else 1
```

Now, we need to use the `step()` method, which returns the new states in response to the actions with which we call it. The action passed to the method is the one we have just decided on:

```
observation, reward, done, info = env.step(action)
```

Finally, we print the step number and the action that's been decided on for visual control of the flow. By running the proposed code, we can verify that, after the training phase, the system is able to keep the pole in equilibrium for 100 time steps.

Deep Q-learning solution

As we said in the *Deep Q-learning* section, Deep Q-learning identifies a reinforcement learning method of the approximation of a function. It therefore represents an evolution of the basic Q-learning method since the state-action table is replaced by a neural network, with the aim of approximating the optimal value function.

Compared to the previous approaches, where it was used to structure the network in order to request both input and action, and provided its expected return, Deep Q-learning revolutionizes the structure to request only the state of the environment and supply as many status-action values as there are actions that can be performed in the environment.

In the following code, a Deep Q-learning solution for the CartPole problem is proposed:

```
import numpy as np
import gym
from keras.models import Sequential
from keras.layers import Dense, Activation, Flatten
from keras.optimizers import Adam
from rl.agents.dqn import DQNAgent
from rl.policy import BoltzmannQPolicy
from rl.memory import SequentialMemory
ENV_NAME = 'CartPole-v0'
env = gym.make(ENV_NAME)
np.random.seed(1)
env.seed(1)
nb_actions = env.action_space.n
model = Sequential()
model.add(Flatten(input_shape=(1,) + env.observation_space.shape))
model.add(Dense(16))
model.add(Activation('relu'))
model.add(Dense(16))
model.add(Activation('relu'))
model.add(Dense(16))
model.add(Activation('relu'))
model.add(Dense(nb_actions))
model.add(Activation('linear'))
print(model.summary())
memory = SequentialMemory(limit=50000, window_length=1)
policy = BoltzmannQPolicy()
dqn = DQNAgent(model=model, nb_actions=nb_actions, memory=memory,
               nb_steps_warmup=10, target_model_update=1e-2,
               policy=policy)
dqn.compile(Adam(lr=1e-3), metrics=['mae'])
dqn.fit(env, nb_steps=1000, visualize=True, verbose=2)
dqn.save_weights('dqn_{}_weights.h5f'.format(ENV_NAME), overwrite=True)
dqn.test(env, nb_episodes=5, visualize=True)
```

As we've done in all of the examples that we've proposed so far, we will analyze this code line by line to understand its operating principle. The first part of this code is used to import the necessary libraries:

```
import numpy as np
import gym
```

First, we import the `numpy` library, which will be used to set the seed value. Therefore, we need to import the `gym` library that will help us define the environment. Having done this, we import some functions of the `keras` library to build a neural network model:

```
from keras.models import Sequential
from keras.layers import Dense, Activation, Flatten
from keras.optimizers import Adam
```

First the `Sequential` model is imported; the `Sequential` model is a linear stack of layers. Then, some Keras layers are imported: `Dense`, `Activation`, and `Flatten`. A dense model is a fully connected neural network layer. The `Activation` layer applies an activation function to an output. The `Flatten` layer flattens the input; it does not affect the batch size. Finally, the Adam optimizer is imported. Let's move on to importing the `Keras-RL` library:

```
from rl.agents.dqn import DQNAgent
from rl.policy import BoltzmannQPolicy
from rl.memory import SequentialMemory
```

The `Keras-RL` library implements some state-of-the art deep reinforcement learning algorithms in Python and seamlessly integrates with the deep learning `keras` library. `DQNAgent`, a policy, and a memory model are imported. Now, we will define the environment:

```
ENV_NAME = 'CartPole-v0'
```

In this way, we have set the name of the environment. Let's proceed and obtain it:

```
env = gym.make(ENV_NAME)
```

To set the seed value, the `numpy` library's `random.seed()` function is used:

```
np.random.seed(1)
```

The `seed()` function sets the seed of the random number generator, which is useful for creating simulations or random objects that can be reproduced. You have to use this function every time you want to get a reproducible random result. The seed must also be set for the environment:

```
env.seed(1)
```

Now, we will extract the actions that are available to the agent:

```
nb_actions = env.action_space.n
```

The `nb_actions` variable now contains all of the actions that are available in the selected environment. The Gym will not always tell you what these actions mean, only which ones are available. Now, we will build a simple neural network model using the `keras` library:

```
model = Sequential()
model.add(Flatten(input_shape=(1,) + env.observation_space.shape))
model.add(Dense(16))
model.add(Activation('relu'))
model.add(Dense(16))
model.add(Activation('relu'))
model.add(Dense(16))
model.add(Activation('relu'))
model.add(Dense(nb_actions))
model.add(Activation('linear'))
print(model.summary())
```

The following information is returned:

Layer (type)	Output Shape	Param #
flatten_3 (Flatten)	(None, 4)	0
dense_9 (Dense)	(None, 16)	80
activation_9 (Activation)	(None, 16)	0
dense_10 (Dense)	(None, 16)	272
activation_10 (Activation)	(None, 16)	0
dense_11 (Dense)	(None, 16)	272
activation_11 (Activation)	(None, 16)	0
dense_12 (Dense)	(None, 2)	34
activation_12 (Activation)	(None, 2)	0

```
Total params: 658
Trainable params: 658
Non-trainable params: 0
```

Now that the neural network model is ready to use, let's configure and compile our agent. One problem with using the DQN is that the neural network used in the algorithm tends to forget previous experiences because it overwrites them with new experiences. Therefore, we need a list of previous experiences and observations to reform the model with previous experiences. For this reason, a `Memory` variable is defined, which will contain the previous experiences:

```
memory = SequentialMemory(limit=50000, window_length=1)
```

Now, we will set the `policy` variable:

```
policy = BoltzmannQPolicy()
```

Then, we just have to define the agent:

```
dqn = DQNAgent(model=model, nb_actions=nb_actions, memory=memory,
               nb_steps_warmup=10, target_model_update=1e-2,
               policy=policy)
```

Let's move on to compile the model:

```
dqn.compile(Adam(lr=1e-3), metrics=['mae'])
```

The preceding command compiles an agent and the underlying models to be used for training and testing. Now that the agent is ready, we can train it:

```
dqn.fit(env, nb_steps=1000, visualize=True, verbose=2)
```

The `fit()` function trains the agent on the given environment. At the end of the training, it is necessary to save the obtained weights:

```
dqn.save_weights('dqn_{}_weights.h5f'.format(ENV_NAME), overwrite=True)
```

Saving the weight of a network or an entire structure takes place in an `HDF5` file, which is an efficient and flexible storage system that supports complex multidimensional datasets. Finally, we will evaluate our algorithm for 10 episodes:

```
dqn.test(env, nb_episodes=5, visualize=True)
```

In this way, the balance of the system is assured.

Summary

In this chapter, we learned about the basic concepts of reinforcement learning and how to use these techniques to control a mechanical system. To start with, an overview of robot control was addressed.

Then, the OpenAI Gym library was introduced, which helps us to implement algorithms based on reinforcement learning. It includes a growing collection of benchmark issues that expose a common interface, and a website where people can share their results and compare algorithm performance. We explored the different environments that are available and how to install the library.

Finally, the CartPole system was used to implement Q-learning and Deep Q-learning algorithms. The CartPole system is a classic problem of reinforced learning. The system consists of a pole (which acts like an inverted pendulum) that's attached to a cart via a joint. The system is controlled by applying a force of +1 or -1 to the cart. The force that's applied to the cart can be controlled, and the objective is to swing the pole upward and stabilize it.

In the next chapter, we will learn about the basics of **natural language processing** (**NLP**), text classification concepts, and how Keras sequential layers work. Then, we will gain an understanding of training and validation procedures, and finally, learn how to implement a DNN model for labeling sentences.

10
Reuters Newswire Topics Classifier in Keras

Natural language processing (**NLP**) is the process of automatic processing of information written or spoken in a natural language using an electronic calculator. This is made particularly difficult and complex due to the intrinsic characteristics of the ambiguity of human language. When it's necessary to make the machine learn methods of interaction with the environment typical of man, the question isn't so much that of storing data, but that of letting the machine learn how this data can be translated simultaneously to create a concept. Natural language interacts with the environment generating predictive knowledge.

In this chapter, Keras layers are used to build a model to classify Reuter's newswire topics. Data is available from a dataset that contains 11,228 newswires from Reuters with 46 labeled topics. This dataset is from Keras, and each wire is encoded as a sequence of word indexes.

The following topics will be covered in this chapter:

- Natural language processing
- The Natural Language Toolkit
- Corpora
- Word and sentence tokenize
- Implementing a DNN to label sentences

In this chapter, we'll learn how to analyze, understand, and generate texts using Natural Language Toolkit. Then, we will analyze the most frequent applications using natural language processing. We'll learn about Keras sequential layers and understand training and validation procedures. Finally, we will explore a practical case: how to label sentences contained in the Reuters newswire topics dataset using a Keras Deep Neural Network.

Natural language processing

NLP aims to implement IT tools to analyze, understand, and generate texts that people can understand naturally, as if they were communicating with another human interlocutor and not a computer. By natural language, we mean the language that we use in everyday life, such as English, Chinese, or Arabic, and that's synonymous with human language, mainly to distinguish it from formal language, including computer language. Natural language is the most natural and common form of communication, not only in its spoken version, but also in its written one. Compared to formal language, natural language is much more complex and often contains implications and ambiguities, which makes it very difficult to elaborate. Two goals can be pursued: text analysis and text generation. These characteristics define the following disciplines:

- **Natural language analysis** (**NLA**): This aims to study the understanding of natural language by machines. Deals with the reduction of a text in natural language in a formal and univocal representation.

- **Natural language generation** (**NLG**): This aims to study how machines can generate sentences in natural language. It deals with the construction of applications capable of producing correct sentences in a specific language.

These activities have a certain complexity and require different types of skills ranging from computer science to linguistics.

NLP phases

NLP involves several phases in the text analysis that make it a layered structure. The fundamental levels on which the analysis of a sentence is based are listed in the following:

- Morphology analysis
- Syntax analysis
- Semantic analysis
- Pragmatic analysis

Let's understand in depth about each layer.

Morphology analysis

The purpose of this phase is to subdivide the language input strings into sets of tokens corresponding to discrete words, sub-words, and punctuation forms. The text is then fragmented through a tokenization process, forming a series of tokens—each token is associated with a word of the text. In this phase, two terms assume relevance: stem and lemma. The stem is the root of a word, obtainable by removing from its flexed form (for example the conjugation of a verb or the plural of a noun) the ending. The lemma is instead the canonical form of the word, which is the one that's conventionally chosen to represent all of the inflected forms.

This phase has the task of identifying the stem and lemma of each word through two different operations, stemming and lemmatization respectively. This information will then be used in the subsequent analysis phases; in fact, it's much less expensive, in terms of memory, to maintain rules based on the parts that make up a word and how their combinations go to form certain inflected forms, rather than managing each word as an atomic element within a huge inventory.

Syntax analysis

To understand the meaning of a sentence, it's not enough to know the meaning of the words that compose it, but it's also essential to know how they relate to each other. This phase deals with the syntactic analysis of the text placed in input. All parts of the speech are identified, understood as verbs, nouns, adjectives, adverbs, prepositions, and pronouns. The process that deals with marking each word with its own part of the speech is called **Part-of-Speech Tagging**.

The process is divided into two sub-processes: the first, called **shallow parsing**, produces a binary tree in which the elementary parts are identified—that is, the **nominal part** (**NP**) and the **verbal part** (**VP**). The second, called **full parsing**, produces a syntactic tree in which each word is marked with its syntactic role within the sentence.

Semantic analysis

The semantic analysis phase exploits the information obtained from the previous analysis steps concerning the meanings of the single words and the relationships between them to interpret the meaning of the sentence in the complex. The named entity recognition process is used to search for and identify groups of words that can form an entity, understood as personal names, countries, events, and so on. Semantic processing determines the possible meaning of a sentence, focusing on the interactions between the meanings of the words in the sentence under examination.

This level of processing can include the semantic disambiguation of words with multiple meanings (**word sense disambiguation (WSD)**), similar to how the disambiguation of words that can act as multiple parts of the syntactic discourse is realized. Various methods can be implemented to realize disambiguation, some of which require information on the frequency with which each sense occurs in a particular corpus of interest, others require consideration of the local context, and others still use the pragmatic knowledge of the document domain.

Pragmatic analysis

This phase deals with identifying the context in which the text is placed and to elaborate and use it accordingly. More specifically, pragmatics deals with how the context affects the interpretation of meanings. In this case, by context we mean situation, such as the set of extra linguistic factors (social, environmental, and psychological) that influence linguistic acts. In fact, human language is based not only on its morphological, syntactic, and semantic characteristics, but also on external knowledge, linked to the context in which a sentence is inserted.

In pragmatic analysis, we tend to distinguish between the meaning of the utterance and the speaker's intention. The meaning of the utterance is its literal meaning, while the speaker's intention is the concept that the speaker attempts to convey.

In order to correctly interpret the message of a communication, it may be necessary, for example, to have the following:

- Knowledge of the role and status of the interlocutors
- Spatio-temporal location of the situation
- Knowledge of the subject matter

The ability to understand the meaning inferred by another speaker is called **pragmatic competence.** Even this type of analysis is still not detailed in the literature, mainly because of the great difficulties it presents.

Automatic processing problems

From the point of view of automatic processing, the syntactic level is the least problematic. It's possible to analyze even very complex sentences, to recognize their grammatical correctness, and to reconstruct their syntactic structure.

The semantic level is much more difficult. In the simplest cases, we can proceed as follows:

- Sentence meaning is obtained from the meaning of the single words, once the syntactic structure of the sentence is known.
- The meaning of individual words is defined from an automatically accessible dictionary.

However, there are several problems. First of all, the same word can have different meanings in different contexts. Then, the syntactic structure of a sentence can be ambiguous. In other words, different structures can sometimes be attributed to the same succession of words. Finally, the meaning of certain idiomatic phrases is different from the literal meaning that's obtained by composing the meanings of the individual words. Artificial intelligence attempts to solve these problems by using an appropriate knowledge base which the language processing program is able to access.

The pragmatic level is even more difficult. The main problem is due to the fact that, when we talk, we're able to predict the mental states of our interlocutors. In other words, to communicate properly, it's necessary to represent the intentions of the interlocutors, which are only partially reflected in their words.

NLP applications

Any application that uses text is an NLP application. As the amount of information available online increases day by day, the need to access and process them becomes essential. For example, to translate information from one language to another, you can use machine translation, which is the most used NLP application and allows you to overcome language barriers. The most frequent applications using NLP include the following.

Information retrieval

Information retrieval (**IR**) is a set of techniques used to retrieve information in electronic format that's relevant to user requests. Information refers to all documents, metadata, or files in databases or on the World Wide Web. There's the possibility of carrying out information retrieval even without carrying out significant NLP operations, as many search engines continue to do. However, the trend that emerged from the 90s to the present day is that of a process of indexing, identification, and presentation of documents, which is increasingly complex and strictly dependent on the linguistic analysis of contents. Many Universities and public libraries use IR systems to provide access to publications, books and other documents.

Information extraction

Information extraction (**IE**) concerns the creation of a structured representation of the relevant information present in an unstructured machine-readable document. A machine-readable document is a document the content of which can be readily processed by computers. When applied to text documents, IE is therefore a technology that aims to extract salient elements related to a particular context, such as entities or relationships. It differs from IR because the purpose of the IR is to find documents that already contain the answer to the user's question: given a collection of documents, the IR system that receives a query (set of keywords) as input selects a subset of the documents that're relevant to the query. The user will then navigate the list of documents and look for the information that interests them most. Instead, the IE system, given a selection of documents, seeks to extract the relevant information in a structured way according to the needs provided in input. Multimedia document processing like automatic annotation and content extraction out of images/audio/video are real world examples of information extraction activities.

Question-answering

Unlike IR, which provides a list of potentially relevant documents in response to a user query, **question-answering** (**QA**) provides the user with only the text of the response or the steps that provide the response. To find the answer to a question, a QA program can use a knowledge base or a collection of documents in natural language (a corpus such as the World Wide Web or other local collections). Researchers try to deal with a wide range of question types such as facts, lists, definitions, how, why, hypothetical, and semantically constrained. Research collections vary from small corpora to news collections to the World Wide Web. QA requires more complex natural language processing techniques than other types of information retrieval such as document retrieval. Unlike current search engines, **QA** systems do not search for entire documents but provide specific answers located in small fragments of text. This functionality makes research much slower, but also more precise and timely.

Automatic summarization

Automatic summarization is related to the creation of summarized versions of a text in such a way that only the most important points of the original text are kept. This operation differs from IE due to the fact that the recovered information is not necessarily formatted so that it can be processed by further applications.

We can consider the automatic summarization as a process characterized by three phases that can be roughly described as follows:

1. **Analysis of the source text**: The objective of this phase is to process the text and characterize it in such a way as to allow the identification of the contents of the information.
2. **Determining the salient pieces of the text**: This step is necessary to calculate the measure of relevance for the information contained in the document.
3. **Synthesizing an appropriate output**: This last phase is characterized both by the need to organize the information extracted legibly and by the need to represent the information as accurately as possible.

The process described through these three phases is shared by almost all automatic summary generation systems, but these systems are different for many peculiarities.

Automatic translation

Automatic translation, of which many online examples already exist, exploits the treatment of natural language to translate from one language into another not simply by substituting a word with the relative translation, but by checking if there're any linguistic anomalies such as, for example, idioms or proverbs that would have no meaning if translated word for word. There're three important types of automatic translation:

- **Rule-based translation**: This includes translation based on the transfer principle and the one based on the use of an Interlingua (or pivot language) is nowadays the prevailing paradigm for machine translation. Words are translated according to a purely linguistic point of view, choosing the most appropriate linguistic equivalents. Rule-based machine translation typically uses a translation process divided into three phases: text sentence parsing, transfer phase, and generation or synthesis phase.
- **Translation via corpora**: This uses parallel linguistic corpora and is based on the analysis of real samples and their corresponding translations. Among these systems, the main one is **statistical machine translation** (**SMT**). The goal of this technology is to generate translations based on statistical methods based on corpora of bilingual and monolingual texts.

- **Context-based translation**: This is based on the search for the best translation of a word taking into consideration the rest of the words surrounding it. The system divides a text into units of four to eight words and proposes translations of each sequence into the target language by deleting translations that contain nonsense phrases. This filtering uses a corpus in the target language, in which the search phrase is counted a number of times. The sequence created is then moved one position (one word), retranslating most of the words and filtering the text again in order to leave only the coherent sentences. This procedure is repeated throughout the text. In the final phase, the results of each sequence are concatenated so as to obtain a single translation of the text.

Automatic translators cannot replace human translators, but they can help to organize a larger amount of work in an organized way and are still useful for grasping the general sense of a text and for checking whether the content is of interest.

Sentiment analysis

As we saw in the `Chapter 6`, *Movie Reviews Sentiment Analysis Using Recurrent Neural Network* and the term sentiment analysis refers to the set of natural language processing techniques, text analysis, and computational linguistics to identify and extract subjective information in written or spoken text sources. If this subjective information is taken from large amounts of data, and therefore from the opinions of large groups of people, the sentiment analysis can also be called **opinion mining**.

NLP methods

At the beginning of this chapter, we said that natural language processing involves several phases in text analysis that make it a layered structure. In each of these phases, the operations necessary for the treatment of the text follow precise procedures that we analyze in detail.

Sentence splitting

Sentence splitting is the process of breaking down the text into sentences. This module, starting from the initial document, returns a set of strings, where each element represents a sentence. A problem that should not be underestimated is the fact that strong punctuation symbols, such as ., !, and ?, are in general a necessary but not sufficient condition to say that the sentence is finished. In fact, the character can be found in correspondence of abbreviations of URLs, email addresses, numbers, and so on.

Tokenization

In the tokenization phase, within each single sentence, atomic elements called tokens are identified; based on the token identified, it's possible to carry out an analysis and evaluation of the sentence itself. Therefore, during the tokenization phase, not only are these elements recognized and evaluated, but in some cases there's the conversion of negative constructs. Hence, the text is subdivided into tokens—that is, into a series of "indivisible" units. It's relatively simple for languages that use spaces to delimit words and very complex for languages with a continuous spelling system. Limiting ourselves to languages such as English—that is, part of the first case—the token can be defined simply as any sequence of characters bounded by spaces; however, this definition leaves room for numerous exceptions. In languages where word boundaries aren't explicitly marked in writing, tokenization is also called **word segmentation**.

In general, in the process of tokenization, several problems must be addressed:

- There are no spaces that separate words from punctuation that follows (precedes)
- There are sequences of characters not separated by spaces that correspond to two tokens
- Sequences of characters separated by spaces can form a single token
- Upper- and lowercase management
- There are space of variability of spelling conventions

At the end of the procedure, a string with an assigned meaning is identified (token). The token is structured as a pair consisting of a token name and an optional token value.

Part-of-speech tagging

Part-of-speech tagging (**PoS tagging**) is the process of labeling text words that correspond to particular lexical categories. The common linguistic categories include nouns, verbs, adjectives, articles, pronouns, adverbs, conjunctions, and so on. Within the NLP, we can distinguish two approaches in addressing the problem of PoS tagging:

- An approach based on the definition of rules useful for distinguishing individual classes
- An approach based on machine learning models

The models of machine learning used in literature are many; all tackle the problem with a supervised training approach using collections of annotated documents called **corpora**. Many statistical systems use corpora to obtain probabilistic data and rules for the problem of PoS tagging. A first difficulty of this approach arises when we must classify unknown words—that is, that weren't present in the training set and for which we don't have statistical data on their belonging to certain classes.

Shallow parsing

Shallow parsing (also chunking) is the analysis of a proposition, which is formed in simple form by a subject and a predicate. The subject is typically a noun phrase while the predicate is a verbal phrase formed by a verb with zero or more complements and adverbs. A chunk is made up of one or more adjacent tokens.

There're numerous approaches to the problem of chunking. For example, in the assigned task, a chunk is represented as a group of words delimited by square brackets for which a tag representing the type of chunk is indicated. The dataset used was derived from a given corpora by taking the part related to journal articles and extracting chunk information from syntactic trees of the corpora.

Named entity recognition

The named entity recognition process is used to search for and identify groups of words that can form an entity, understood as personal names, countries, events, and so on. The extraction of entities within a text implies two main tasks:

- **Segmentation**: The phase in which the boundaries of an entity must be identified
- **Classification**: The assignment of relevant semantic information to the identified segments

The possible approaches to the two problems can be of three types:

- **Based on lookup list**, then on the recognition of parts of the text within predefined lists divided by categories. It's a simple system, but it requires extremely complex and extensive lists of possible entities, which are difficult to compile and manage.

- **Rule-based**, in which the text is analyzed according to a set of rules that determine the presence of entities within a text and define its semantic information. The rules used generally make use of orthographic and syntactic information. The complexity of the language makes it very difficult to set up an effective set of rules if the context is complex enough, but with a good work of study and testing it's possible to reach a high level of precision.
- **Statistical-based**, generally through the use of machine learning techniques, this approach consists of identifying patterns in the input data to determine probabilistically where an entity might be present.

Given the complexity of the problem and the presence of various techniques for its resolution, it's important to be able to evaluate the performance of a system, to understand if it can represent a valid approach.

Syntactic parsing

Syntactic parsing is a process that analyzes a continuous flow of input data (input read, for example, from a file or a keyboard) in order to determine its structure thanks to a given formal grammar. A parser is a program that performs this task. Usually, parsers aren't written by hand, but made through parser generators. In most languages, syntactic analysis operates on a token sequence in which the lexical analyzer splits the input.

Semantic role labeling

Semantic role labeling takes a set of input phrases and for each of them starts to determine the various components that could play a semantic role. A component of a proposition that plays a semantic role is defined as constituent. Once the possible candidates are determined, machine learning techniques are used to label them with the right role. With semantic role we mean the meaning that this component has with respect to the verb. This meaning goes beyond the syntax, but doesn't include the meaning of the component, but only of its role. You can write syntactically correct sentences, but without meaning.

Natural language processing tools

Getting information is a complex process, both because the data are often not structured, and because the collections of documents are becoming more extensive, not to mention that in some cases the information is duplicated or inaccurate. The speed with which the collections are enlarged, the heterogeneity and complexity that characterize them, as well as the increasingly demanding requests of the user seem to make this work more and more complex. Despite this, the researchers' work is greatly facilitated by various tools that are available. As research in the field progresses, the availability of platforms for NLP task execution is growing even greater.

Currently, there're many tools for processing the natural language and the open source world offers high quality libraries for solving the most common problems in the processing of texts such as sentiment analysis, topic identification, and self-logging of content. Many of these can be considered as libraries that provide the basic blocks for much more complex and innovative solutions that allow focusing exclusively the application logic. In the next sections, we'll analyze the most used tools.

The Natural Language Toolkit

The **Natural Language Toolkit** (**NLTK**) is a collection of tools for natural language processing, developed with the Python programming language. This toolkit offers access to over 100 corpora in numerous languages. This tool is also able to carry out different types of textual elaborations such as PoS tagging, parsing, and tokenization (that is, the classification of word roots, a preparatory passage often used for natural language processing) and the possibility to summarize texts, operation called wrapping. The NLTK also includes an introduction to programming and extensive documentation, making it a program suited to the needs of students, faculty and researchers.

 The official project page is available at the following URL:
https://www.nltk.org/

The Stanford NLP Group software

The Stanford NLP Group is one of the most important research groups in the field of natural language processing and offers several valuable tools. With these tools, it's possible to distinguish and classify the derivations of words (tokenization), their function (parts of speech tagging), and the structure of propositions (parsing). In addition, there're tools for more complicated processes such as deep learning, through which the focus is placed on the context of propositions. All of the most important basic functions can be found in the Stanford Core NLP. All Stanford NLP Group programs are written in Java and are available in several languages.

> The official project page is available at the following URL:
> https://nlp.stanford.edu/software/

Apache OpenNLP

Apache OpenNLP is a library licensed under Apache and supports the most common tasks of the NLP such as tokenization, sentence segmentation, PoS Tagging, and parsing and therefore allows the implementation of a complete annotation pipeline. It offers a diametrically opposite approach to the Standford suite as it's based on machine learning and training of models for NLP; in fact, it provides a wide range of pre-built models for different languages as well as the resources from which these models were generated (annotated texts).

The OpenNLP language detector, a component whose model is available for public download, can recognize up to 103 languages. The language detector model recognizes languages in the ISO 639-3 standard and has been trained through the Leipzig corpus, allowing 98.81% accuracy and accuracy of 1 in phrase recognition.

> The official project page is available at the following URL:
> https://opennlp.apache.org/

GATE

GATE is an open source software developed by the University of Sheffield since 1995; it's composed of a suite of tools for the resolution of various problems related to NLP. One of the main components of GATE is ANNIE, a system that provides basic functionality for IE. GATE isn't just a set of software tools, it's a wide-ranging project that includes several solutions dedicated to NLP activities.

 The official project page is available at the following URL: https://gate.ac.uk/

The Natural Language Toolkit

The NLTK is a suite of libraries and programs for symbolic and statistical analysis in the field of natural language processing, mainly in the English language, written in Python language. It was developed by Steven Bird and Edward Loper at the University of Pennsylvania's Department of Computer and Information Science. The NLTK includes graphical tools and sample data and is accompanied by a book that exposes the concepts behind natural language problems solved by the toolkit programs, as well as a cookbook for the most common procedures.

NLTK aims to support the research and teaching of NLP and other related fields, such as linguistics, cognitive science, artificial intelligence, information retrieval, and machine learning. NLTK has been used successfully as an aid to teaching, as a tool for individual study, and as a platform for prototyping and developing research tools. NLTK has been used in university courses held in 32 US institutions and in 25 countries. The procedures supported by NLTK include classification, tokenization, stemming and tagging, parsing, and semantic reasoning.

Getting started with the NLTK

The first thing to do is to install the NLTK library. To install the NLTK, we can use the `pip` package manager. When you use `pip` to install packages, it connects to PyPI and searches for and downloads the required package. For this, you naturally need your shell to have access to the internet. Then, we type the following command:

```
pip install nltk
```

For the correct installation of `nltk`, it's necessary that the `numpy` library has been previously installed. The following screenshot is returned:

```
C:\pythonscript\KDL>pip install nltk
Collecting nltk
  Downloading https://files.pythonhosted.org/packages/6f/ed/9c755d357d33bc1931e157f537721efb5b88d2c583fe593cc09603076cc3/nltk-3
.4.zip (1.4MB)
    100% |                                        | 1.4MB 1.3MB/s
Requirement already satisfied: six in c:\python36\lib\site-packages (from nltk) (1.11.0)
Collecting singledispatch (from nltk)
  Downloading https://files.pythonhosted.org/packages/c5/10/369f50bcd4621b263927b0a1519987a04383d4a98fb10438042ad410cf88/single
dispatch-3.4.0.3-py2.py3-none-any.whl
Building wheels for collected packages: nltk
  Running setup.py bdist_wheel for nltk ... done
  Stored in directory: C:\Users\lavoro\AppData\Local\pip\Cache\wheels\4b\c8\24\b2343664bcceb7147efeb21c0b23703a05b23fcfeaceaa2a
1e
Successfully built nltk
Installing collected packages: singledispatch, nltk
Successfully installed nltk-3.4 singledispatch-3.4.0.3

C:\pythonscript\KDL>_
```

To check the presence of the package in our installation, just type the following (Python shell):

```
import nltk
```

Along with the `nltk` package are provided many corpora, toy grammars, trained models, and so on.

 For a complete list of available data, refer to the following URL:
http://www.nltk.org/nltk_data/

To use this data, it's necessary to proceed with the relative download through the following command:

```
nltk.download()
```

The following window is opened (**NLTK Downloader**):

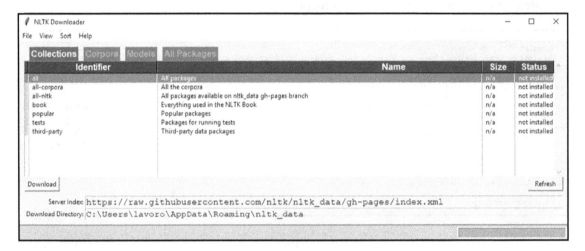

In **NLTK Downloader**, four navigation tabs are available: **Collections**, **Corpora**, **Models**, and **All Packages**.

You can download the entire collection (using **all**), or just the corpora and no grammars or trained models (using **all-corpora**). Of course, it's also possible to download a single package after selecting it and clicking on the **Download** button at the bottom-left of the **NLTK Downloader** screen.

Corpora

Linguistic corpora are collections, mostly large, of oral or written texts produced in real communication contexts (recordings of speeches or newspaper articles), stored in electronic format and often accompanied by computerized consultation tools.

Corpora allow to observe the actual use of a language and to verify general trends on a statistical basis. They're of fundamental importance in contemporary lexicography, within which they're used among other things to select lemmas based on their frequency of use, to identify the typical constructions in which a word is needed, and to grasp the nuances of meaning in based on contexts.

Corpora are also an important tool in the development of language technologies such as automatic translation and automatic speech recognition, in which they're used to build statistical models of the language. They're also used in the teaching of languages, where they can be a subsidy for the construction of teaching materials and allow, above all advanced learners, to infer properties of words and constructions by observing their use contexts.

nltk contains a collection of corpus reader classes ready to use (nltk.corpus). Through this package, it's possible to access the contents of a diversified set of corpora.

 To get a list of the available corpora, refer to the following URL:
http://www.nltk.org/nltk_data/

To use a specific corpora just use the **NLTK Downloader**, as we saw in the *Getting started with NLTK* section, and to preview the contents of a corpora, it's advisable to consult the README file included in each corpus.

Brown corpus

In the list of corpora, at number 98, it's possible to find the brown corpus. The Brown University Standard Corpus of Present-Day American English (or simply, the brown corpus) is a corpus compiled in the 1960s by Henry Kucera and W. Nelson Francis at Brown University, Providence (Rhode Island). It contains 500 text extracts in English obtained from works published in the United States of America in 1961, for a total of about one million words.

To import the brown corpus, simply type the following:

```
from nltk.corpus import brown
```

Now we can access the corpus content. We said that it contains about a million words, so let's check it out:

```
len(brown.words())
```

The following result is returned:

```
1161192
```

To know the number of judgments contained in the dataset, we can use the `sents()` function as follows:

```
len(brown.sents())
```

The following result is returned:

57340

We then display the first sentence:

```
brown.sents()[0]
```

The following sentence is returned:

```
['The', 'Fulton', 'County', 'Grand', 'Jury', 'said', 'Friday', 'an',
'investigation', 'of', "Atlanta's", 'recent', 'primary', 'election',
'produced', '``', 'no', 'evidence', "''", 'that', 'any', 'irregularities',
'took', 'place', '.']
```

As can be verified, each element of the sentence has been identified. We can also recover the tags of each element. We'll do it for the first ten words contained in the sentence:

```
brown.tagged_words()[0:10]
```

In the following list, the couple word-tags are returned:

```
[('The', 'AT'),
('Fulton', 'NP-TL'),
('County', 'NN-TL'),
('Grand', 'JJ-TL'),
('Jury', 'NN-TL'),
('said', 'VBD'),
('Friday', 'NR'),
('an', 'AT'),
('investigation', 'NN'),
('of', 'IN')]
```

To extract a list of the tags available with a short description, simply type the following:

```
nltk.help.brown_tagset()
```

In the following screenshot, the tail of the list is shown:

```
WPS+BEZ: WH-pronoun, nominative + verb 'to be', present, 3rd person singular
    that's who's
WPS+HVD: WH-pronoun, nominative + verb 'to have', past tense
    who'd
WPS+HVZ: WH-pronoun, nominative + verb 'to have', present tense, 3rd person singular
    who's that's
WPS+MD: WH-pronoun, nominative + modal auxillary
    who'll that'd who'd that'll
WQL: WH-qualifier
    however how
WRB: WH-adverb
    however when where why whereby wherever how whenever whereon wherein
    wherewith wheare wherefore whereof howsabout
WRB+BER: WH-adverb + verb 'to be', present, 2nd person singular or all persons plural
    where're
WRB+BEZ: WH-adverb + verb 'to be', present, 3rd person singular
    how's where's
WRB+DO: WH-adverb + verb 'to do', present, not 3rd person singular
    howda
WRB+DOD: WH-adverb + verb 'to do', past tense
    where'd how'd
WRB+DOD*: WH-adverb + verb 'to do', past tense, negated
    whyn't
WRB+DOZ: WH-adverb + verb 'to do', present tense, 3rd person singular
    how's
WRB+IN: WH-adverb + preposition
    why'n
WRB+MD: WH-adverb + modal auxillary
    where'd
```

Moreover, in the `brown` corpus, the sentences are divided by category. To view the list of available categories, we'll use the following code:

```
brown.categories()
```

The following list is returned:

```
['adventure',
 'belles_lettres',
 'editorial',
 'fiction',
 'government',
 'hobbies',
 'humor',
 'learned',
 'lore',
 'mystery',
 'news',
 'religion',
 'reviews',
 'romance',
 'science_fiction']
```

For example, to view only the sentence in the news category, we'll type the following:

```
brown.words(categories='news')
```

We'll obtain the following:

```
['The', 'Fulton', 'County', 'Grand', 'Jury', 'said', ...]
```

The list of the sentence is truncated (...) to conserve space.

Word and sentence tokenize

So far, we've used the `brown` corpus, which represents a source of data already correctly processed. Let's see what happens when we treat a new data source introduced by the user. As a source, I used a passage based on the novel *The Adventures of Huckleberry Finn* by Mark Twain:

> *We catched fish, and talked, and we took a swim now and then to keep off sleepiness. It was kind of solemn, drifting down the big still river, laying on our backs looking up at the stars, and we didn't ever feel like talking loud, and it warn't often that we laughed, only a kind of low chuckle. We had mighty good weather, as a general thing, and nothing ever happened to us at all, that night, nor the next, nor the next.*

Text data can be split into words using the `word_tokenize()` method, as follows:

```
from nltk.tokenize import word_tokenize
TextData="We catched fish, and talked, and we took a swim now and then to
keep off sleepiness. It was kind of solemn, drifting down the big still
river, laying on our backs looking up at the stars, and we didn't ever feel
like talking loud, and it warn't often that we laughed, only a kind of low
chuckle. We had mighty good weather, as a general thing, and nothing ever
happened to us at all, that night, nor the next, nor the next."
```

The first command imports the `word_tokenize()` method: This method tokenizes a string to split off punctuation other than periods. The last command sets a piece of text as the `TextData` variable (str type). When tokenizing the text, you can specify a language other than English, which is adopted by default. Now we can tokenize this data:

```
TextDataWords=word_tokenize(TextData)
```

To see the result, let's `print` it:

```
print(TextDataWords)
```

The following results are returned:

```
['We', 'catched', 'fish', ',', 'and', 'talked', ',', 'and', 'we', 'took',
'a', 'swim', 'now', 'and', 'then', 'to', 'keep', 'off', 'sleepiness', '.',
'It', 'was', 'kind', 'of', 'solemn', ',', 'drifting', 'down', 'the', 'big',
'still', 'river', ',', 'laying', 'on', 'our', 'backs', 'looking', 'up',
'at', 'the', 'stars', ',', 'and', 'we', 'didn', "'", 't', 'ever', 'feel',
'like', 'talking', 'loud', ',', 'and', 'it', 'warn', "'", 't', 'often',
'that', 'we', 'laughed', ',', 'only', 'a', 'kind', 'of', 'low', 'chuckle',
'.', 'We', 'had', 'mighty', 'good', 'weather', ',', 'as', 'a', 'general',
'thing', ',', 'and', 'nothing', 'ever', 'happened', 'to', 'us', 'at',
'all', ',', 'that', 'night', ',', 'nor', 'the', 'next', ',', 'nor', 'the',
'next', '.']
```

As we can see, all of the elements have been identified; not only words but also punctuation and special characters have been treated as separate tokens. Let's count the number of identified elements:

```
len(TextDataWords)
```

We obtain the following:

```
102
```

In a similar way, we can proceed to identify the sentences:

```
from nltk.tokenize import sent_tokenize
```

This time, we import the `sent_tokenize()` method which returns a sentence-tokenized copy of text, using NLTK's recommended sentence tokenizer. Now we can use this method:

```
TextDataSent = sent_tokenize(TextData)
```

The following results are returned:

```
['We catched fish, and talked, and we took a swim now and then to keep off
sleepiness.', 'It was kind of solemn, drifting down the big still river,
laying on our backs looking up at the stars, and we didn't ever feel like
talking loud, and it warn't often that we laughed, only a kind of low
chuckle.', 'We had mighty good weather, as a general thing, and nothing
ever happened to us at all, that night, nor the next, nor the next.']
```

In this case, I can clearly distinguish the phrases identified by the method. Let's see how many we count:

```
len(TextDataSent)
```

Only three sentences are split:

```
3
```

The two variables we've just created (`TextDataWords` and `TextDataSent`) represent lists. To extract a single sentence, we can work as follows:

```
print(TextDataSent[0])
```

The following result is returned:

```
'We catched fish, and talked, and we took a swim now and then to keep off
sleepiness.'
```

Hence, each sentence can be used to perform analyses.

Part-of-speech tagger

As we said in the *Part-of-speech tagging* section, **PoS tagging** is the process of labeling text words that correspond to particular lexical categories. The common linguistic categories include nouns, verbs, adjectives, articles, pronouns, adverbs, conjunctions, and so on. To automatically label each word of a text automatically with its word class, the `nltk` package has a specific method: `pos_tag`. This method contains classes and interfaces for part-of-speech tagging, or simply tagging. A tag is a case-sensitive string that specifies some property of token, such as its part of speech. Tagged tokens are encoded as tuples (tag, token). First, we need to import the method:

```
from nltk import pos_tag
```

After importing the `pos_tag()` method in the Python interpreter, you should use `word_tokenize` before PoS Tagging, which is referred to as the `pos_tag` method. This operation has already been performed in the *Word and sentence tokenize* section. On that occasion, we kept the result in the `TextDataWords` variable. To avoid repeating the operation, we'll refer to this variable:

```
TextDataPT = pos_tag(TextDataWords)
```

Let's print the results:

```
print(TextDataPT)
```

The following results are printed:

```
[('We', 'PRP'), ('catched', 'VBD'), ('fish', 'JJ'), (',', ','), ('and',
'CC'), ('talked', 'VBD'), (',', ','), ('and', 'CC'), ('we', 'PRP'),
('took', 'VBD'), ('a', 'DT'), ('swim', 'NN'), ('now', 'RB'), ('and', 'CC'),
('then', 'RB'), ('to', 'TO'), ('keep', 'VB'), ('off', 'RP'), ('sleepiness',
'NN'), ('.', '.'), ('It', 'PRP'), ('was', 'VBD'), ('kind', 'NN'), ('of',
'IN'), ('solemn', 'NN'), (',', ','), ('drifting', 'VBG'), ('down', 'RP'),
('the', 'DT'), ('big', 'JJ'), ('still', 'RB'), ('river', 'NN'), (',', ','),
('laying', 'VBG'), ('on', 'IN'), ('our', 'PRP$'), ('backs', 'NNS'),
('looking', 'VBG'), ('up', 'RP'), ('at', 'IN'), ('the', 'DT'), ('stars',
'NNS'), (',', ','), ('and', 'CC'), ('we', 'PRP'), ('didn', 'VBP'), (''',
'JJ'), ('t', 'NN'), ('ever', 'RB'), ('feel', 'VBP'), ('like', 'IN'),
('talking', 'VBG'), ('loud', 'JJ'), (',', ','), ('and', 'CC'), ('it',
'PRP'), ('warn', 'VBD'), (''', 'NNP'), ('t', 'NNS'), ('often', 'RB'),
('that', 'IN'), ('we', 'PRP'), ('laughed', 'VBD'), (',', ','), ('only',
'RB'), ('a', 'DT'), ('kind', 'NN'), ('of', 'IN'), ('low', 'JJ'),
('chuckle', 'NN'), ('.', '.'), ('We', 'PRP'), ('had', 'VBD'), ('mighty',
'VBN'), ('good', 'JJ'), ('weather', 'NN'), (',', ','), ('as', 'IN'), ('a',
'DT'), ('general', 'JJ'), ('thing', 'NN'), (',', ','), ('and', 'CC'),
('nothing', 'NN'), ('ever', 'RB'), ('happened', 'VBD'), ('to', 'TO'),
('us', 'PRP'), ('at', 'IN'), ('all', 'DT'), (',', ','), ('that', 'WDT'),
('night', 'NN'), (',', ','), ('nor', 'CC'), ('the', 'DT'), ('next', 'JJ'),
(',', ','), ('nor', 'CC'), ('the', 'DT'), ('next', 'JJ'), ('.', '.')]
```

A POS-tagger processes a sequence of words, and attaches a part of speech tag to each word. The default tagger of `nltk.pos_tag()` adopts the Penn Treebank Tag Set. The following table lists part-of-speech tags used, in alphabetical order:

Tag	Description	Tag	Description
CC	Coordinating conjunction	PRP$	Possessive pronoun
CD	Cardinal number	RB	Adverb
DT	Determiner	RBR	Adverb, comparative
EX	Existential there	RBS	Adverb, superlative
FW	Foreign word	RP	Particle
IN	Preposition or subordinating conjunction	SYM	Symbol
JJ	Adjective	TO	to
JJR	Adjective, comparative	UH	Interjection
JJS	Adjective, superlative	VB	Verb, base form
LS	List item marker	VBD	Verb, past tense
MD	Modal	VBG	Verb, gerund or present participle

NN	Noun, singular or mass	VBN	Verb, past participle
NNS	Noun, plural	VBP	Verb, non-3rd person singular present
NNP	Proper noun, singular	VBZ	Verb, 3rd person singular present
NNPS	Proper noun, plural	WDT	Wh-determiner
PDT	Predeterminer	WP	Wh-pronoun
POS	Possessive ending	WP$	Possessive wh-pronoun
PRP	Personal pronoun	WRB	Wh-adverb

Let's see how many tags have been identified. To get a frequency distribution of a set of documents using Python, we'll use the `nltk.probability.FreqDist` method. Conditional frequency distributions are used to record the number of times each sample occurred, given the condition under which the experiment was run. Formally, a conditional frequency distribution can be defined as a function that maps from each condition to `FreqDist` for the experiment under that condition. First, let's import the library:

```
from nltk.probability import FreqDist
```

At this point, we apply the method to the variable in which we put the results of PoS Tagging (`TextDataPT`):

```
TagFrequency = FreqDist(tag for (word, tag) in TextDataPT)
```

Finally, we print the results:

```
print(TagFrequency.most_common())
```

The `most_common()` function returns a list of the *n* most common elements and their counts from the most common to the least. If n is omitted or `None`, `most_common()` returns all elements in the counter. Elements with equal counts are ordered arbitrarily. The following are the results:

```
[(',', 12), ('NN', 12), ('JJ', 9), ('PRP', 8), ('VBD', 8), ('CC', 8),
('DT', 8), ('IN', 8), ('RB', 7), ('VBG', 4), ('RP', 3), ('.', 3), ('NNS',
3), ('TO', 2), ('VBP', 2), ('VB', 1), ('PRP$', 1), ('NNP', 1), ('VBN', 1),
('WDT', 1)]
```

In this way, we could retrieve a list with the most used grammatical elements in the text extracted from Mark Twain's masterpiece.

Stemming and lemmatization

As we said in the *Morphology analysis* section, the stem is the root of a word, obtainable by removing the ending from its flexed form (for example the conjugation of a verb or the plural of a noun). The lemma is instead the canonical form of the word, which is the one that's conventionally chosen to represent all of the inflected forms.

Stemming

Stemming is the process of reducing the inflected form of a word to its root form, called the stem. The stem doesn't necessarily correspond to the morphological root (lemma) of the word: it's normally sufficient that the related words are mapped to the same stem, even if the latter isn't a valid root for the word. The creation of a stemming algorithm has been a long-standing problem in computer science. The stemming process is used in search engines for query expansion and other natural language processing problems.

The `nltk.stem` package offers a processing interface for removing morphological affixes from words. Different stemmers for different languages are available. For the English language, you can choose between `PorterStammer` or `LancasterStammer`. `PorterStemmer` is the oldest one originally developed in 1979. `LancasterStemmer` was developed in 1990 and uses a more aggressive approach compared to its predecessor.

> In the following link, there is the official home page for distribution of the Porter Stemming Algorithm, written and maintained by its author, Martin Porter: https://tartarus.org/martin/PorterStemmer/

In the following example, we'll use `PorterStemmer` to extract the stems from the first sentence of the passage extracted from the novel *The Adventures of Huckleberry Finn* by Mark Twain. Start by importing the method:

```
from nltk.stem import PorterStemmer
```

Now, we'll create a new `PorterStemmer`:

```
PtSt = PorterStemmer()
```

Then, we'll test the stemmer on the first sentence of the novel. The sentence must first be tokenized using the `word_tokenize()` method. This operation has already been performed in the *Word and sentence tokenize* section, creating the `TextDataWords` variable. The first sentence contains 20 words, so we'll use only these:

```
for word in TextDataWords[0:20]:
    print(word + ":" + PtSt.stem(word))
```

The following results are returned:

```
We:We
catched:catch
fish:fish
,:,
and:and
talked:talk
,:,
and:and
we:we
took:took
a:a
swim:swim
now:now
and:and
then:then
to:to
keep:keep
off:off
sleepiness:sleep
.:.
```

In each row, we have the original word and the stemmed word separated by the colon. Only a few words have been stemmed. The techniques of stemming cut the tails of the terms according to syntactic and empirical rules only partially dependent on the language. The stemming produces good results for many terms, but different imperfections.

Lemmatization

Lemmatization is the process of reducing a word's inflected form to its canonical form, called a lemma. In the processing of natural language, lemmatization is the algorithmic process that automatically determines the word of a given word. The process may involve other language processing activities, such as morphological and grammatical analysis. In many languages, words appear in different inflected forms. The combination of the canonical form with its part of the speech is called the **lexeme of the word**. A lexeme is, in structural lexicology, the minimal unit that constitutes the lexicon of a language. Hence, every lexicon of a language may correspond to its registration in a dictionary in the form of a lemma.

In NLTK, for lemmatization, WordNet is available, but this resource is limited to the English language. It's a large lexical database of the English language. In this package, names, verbs, adjectives, and adverbs are grouped into sets of cognitive synonyms (synsets), each of which expresses a distinct concept. The synsets are interconnected by means of semantic and lexical conceptual relationships. The resulting network of significantly related words and concepts can be navigated with the browser. WordNet groups words according to their meanings, connecting not only word forms, strings of letters, but specific words. Hence, the words that are in close proximity to each other in the network are semantically disambiguated. In addition, WordNet labels the semantic relationships between words.

In the next example, we'll use this package to derive the singular term from a list of plurals, many of them irregularly shaped. Start by importing the method:

```
from nltk.stem import WordNetLemmatizer
```

Instance a new object of the `WordNetLemmatizer` class:

```
WnetLem = WordNetLemmatizer()
```

We set up a new list containing a series of words in the plural:

```
Plurals =['buses','wishes','pitches', 'boxes', 'pennies', 'children',
'potatoes', 'boats', 'cats', 'analyses', 'theses', 'phenomena']
```

At this point, we can execute the lemmatization:

```
for word in Plurals:
    print(word + ":" + WnetLem.lemmatize(word))
```

The following results are returned:

```
buses:bus
wishes:wish
pitches:pitch
boxes:box
pennies:penny
children:child
potatoes:potato
boats:boat
cats:cat
analyses:analysis
theses:thesis
phenomena:phenomenon
```

In each row, we have the original word and the lemmatized word separated by the colon. As a rule, lemmatization implies that the forms of the verbs are traced back to the present infinite, those of nouns and adjectives to the masculine singular, those of the prepositions articulated to their form without an article, and so on.

Implementing a DNN to label sentences

To labeling sentences, we'll use the Reuters newswire topics dataset. This is a dataset of 11,228 newswires from Reuters, labeled over 46 topics, published by Reuters in 1986. As with the IMDB dataset used in Chapter 6, *Movie Reviews Sentiment Analysis Using Recurrent Neural Network*, each wire is encoded as a sequence of word indexes.

 Just as MNIST, Fashion-MNIST, and IMDB already used in the previous chapters, the Reuters dataset comes packaged as part of the Keras distribution, where there's also a detailed description of its content, as shown at the following link: https://keras.io/datasets/.

To import the Reuters dataset in the Python environment, the following code must be used:

```python
from keras.datasets import reuters
(XTrain, YTrain), (XTest, YTest) = reuters.load_data(path="reuters.npz",
                            num_words=None,
                            skip_top=0,
                            maxlen=None,
                            seed=113,
                            start_char=1,
                            oov_char=2,
                            index_from=3)
```

Here are the following variables from the preceding code:

- `path`: If you don't have the data locally (at ~/.keras/datasets/ + path), it'll be downloaded to this location.

- `num_words`: This is an integer or `None`. This shows the top most frequent words to consider. Any less frequent word will appear as an `oov_char` value in the sequence data.

- `skip_top`: This is an integer. It represents the top most frequent words to ignore (they'll appear as `oov_char` value in the sequence data).

- `maxlen`: This is an integer. This is the maximum sequence length. Any longer sequence will be truncated.

- `seed`: This is an integer. This is the seed for reproducible data shuffling.

- `start_char`: This is an integer. The start of a sequence will be marked with this character. It's set to 1 because 0 is usually the padding character.

- `oov_char`: This is an integer. Words that were cut out because of the `num_words` or `skip_top` limit will be replaced with this character.

- `index_from`: This is an integer. Index actual words with this index and higher.

The following data is returned:

- `XTrain`, `XTest`: This is a list of sequences, which are lists of indexes (integers). If the `num_words` argument was specific, the maximum possible index value is `num_words`-1. If the `maxlen` argument was specified, the largest possible sequence length is `maxlen`.

- `YTrain`, `YTest`: This is a list of integer labels (1 or 0).

The label contained in the output (`YTrain` and `YTest`) is an integer value of either 1 or 0, where 1 stands for positive review and 0 stands for negative review.

Exploratory analysis

As anticipated, the dataset is already available in the Keras library. So we have loaded the appropriate library and then loaded the data:

```
from keras.datasets import reuters
(XTrain, YTrain),(XTest, YTest) = reuters.load_data(num_words=None,
test_split=0.3)
```

The following information is returned:

```
Downloading data from https://s3.amazonaws.com/text-datasets/reuters.npz
2113536/2110848 [==============================] - 2s 1us/step
```

Now, let's check the contents of the four objects we imported. First, we get the type of the objects. To do this, we'll use the built-in function `type()`, as follows:

```
print('XTrain class = ',type(XTrain))
print('YTrain class = ',type(YTrain))
print('XTest shape = ',type(XTest))
print('YTest shape = ',type(YTest))
```

If a single argument (object) is passed, the type of the given object is returned. If three arguments (name, bases, and dictionary) are passed, a new type object is returned. The following results are obtained:

```
XTrain class = <class 'numpy.ndarray'>
YTrain class = <class 'numpy.ndarray'>
XTest shape = <class 'numpy.ndarray'>
YTest shape = <class 'numpy.ndarray'>
```

So, four `numpy.ndarray` objects are returned. Now we extract the number of elements contained in each array:

```
print('XTrain shape = ',XTrain.shape)
print('XTest shape = ',XTest.shape)
print('YTrain shape = ',YTrain.shape)
print('YTest shape = ',YTest.shape)
```

The shape attribute for `numpy` arrays returns the dimensions of the array. The following results are obtained:

```
XTrain shape = (7859,)
XTest shape = (3369,)
YTrain shape = (7859,)
YTest shape = (3369,)
```

As we anticipated, the Reuters dataset consists of 11,228 items. These items have been split in 7,859 (train data) and 3,369 (test data) as set with the `test_split=0.3` option, that is, 70% for training and 30% for testing. Now let's see what's contained in the output data:

```
import numpy as np
print('YTrain values = ',np.unique(YTrain))
print('YTest values = ',np.unique(YTest))
```

To extract the output values, the `numpy.unique()` function was used, which find the unique elements of an array. This function returns the sorted unique elements of an array. There are three optional outputs in addition to the unique elements: the indexes of the input array that give the unique values, the indexes of the unique array that reconstruct the input array, and the number of times each unique value comes up in the input array. The following results are returned:

```
YTrain values = [ 0  1  2  3  4  5  6  7  8  9 10 11 12 13 14 15 16 17 18 19 20 21
22 23
24 25 26 27 28 29 30 31 32 33 34 35 36 37 38 39 40 41 42 43 44 45]
YTest values = [ 0  1  2  3  4  5  6  7  8  9 10 11 12 13 14 15 16 17 18 19 20 21 22
23
24 25 26 27 28 29 30 31 32 33 34 35 36 37 38 39 40 41 42 43 44 45]
```

In this way, we've confirmed that the data output is labeled by 46 topics. It may be useful to analyze the distribution of the two values in the available arrays. To start, we count the number of occurrences:

```
unique, counts = np.unique(YTrain, return_counts=True)
print('YTrain distribution = ',dict(zip(unique, counts)))
unique, counts = np.unique(YTest, return_counts=True)
print('YTrain distribution = ',dict(zip(unique, counts)))
```

The `numpy.unique()` function was once again applied: in this case, the `return_counts` attribute was added, which if set to `True`, also returns the number of times that unique items appear. Then, the `dict()` function was applied, which creates a new dictionary, while the `zip()` function makes an iterator that aggregates elements from each of the iterables. It returns an iterator of tuples, where the *i-th* tuple contains the *i-th* element from each of the argument sequences or iterables. The iterator stops when the shortest input iterable is exhausted. The following results are shown:

```
YTrain distribution = {0: 50, 1: 378, 2: 66, 3: 2769, 4: 1701, 5: 14, 6:
39, 7: 15, 8: 126, 9: 93, 10: 114, 11: 337, 12: 40, 13: 149, 14: 18, 15:
19, 16: 387, 17: 33, 18: 59, 19: 475, 20: 238, 21: 91, 22: 10, 23: 36, 24:
56, 25: 77, 26: 18, 27: 13, 28: 43, 29: 19, 30: 38, 31: 34, 32: 30, 33: 9,
34: 43, 35: 10, 36: 46, 37: 17, 38: 16, 39: 20, 40: 32, 41: 28, 42: 10, 43:
19, 44: 10, 45: 14}
YTrain distribution = {0: 17, 1: 159, 2: 28, 3: 1203, 4: 722, 5: 8, 6: 23,
```

```
7: 4, 8: 51, 9: 33, 10: 40, 11: 136, 12: 22, 13: 60, 14: 10, 15: 10, 16:
156, 17: 18, 18: 27, 19: 207, 20: 101, 21: 36, 22: 12, 23: 17, 24: 25, 25:
46, 26: 14, 27: 6, 28: 15, 29: 4, 30: 19, 31: 18, 32: 12, 33: 7, 34: 14,
35: 6, 36: 14, 37: 4, 38: 6, 39: 9, 40: 14, 41: 10, 42: 6, 43: 8, 44: 7,
45: 5}
```

To understand the distribution of the topics better, we trace the histogram:

```
import matplotlib.pyplot as plt
plt.figure(1)
plt.subplot(121)
plt.hist(YTrain, bins='auto')
plt.xlabel("Classes")
plt.ylabel("Number of occurrences")
plt.title("YTrain data")

plt.subplot(122)
plt.hist(YTest, bins='auto')
plt.xlabel("Classes")
plt.ylabel("Number of occurrences")
plt.title("YTest data")
plt.show()
```

To compare the results obtained on both output datasets (`YTrain` and `YTest`), two histograms were traced and side by side, as shown in the following figure:

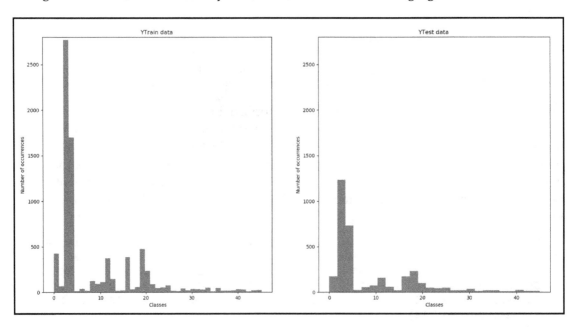

As seen previously, the classes aren't equally represented in both datasets. Now, let's see what's inside the data. We print the second record of the data we'll use for the training:

```
print(XTrain[1])
```

The following result is returned:

```
[1, 3267, 699, 3434, 2295, 56, 16784, 7511, 9, 56, 3906, 1073, 81, 5, 1198,
57, 366, 737, 132, 20, 4093, 7, 19261, 49, 2295, 13415, 1037, 3267, 699,
3434, 8, 7, 10, 241, 16, 855, 129, 231, 783, 5, 4, 587, 2295, 13415, 30625,
775, 7, 48, 34, 191, 44, 35, 1795, 505, 17, 12]
```

The sequence of integers returned by the previous command then represents the sequence of words contained in the first newswire. The newswires are different in content but also in length (number of words). Let's see, for example, how many words are contained in the first newswire, the one we have just printed:

```
len(XTrain[1])
```

The following result is obtained:

```
56
```

To mean that 56 words are contained in the first newswire. To understand how the dataset has been encoded, we follow the backward path: from a coded newswire, we try to get the original newswire. To do this, we need the list containing the pairs: word, integer index. As we said, this information is included in the original dataset, we only need to load it to our environment:

```
WordIndex = reuters.get_word_index(path="reuters_word_index.json")
```

Let's see how many words have been coded:

```
print(len(WordIndex))
```

The following result is obtained:

```
30979
```

So, 30,979 words are contained in the dictionary. The values returned from the first record of the training dataset (XTrain) represent the values of the dictionary. So, to get the words associated with this integer index we'll have to extract the key associated with it from the dictionary:

```
IndexToWord = {}
for key, value in WordIndex.items():
    IndexToWord[value] = key
```

The `items()` method returns a view object that displays a list of dictionary's (key, value) tuple pairs. To decode the second newswire contained in the dataset, we'll proceed as follows:

```
print(' '.join([IndexToWord[x] for x in XTrain[1]]))
```

The following result is returned:

```
the termination payment airport takes 6 visibility geological 3 6 602 begin
up said fully bank expects commodity total is giant a recreation this takes
leroy series termination payment airport mln a for capital 1 pre 50
american east said in council takes leroy recommend's france a but u any 4
s 1st losses pct dlrs
```

We also print the label associated with this newswire:

```
print(YTrain[1])
```

We obtain the following result:

```
4
```

Now the content of the dataset is clear enough, and we can focus on building the model.

Data preparation

Before proceeding, it's necessary to tokenize the data appropriately. To do it, we'll use `Keras Tokenizer` as follows:

```
from keras.preprocessing.text import Tokenizer
```

This is a text tokenization utility class. This class allows to vectorize a text corpus, by turning each text into either a sequence of integers (each integer being the index of a token in a dictionary) or into a vector where the coefficient for each token could be binary.

The following arguments are accepted:

- `num_words`: Thi

    - s is the maximum number of words to keep, based on word frequency. Only the most common `num_words` words will be kept.

- `filters`: This is the string where each element is a character that'll be filtered from the texts. The default is all punctuation, plus tabs, and line breaks, minus the ' character.
- `lower`: `boolean`. This determines whether to convert the texts into lowercase.
- `split`: `str`. This is a separator for word splitting.
- `char_level`: If `True`, every character will be treated as a token.
- `oov_token`: If given, it'll be
- added to `word_index` and used to replace out-of-vocabulary words during `text_to_sequence` calls.

By default, all punctuation is removed, turning the texts into space-separated sequences of words (words maybe include the character). These sequences are then split into lists of tokens. They'll then be indexed or vectorized.

First, we limit the number of words to use:

```
MaxWords = 10000
```

Let's create the `Tokenizer`:

```
Tok = Tokenizer(num_words=MaxWords)
```

Finally, we can perform the tokenization operation:

```
XTrain = Tok.sequences_to_matrix(XTrain, mode='binary')
XTest = Tok.sequences_to_matrix(XTest, mode='binary')
```

The `sequences_to_matrix()` function convert a list of sequences into a matrix. The following arguments are accepted:

- **Tokenizer**: This is the tokenizer.

- **Sequences**: This is a list of sequences (a sequence is a list of integer word indexes).

- **Mode**: It's one of the following: `binary`, `count`, `tfidf`, or `freq`.

This function creates a vector for each newswire. The length of the vectors is the total size of the vocabulary. Now it's necessary to rebuild each vector so that it can represent one of the 46 labeled classes. So we fix the number of classes:

```
NumClasses = max(YTrain) + 1
```

We carry out the conversion:

```
from keras.utils import to_categorical
YTrain = to_categorical(YTrain, NumClasses)
YTest = to_categorical(YTest, NumClasses)
```

The `keras.utils.to_categorical()` function is used to convert an array of labeled data (from 0 to `NumClasses-1`) into a one-hot vector. It assumes the class values were in string and you will be label encoding them, hence starting every time from 0 to `NumClasses`. Let's see how each vector is changed:

```
print(XTrain[1])
```

The following result is returned:

```
[0. 0. 0. 1. 0. 0. 0. 0. 0. 0. 0. 0. 0. 0. 0. 0. 0. 0. 0. 0. 0. 0. 0. 0.
 0. 0. 0. 0. 0. 0. 0. 0. 0. 0. 0. 0. 0. 0. 0. 0. 0. 0. 0. 0. 0. 0.]
```

Let's see how the length of the vector is changed:

```
print(len(XTrain[1]))
```

The following result is returned:

46

Now, the length of the vector coincides with the number of classes. This will happen for all newswires.

Keras deep neural network model

After exploring the dataset, it's time to build the **deep neural network (DNN)** model to labeling newswire from data recorded in the dataset. To build a model, we'll use the Keras Sequential model. Let's start importing the libraries:

```
from keras.models import Sequential
from keras.layers import Dense
from keras.layers import Dropout
from keras.layers import Activation
```

Four layer classes have been imported: `Sequential`, `Dense`, `Dropout`, and `Activation`. The sequential class is used to define a linear stack of network layers that make up a model. In the following, we'll use the Sequential constructor to create the model, which will then be enriched with layers using the `add()` method. The `Dense` class is used to instantiate a dense layer, which is the basic feed forward fully connected layer. The `Dropout` class applies dropout to the input. `Dropout` consists of randomly setting a fraction rate of input units to 0 at each update during training time, which helps prevent overfitting. The `Activation` layer is used to add an activation function to the sequence of layers. To start, we must set the model type:

```
DNNmodel = Sequential()
```

Next, we have to add the layers:

```
DNNmodel.add(Dense(512, input_shape=(MaxWords,)))
```

The first is the most important because it's the level that defines the input. We've used a completely connected network structure with five layers. Fully connected layers are defined using the `Dense` class. Then, the `Activation` layer is used to set the activation function:

```
DNNmodel.add(Activation('relu'))
```

The **Rectified linear unit (ReLU)** is the most used activation function since 2015. It's a simple condition and has advantages over the other functions. The range of output is between 0 and infinity. Now, we'll add a `Dropout` layer:

```
DNNmodel.add(Dropout(0.5))
```

`Dropout` is a regularization technique in which randomly selected neurons are ignored during training. This technique aims to reduce the complexity of the model to avoid overfitting. With the dropout a part of the neuronal units are deactivated in the training process. The number of deactivated neurons can be set (in our case 50%). By setting a part of the neurons to zero, the network won't apply particular activations in a given feed-forward step; consequently, the network will learn different redundant representations, so the training will be faster. The success of this technique lies in the fact that, if the neurons are randomly ignored by the network during training, the other neurons will have to intervene and manage the representation required to make predictions for the missing neurons. Then, we'll add a new `Dense` layer:

```
DNNmodel.add(Dense(NumClasses))
```

Another feedforward fully connected layer is added with the aim of setting the shape of the output (46). Finally, an `Activation` layer is added:

```
DNNmodel.add(Activation('softmax'))
```

To print a summary of the model, simply type the following:

```
DNNmodel.summary()
```

The following screenshot shows the results:

```
Layer (type)                    Output Shape              Param #
=================================================================
dense_1 (Dense)                 (None, 512)               5120512

activation_1 (Activation)       (None, 512)               0

dropout_1 (Dropout)             (None, 512)               0

dense_2 (Dense)                 (None, 46)                23598

activation_2 (Activation)       (None, 46)                0
=================================================================
Total params: 5,144,110
Trainable params: 5,144,110
Non-trainable params: 0
```

Before training a model, you need to configure the learning process, which is done via the `compile()` method:

```
DNNmodel.compile(loss='categorical_crossentropy',
                 optimizer='adam', metrics=['accuracy'])
```

Three arguments are passed:

- `categorical_crossentropy` **loss function**: We've used categorical crossentropy loss. When using the `categorical_crossentropy` loss, your targets should be in categorical format (we have 10 classes, the target for each sample must be a 10-dimensional vector, that is, all-zeros except for a 1 at the index corresponding to the class of the sample).

- **Adam optimizer**: This an algorithm for first-order gradient-based optimization of stochastic objective functions, based on adaptive estimates of lower-order moments

- **Accuracy metric**: This metric is a function that's used to evaluate the performance of your model during training and testing.

To train the model, the `fit ()` method is used as follows:

```
DNNmodel.fit(XTrain, YTrain, validation_data=(XTest, YTest),
                         epochs=10, batch_size=64, verbose=1)
```

Six arguments are passed:

- `XTrain`: This is an array of input training data.

- `YTrain`: This is an array of target (label) data.

- `validation_data=(XTest, Ytest)`: This is a tuple on which to evaluate the loss and any model metrics at the end of each epoch. The model won't be trained on this data.

- `epochs=10`: This is the number of epochs to train the model. An epoch is an iteration over the entire x and y data provided.

- `batch_size=64`: This is the number of samples per gradient update.

- `verbose=1`: This is an integer. 0, 1, or 2. Verbosity mode where 0 = silent, 1 = progress bar, 2 = one line per epoch.

When the `fit()` function is performed, the loss and the accuracy at the end of each training epoch are displayed on the video, as shown in the following screenshot:

```
Train on 7859 samples, validate on 3369 samples
Epoch 1/10
7859/7859 [==============================] - 19s 2ms/step - loss: 1.4667 - acc: 0.6894 - val_loss: 0.9782 - val_acc: 0.7815
Epoch 2/10
7859/7859 [==============================] - 18s 2ms/step - loss: 0.5885 - acc: 0.8717 - val_loss: 0.8391 - val_acc: 0.8088
Epoch 3/10
7859/7859 [==============================] - 17s 2ms/step - loss: 0.3219 - acc: 0.9284 - val_loss: 0.8517 - val_acc: 0.8071
Epoch 4/10
7859/7859 [==============================] - 16s 2ms/step - loss: 0.2250 - acc: 0.9471 - val_loss: 0.8998 - val_acc: 0.8020
Epoch 5/10
7859/7859 [==============================] - 18s 2ms/step - loss: 0.1814 - acc: 0.9542 - val_loss: 0.9417 - val_acc: 0.7985
Epoch 6/10
7859/7859 [==============================] - 18s 2ms/step - loss: 0.1648 - acc: 0.9550 - val_loss: 0.9280 - val_acc: 0.8059
Epoch 7/10
7859/7859 [==============================] - 17s 2ms/step - loss: 0.1618 - acc: 0.9588 - val_loss: 0.9567 - val_acc: 0.8017
Epoch 8/10
7859/7859 [==============================] - 17s 2ms/step - loss: 0.1544 - acc: 0.9580 - val_loss: 0.9763 - val_acc: 0.8014
Epoch 9/10
7859/7859 [==============================] - 18s 2ms/step - loss: 0.1580 - acc: 0.9578 - val_loss: 0.9762 - val_acc: 0.8074
Epoch 10/10
7859/7859 [==============================] - 17s 2ms/step - loss: 0.1487 - acc: 0.9588 - val_loss: 1.0146 - val_acc: 0.7991
```

To evaluate the performance of the model we've just adapted, we use the `evaluate()` function as follows:

```
Scores = DNNmodel.evaluate(XTest, YTest, verbose=1)
```

This function returns the loss value and metrics values for the model in test mode. Computation is done in batches. Let's print `loss` and `accuracy`:

```
print('Test loss:', Scores[0])
print('Test accuracy:', Scores[1])
```

The following results are printed:

```
Test loss: 1.0145923152243075
Test accuracy: 0.7990501632620369
```

The accuracy obtained confirms that a deep neural network is able to label sentences contained in the Reuters newswire topics dataset with good results.

Summary

In this chapter, we addressed natural language processing basics. Natural language processing aims to implement tools to analyze, understand, and generate texts that people can understand naturally, as if they were communicating with another human interlocutor and not a computer. To begin with, we saw the different phases of text analysis that make it a multilevel structure. The fundamental levels on which the analysis of a sentence is based were addressed. Then, the most frequent applications using natural language processing were analyzed. So the procedures necessary for the treatment of the text were examined.

In the second part of this chapter, we focused on the Natural Language Toolkit, which is a suite of libraries and programs for symbolic and statistical analysis in the field of natural language processing mainly in the English language written in the Python language. We saw how to install this useful tool and how to download all of the packages needed to use it. So we saw the basic commands to start analyzing a simple text.

In the last part of this chapter, we analyzed a practical case: how to label sentences contained in the Reuters newswire topics dataset using a Keras Deep Neural Network. We learned how to train the model and how to evaluate the model performance.

In the next chapter, we'll see a review of deep neural network models, discover ultimate Keras applications in real life, and learn about the **differentiable neural computer** (**DNC**). We'll understand **Genetic Programming** and **Evolutionary Strategies** (**ES**) and discover **Probabilistic relational programming language** (**PRPL**).

11
What is Next?

method, according to the following formula

In this chapter, we will summarize what has been covered in this book so far, and what the next steps are from this point onward. You will look at how to apply the skills you have gained to other projects, real-life challenges in building and deploying Keras deep learning models, and other common technologies that data scientists often use. By the end of this chapter, you will have a better understanding of the real-life challenges in building and deploying deep learning models and the additional resources and technologies you will need to sharpen your deep learning skills. In addition, you'll find out what some of the challenges are that await deep learning researchers in the near future.

We will cover the following topics in this chapter:

- Deep learning methods
- Automated machine learning
- Differentiable neural computers
- Genetic programming and evolutionary strategies
- Inverse reinforcement learning

In the following sections, we will also review the deep neural networks.

Deep learning methods

Deep learning is a field of machine learning based on multi-level machine learning. Each level takes the output data of the previous level as input, extracting more and more information as the depth increases. This sequence of learning levels is inspired by the way the mammalian brain processes information and learns by responding to external stimuli. Each level of learning corresponds to one of the different areas that make up the cerebral cortex.

Generic machine learning algorithms behave well on a large number of tasks, managing to solve many important problems. However, they are often not successful in solving central problems concerning the field of artificial intelligence development. The development of deep learning is motivated by the failure of traditional algorithms to perform these tasks.

One area in which deep learning has become more widespread is artificial neural networks. As we saw in Chapter 4, *Concrete Quality Prediction Using Deep Neural Networks*, a three-level neural network (an input layer, a hidden layer, and an output level) is able to distinguish between arbitrarily complex regions and offers particularly interesting results.

In the following diagram, a three-level neural network architecture is shown:

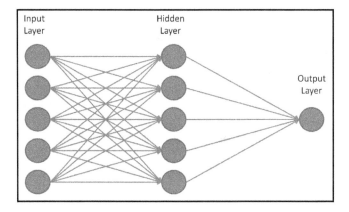

Despite this, in a three-level network, the complexity of the region to be recognized is limited by the number of nodes in the hidden layer. Consequently, to obtain appreciable results in some cases, it is necessary to use a considerable number of nodes. The growth in the number of nodes follows an exponential law with the size of the input. The increase of the nodes causes a high computational cost and a considerable use of memory, which are some of the key reasons that advise against the adoption of such a network architecture.

Another problem that needs to be addressed concerns input data. There are cases in which input data contains many variables. In these cases, as we mentioned previously, the number of nodes of the hidden layer increases exponentially, as does the number of examples needed to train the system. Moreover, as the variables increase, the predictive capacity of the system also decreases with a consequent deterioration in performance. In deep learning, feature representation levels are not designed or built directly by humans, but are learned automatically from the data.

Compared to a simple three-layer architecture, a multi-layer architecture allows for better distribution of the number of nodes on several layers. In this way, a significant reduction of the computational cost is obtained compared to the case in which such nodes are placed in a single hidden layer. Furthermore, a strong reduction in memory usage is guaranteed.

The types of architecture in deep learning are many and are based on different assumptions. In the following sections, we will review the most used ones.

Deep feedforward network

The typical structure of a three-level neural network, the first of which receives the input signals and the last returns the output signals, is a good example of a network in which the signal flow proceeds in one direction. These networks are usually identified as feedforward neural networks.

Feedforward neural networks lend themselves to being used for function approximation and interpolation. The extreme simplicity of an artificial neuron seems to hide the fact that a neural network can represent very complex situations well. However, if we count the number of variables that come into play, even for neural networks consisting of a limited number of neurons arranged in a few layers, we realize that it is an extremely flexible and also heavily redundant structure.

In a neural network, the way in which the weights of the connections between neurons are updated is essential. In the backpropagation algorithm, we compare the output value of the system with the desired value (objective). On the basis of the difference of the calculated error, the algorithm modifies the synaptic weights of the neural network, progressively converging the set of output values toward the desired ones.

In the following diagram, a flowchart of the training phase is shown:

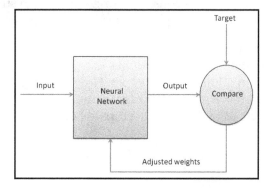

Updating the weights during the learning phase is carried out using the **stochastic gradient descent (SGD)**

method, according to the following formula:

$$w_{i+1} = w_i - \eta * \nabla Q_i(w_i)$$

In the previous formula, we can see the following:

- **w**: Weight
- **η**: Learning rate
- **Q$_i$**: Loss function

These networks are used in language modeling, object recognition, and more generally for modeling non-linear relationships. Some limits of this type of network are the high execution time of the learning phase, and the risk of overfitting.

Convolutional neural networks

The layer of neurons that deals with convolution divides the input data into various overlapping fragments, which are then analyzed to identify the particularities that characterize it, transferring the information to the following layer in the form of a feature map containing the relations between neurons and particularities. As we saw in `Chapter 5`, *Fashion Article Recognition Using Convolutional Neural Networks*, in a **convolutional neural network (CNN)**, the connection pattern between neurons is inspired by the structure of the visual cortex in the animal world. The individual neurons that are present in this part of the brain (visual cortex) respond to certain stimuli in a narrow region of the observation, called the receptive field. The receptive fields of different neurons are partially overlapped to cover the entire field of vision. The response of a single neuron to stimuli taking place in its receptive field can be mathematically approximated by a convolution operation.

Everything related to the training of a neural network, that is, forward or backward propagation and updating the weight, also applies in this context. Moreover, a whole CNN always uses a single function of differentiable cost. However, CNNs make a specific assumption that their input has a precise data structure, such as an image, and this allows them to take specific properties in their architecture to better process such data.

Typically, a CNN consists of several alternative convolution and subsampling levels (**pooling**), followed by one or more **fully connected** (**FC**) final levels in the case of classification. In the following diagram, an example of a CNN architecture is shown:

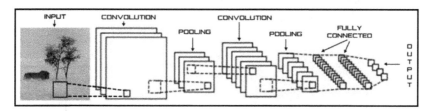

The gain in efficiency compared to the convolution-free techniques is very significant. For input m and output n, a matrix product would require $m \cdot n$ parameters, and the algorithm would have a processing time of O $(m \cdot n)$. Limiting the connection number for each output to a smaller k number of m would require only $k \cdot n$ parameters and a processing time of O $(k \cdot n)$. The gain in efficiency becomes extremely important with k smaller than m of many orders of magnitude.

Recurrent neural networks

Recurrent neural networks (**RNNs**) are a type of neural network that specialize in the processing of sequential data. This type of network is therefore highly optimized for tasks related to speech and facial recognition. As we saw in Chapter 6, *Movie Review Sentiment Analysis Using Recurrent Neural Networks*, the RNN is a neural model in which a bidirectional flow of information is present. In other words, while the propagation of signals in feedforward networks takes place only in a continuous manner in a direction from inputs to outputs, recurrent networks are different. Here, this propagation can also occur from a neural layer following a previous one, or between neurons belonging to the same layer, and even between a neuron and itself.

Recurrent networks are distinguished from feedforward networks thanks to the feedback loop linked to their past decisions, thus accepting their output momentarily as inputs. This feature can be emphasized by saying that recurrent networks have memory. Adding memory to neural networks has a purpose—there is information in the sequence itself, and recurrent networks use it to perform the tasks that feedforward networks cannot.

A typical RNN with connections between the output layer and the hidden layer is represented in the following diagram:

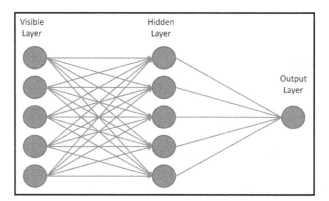

During the input-processing phase, the RNNs maintain a vector in their hidden layers. This contains information on the history of all of the elements of the sequence's past, that is, the previous time instants. Considering the output of the hidden layers at different times of the sequence as outputs of different neurons of a deep multi-layer neural network, it becomes easy to apply backpropagation to train the network. However, although the RNNs are powerful dynamic systems, the training phase often proves to be problematic because the gradient obtained with backpropagation increases or decreases at any discrete time, so after a while, it may either become too large or become somewhat insignificant.

Long short-term memory

As we saw in `Chapter 7`, *Stock Volatility Forecasting Using Long Short-Term Memory*, **long short-term memory** (**LSTM**) is a particular architecture of RNN that was recently rediscovered in the context of deep learning. It is free from the problem of vanishing gradient and in practice offers excellent results and performance.

The vanishing-gradient problem affects the training of **artificial neural networks** (**ANNs**) with gradient-based learning methods. In gradient-based methods such as backpropagation, weights are adjusted proportionally to the gradient of the error. Because of the way in which the aforementioned gradients are calculated, we obtain the effect that their module decreases exponentially, proceeding toward the deepest layers. The problem is that in some cases, the gradient will be significantly small, effectively preventing the weight from changing its value. In the worst case, this may completely stop the neural network from further training.

A LSTM network consists of cells (LSTM blocks) that are linked together. Each cell is, in turn, composed of three types of ports—input gate, output gate, and forget gate. They implement the write, read, and reset functions on the cell memory, respectively. The ports are not binary but analogical (generally managed by a sigmoid activation function mapped in a range (0, 1), where zero indicates total inhibition, and 1 indicates total activation), and they are multiplicative.

The following diagram shows an LSTM unit:

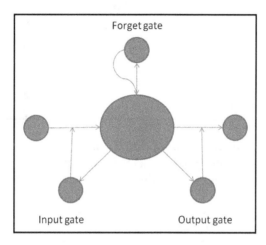

The forget gate layer decides what information is entered into the flow of the network. The input gate layer decides what values must be updated immediately, after which a hyperbolic tangent layer creates a vector that has the new candidate values to be added to the state as elements. Finally, the output gate decides what part of the state vector must be returned to the output.

Restricted Boltzmann machine

The **restricted Boltzmann machine** (**RBM**) has a single hidden layer, and there is no connection among nodes in a group. It is a simple **multilayer perceptron** (**MLP**) model of neural networks. In practice, a Boltzmann machine is a model (including a certain number of parameters) that, when applied to a data distribution, is able to provide a representation. This model can be used to extract important aspects of an unknown distribution (target distribution), starting only from a sample of the latter. The data samples referred to by a Boltzmann machine is also called training data.

In the RBM graph, every neuron is connected to all the neurons of the other level, while there are no connections between neurons of the same level; it is precisely this restriction that gives the RBM its name, as shown in the following diagram:

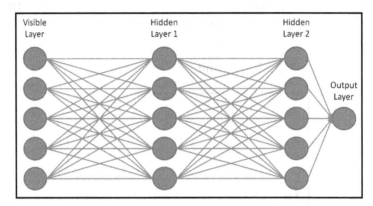

Training a Boltzmann machine means adapting its parameters so that the probability distribution represented by it interpolates the training data as well as possible. The training of a Boltzmann machine is a rather demanding job from a computational point of view.

However, this problem can be made easier by imposing restrictions on the topology of the network on which you are working; this defines RBMs. RBMs were covered in `Chapter 8`, *Reconstruction of Handwritten Digit Images Using Autoencoder*.

Deep belief network

This is typically a feedforward network in which data flows from one layer to another without looping back. There is at least one hidden layer, although there can be many, increasing the complexity of the network. **Deep belief networks (DBNs)** are probabilistic graphic models that present a layer of visible units and multiple hidden layers that are stacked on top of each other. The idea behind a DBN is that it is possible to stack more RBMs on top of each other by building a deep network, which presents the ability to extract a hierarchical representation of the input at multiple levels of abstraction. One of the biggest problems of such an extensive model is learning. In fact, due to the number of layers, the backpropagation method is ineffective. It is, however, true that these models have the advantage of being able to perform a greedy type of training, thus allowing for the training of each layer of the network, as if it were a single RBM. The probability distribution of a DBN is defined by the connection of each layer with the next, excluding the last two levels, which have a structure connected in both directions.

This allows for the calculation of the conditional probability, as shown in the following diagram:

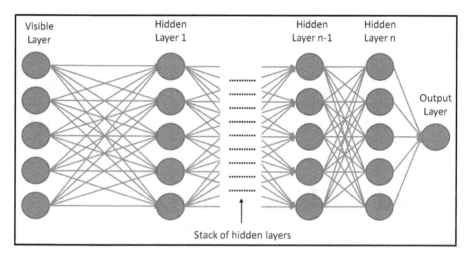

Network training follows these steps:

1. We start from the visible layer and from the first hidden layer (to which it is connected), and we apply contrastive divergence to perform the training as if it were a single RBM.
2. After having trained the first two layers, it is possible to sample the value of the hidden units or use the probabilities of activation of the same relative to the RBM coached in the previous step. The values obtained will be used as input of the second RBM that will be trained. It will be formed by the second and third hidden layers of the DBN.
3. Repeat these two steps for each pair of levels.

This first pre-training phase will be followed by a fine-tuning phase of the network parameters that will usually be performed by means of Stochastic gradient **descent** (**SGD**). The idea is to use a single example to approximate the gradient, and then repeat the process for each example of the training set the update the parameters using an approximation of the gradient relative to the considered example.

Generative adversarial networks

The **generative adversarial network** (**GAN**) is a generative model consisting of two networks that are jointly trained, called the generator and the discriminator. The dynamics between these two networks are such as those between a forger and an investigator. The forger tries to produce faithful imitations of authentic works of art, while the investigator tries to distinguish the fakes from the originals. In this analogy, the forger represents the generator and the investigator represents the discriminator. The generator accepts input values belonging to a fixed distribution and tries to produce images similar to those of the dataset. The discriminator tries to distinguish the data created by the generator from that belonging to the dataset.

Automated machine learning

Automated machine learning (**AutoML**) refers to those applications that are able to automate the end-to-end process of applying machine learning to real-world problems. Generally, scientific analysts must process data through a series of preliminary procedures before submitting them to machine learning algorithms. In previous chapters, we have seen the necessary steps for performing proper analysis of data through these algorithms. We have seen how simple it is to build a model based on deep neural networks using Keras. In some cases, these skills are outside those possessed by analysts, who must seek support from industry experts to solve the problem. AutoML was born from the need to create an application that automates the whole machine learning process, so that the user can take advantage of these services.

Generally, machine learning experts must perform the following tasks:

- Data preparation
- Selection of features
- Selection of an appropriate model class
- Choosing and optimizing model hyperparameters
- Post-processing machine learning models
- Analyzing the results obtained

AutoML automates all these operations. It offers the advantages of producing simpler and faster-to-create solutions that often outperform hand-designed models. There are a number of AutoML frameworks, many of which support Keras. In the following sections, we will see some of them.

Auto-Keras

Auto-Keras is an open source software library for AutoML that aims at providing easy access to deep learning models. Auto-Keras has a number of features that allow you to automatically set up the architecture and parameters of deep learning models. Its ease of use, simple installation, and numerous examples make it a very popular framework. Auto-Keras was developed by DATA Lab at Texas A and M University and community contributors.

In the following screenshot, we can see the website of the project, which is available on the following link: `https://autokeras.com/`:

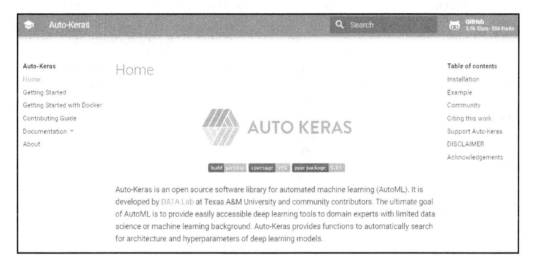

To install the Auto-Keras package, we can use the `pip` command as follows:

```
$ pip install autokeras
```

At the time of writing this book, Auto-Keras is only compatible with Python 3.6.

The following is a brief example of the use of Auto-Keras proposed by official documentation:

```
import autokeras as ak
clf = ak.ImageClassifier()
clf.fit(x_train, y_train)
results = clf.predict(x_test)
```

With only four lines of code, we can achieve a skillful image classifier.

Google Cloud ML Engine

Projects based on machine learning require a lot of resources. From storage to computational power, training models sometimes require resources that can not be found on a simple computer. Physical limitations in terms of storage space have been reduced in recent years. Also, computing power has grown massively; many operations can be performed just on laptops. However, despite all this very rapid evolution, scientific analysts often find themselves in difficulty when it comes to addressing big data problems due to the necessary calculation and space resources. Cloud computing services have been developed to meet these requests for unlimited space and computing power.

The term **cloud computing** indicates a paradigm for the supply of IT resources, such as archiving, and the processing or transmission of data, characterized by availability on demand through the internet starting from a set of pre-existing and configurable resources.

The resources are not fully configured and implemented by the provider for the user, but they are quickly and conveniently assigned, thanks to automated procedures, starting from a set of resources shared with other users, leaving the user part of the configuration burden. When the user releases the resource, it is similarly reconfigured in the initial state and made available in the shared pool of resources, with the same speed and economy for the supplier. One of the advantages of the cloud is that all the resources are accessible from any PC: all that's needed is an internet connection.

Google Cloud Machine Learning (ML) Engine is a managed service that allows developers and data scientists to create higher-quality machine learning models and bring them into production. Cloud ML Engine offers training and forecasting services that can be used together or individually. Cloud ML Engine is a tried and tested service used by companies to solve problems ranging from the identification of clouds in satellite images to the control of food safety.

Google Cloud Machine Learning official website is available at the following link: https://cloud.google.com/ml-engine/

In the following screenshot, the Google Cloud Platform dashboard is shown:

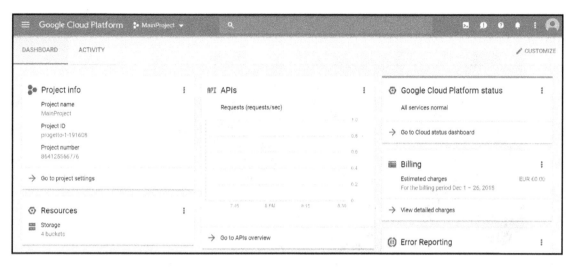

Cloud ML Engine allows us to create models with multiple ML frameworks, including scikit-learn, XGBoost, Keras, and TensorFlow. Cloud ML Engine allows you to automatically design and evaluate model architectures to find intelligent solutions faster and without the help of experts. Cloud ML Engine guarantees the scalability necessary to make the most of all your data. It can train any large-scale model in a managed cluster.

Online training and forecasting enable developers and data scientists to use multiple machine learning frameworks and easily deploy machine learning models into production without having to resort to Docker containers. In addition, users can import models that have been trained anywhere.

Azure Machine Learning Studio

Azure Machine Learning Studio is an interactive programming tool for machine learning analysis. This is the solution offered by Microsoft as a tool to create predictive models automatically without the need to know how the algorithm works. It is a platform in which data, cloud-based tools, and predictive analysis are combined to implement an effective model. The platform also has numerous APIs to help developers build advanced artificial intelligence models. Azure Machine Learning Studio is available at the following link: https://studio.azureml.net/.

The following screenshot shows the welcome page of Azure Machine Learning Studio:

In Azure Machine Learning Studio, building a development model becomes an interactive experience. It's more fun and much easier than the classic methodologies, which involve the implementation/adaptation of algorithms already available in libraries. In fact, thanks to the drag and drop function, it is enough to select the necessary resources: the rest will be provided by Microsoft. Editing, saving a copy, running, converting, and publishing an experiment is just as simple. All this is due to the visual connections available in the development environment, which does not require any programming experience, allowing the user to develop models in a simple and fast manner.

In a time of shared experiences, a sharing place could not be missing even from Azure Machine Learning Studio. This is the Cortana Intelligence Gallery, where users can share and discover solutions. The community also offers the possibility to interact with other developers to arrive at a shared solution to a specific problem.

Work-sharing is not limited to the community offered by the Cortana Intelligence Gallery, in fact, models designed in Azure Machine Learning Studio can be transferred directly to the web for the best visibility possible. In this way, users can use other models and run them with their data. All the changes that will be made to the model will be updated in real time on the version available on the web.

Amazon Web Services

Amazon Web Services (**AWS**) is a set of cloud computing services that make up the on-demand platform offered by Amazon. These services are operational in the 12 geographical regions into which Amazon has divided the globe.

AWS has the widest and deepest set of machine learning and artificial intelligence services for the needs of businesses and individuals. The platform supports the resolution of some of the toughest challenges that prevent machine learning from being in the hands of any developer. It is possible to choose between predefined artificial intelligence services for computerized vision, language, recommendations, and forecasts; Amazon SageMaker, to create, train, and distribute scale machine learning models; and the construction of customized models with support for all the most known open-source structures.

These features are built within a comprehensive cloud platform, optimized for machine learning with high-performance processing and no compromise on security and analysis.

Amazon Machine Learning (**Amazon ML**) offers visualization tools and wizards that help you complete the process of creating machine learning or ML models without having to learn complex ML technologies and algorithms. When your models are ready, Amazon ML makes it easy to get estimates for your application using simple APIs, without having to implement custom code for generating estimates or managing any infrastructure.

In the following screenshot, we can see the setup page for Amazon ML:

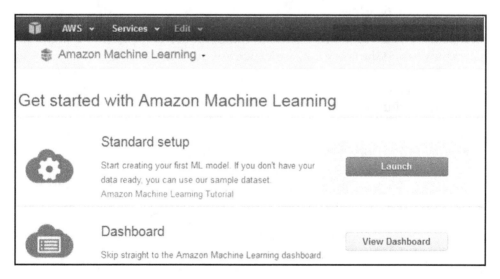

As already mentioned, AWS offers Amazon SageMaker, a fully managed service with advanced features dedicated to development, training, and hosting that allows developers to focus on the scientific approach to data for the development, training, and optimization of machine learning models without having to worry about infrastructure or systems management.

Amazon ML is an effective cloud-based service that allows developers of all levels to easily use machine learning technology. It offers visualization tools and wizards that support the user through the entire process of creating machine learning models, without having to learn complex algorithms and machine learning technology. Once the templates are ready, Amazon ML allows you to easily get application forecasts using simple APIs, without having to implement custom forecasting codes or manage an infrastructure.

Differentiable neural computer

Differentiable neural computer (DNC) refers to a new architecture of computers equipped with artificial intelligence that can access the memory and process it to answer new questions. This machine is therefore able to learn from its memory. This architecture of calculators was presented by its authors (the Google DeepMind team) in 2016 through the following publication: Graves, A., Wayne, G., Reynolds, M., Harley, T., Danihelka, I., Grabska-Barwińska, A., Colmenarejo, SG, Grefenstette, E., Ramalho, T., Agapiou, J., and Badia, AP, 2016. *Hybrid computing using a neural network with dynamic external memory*, Nature, 538 (7626), p.471.

When we, as humans, recall something to our minds from our memories, we take as input all of our memories and the context in which we are, and we return a new interpretation of the memory. Our process of remembering is therefore comparable to the processes of artificial intelligence, which learns to read its own memory as if it were an input, and to produce new output information, which will still be memorized for later use.

The core of the DNC (the controller) is therefore the artificial intelligence trained to process the memory, and is therefore responsible for the reading of the memory, its processing, and the subsequent writing in memory, since the new data processing must be memorized. Memory is a series of locations, each of which can store a vector of information. The controller decides when to write and where to write in the memory, it can choose to write in a new memory space or in an already used one, thus updating the information. If the memory is full, the controller can decide which information to delete and then which locations to free. Each memory location therefore represents a memory, and as such is connected to other locations, as the memories are connected to one another.

In the following diagram is shown the process of data exchange between controller and memory:

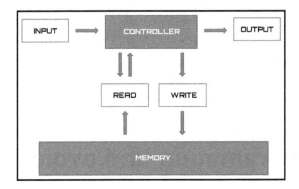

The controller then takes care to read the data it stores: It can scroll through the connections in the order in which they were stored. The very structure of the information stored so far may suggest to the controller how to store new information, so that it is inserted according to logical schemes.

In the following diagram is shown the overall architecture proposed by the authors in the paper mentioned at the beginning of the section:

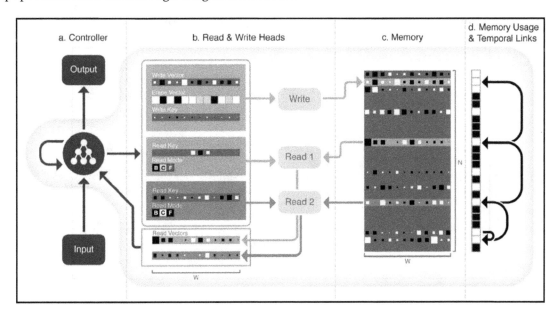

The results obtained with this architecture proved to be truly surprising. The researchers trained the system so as to easily store information and then reinterpret it to extract new complex meanings. In a short time, by creating random graphs, the DNC was trained to interpret them as if it were a metropolitan network. Following a test on the London Underground network, the DNC gave perfect answers to even the most complex questions.

The DeepMind team defines DNC with the following sentence: *Here is a learning machine that, without prior programming, can be organized into information and use those facts to solve problems.*

Genetic programming and evolutionary strategies

In artificial intelligence, genetic algorithms are part of the class of evolutionary algorithms. The characteristic of the latter is the finding of solutions to problems using techniques borrowed from natural evolution. The search for a solution to a problem is entrusted to an iterative process that selects and recombines more and more refined solutions until a criterion of optimality is reached. In a genetic algorithm, the population of solutions is pushed toward a given objective by the evolutionary pressure.

In the following diagram is shown a flowchart of a genetic algorithm:

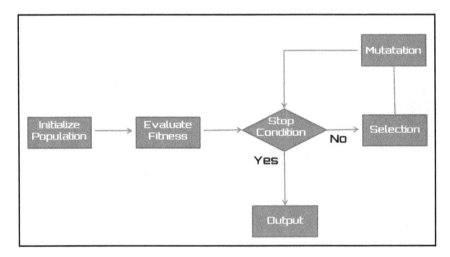

Evolutionary algorithm is obtained through a particular function, called the **fitness function**, which is able to synthesize the quality of the solution in a single parameter. Each solution consists of a set of genes. These genes take part in the recombination and mutation process to generate new solutions. Generally, evolution begins with a population consisting of individuals endowed with random genetic material. At each iteration, the fitness function is evaluated for each unit. The individuals most suitable are selected and recombined with different techniques. The next generation will contain the offspring of the best units from the previous population. Iteratively, the units move toward the solution, guided by the fitness function. Generally, the algorithm ends when a maximum number of generations is reached or an optimality criterion has been reached (a stop condition).

The first prototype genetic algorithm was proposed by J.H. Holland in the early 1960s in order to implement the mechanisms of natural adaptation in computer systems. Holland's genetic algorithm predicts a population of N solutions (chromosomes) of prefixed length L encoded in binary code.

Genetic programming, introduced by John R. Koza, is a problem-solving technique by which computer programs evolve by combining, reproducing, or mutating to give rise to other programs that are better suited to solve a given problem. It represents an extension of the genetic algorithms where each element of the population represents a computer program rather than a string of bits. A program is represented as a tree in which the internal nodes are functions and the leaves are the terminal symbols of the program. The search space consists of all the programs composed of the terminals and the functions defined for a specific problem. The program population evolves using a fitness function, which defines the effectiveness of a program to solve a given problem, and the genetic operators of crossover and mutation adapted to the tree representation.

Genetic programming and evolutionary algorithms generally need large populations to achieve good convergence. This aspect, combined with the fact that calculating the fitness of a single individual requires evaluation on a certain training set, leads to a considerable computational effort.

Today, evolutionary strategy is an expanding field and genetic algorithms solve everyday problems in many areas of study, such as financial market prediction, aerospace engineering, microchip design, biochemistry, molecular biology, airport timetable tables, and assembly lines.

Introducing the genetic algorithm

The functioning of the genetic algorithm is the result of different experiments on the different types of algorithms available. The choice of the parameters to be used proves to be fundamentally important for obtaining good results. First, a method is needed to code potential solutions in a form that the computer understands. A common approach is to encode the solution in the form of a binary string, with sequences of ones and zeros, where each bit represents the value of an aspect of the solution. Another method is to code solutions as lists of integers or real numbers. Finally, we can represent the solution with tree-shaped data structures. In the genetic algorithm the following topics are essential: the fitness function, selection and mutation. In the following sections we will deepen the concepts.

The fitness function

A fitness function is a particular type of objective function that summarizes, in a single measure of merit, how suitable a solution is for solving a problem. The fitness function has the task of estimating the effectiveness of a solution and, depending on the type of problem, it can be changeable or immutable. In the first case, the fitness function changes from generation to generation, as in the case of a genetic algorithm for forecasting stock market trends. In the second case, any evaluation of the function at the same point will always have the same value. This type of fitness function is often used to optimize a multi-variable function.

Selection

Selection is an important phase of the genetic algorithm, because in it the units to be recombined are chosen to form the next generation. There are many selection methods. The most common is the proportional method, which consists of the following steps:

1. The fitness function is evaluated for each unit, and the value is normalized. By normalization, we mean the division of the value by the sum of all the others, so that the sum of the resulting values is 1.
2. The population is sorted in descending order by the value of the fitness function.
3. The normalized cumulative values of fitness are calculated; that is, the fitness of each unit is added to that of all those preceding it.
4. Using a random number generator, a number between 0 and 1 is extracted.
5. The unit that has a normalized cumulative fitness value greater than the extracted number is selected.

An evolution of the proportional selection method is stochastic universal sampling, which uses a single random value to select all solutions in equally distributed intervals.

Mutation

Mutation is an operation used to maintain genetic diversity from one generation to the next. It works by altering the value of one or more genes and is governed by a parameter that specifies the probability of mutation. The mutation must allow the genetic algorithm to exit from the local minima, while avoiding the eventuality of the genetic pool becoming too uniform. For this reason, the probability of mutation should not be too low but also not too high, because it would transform the genetic algorithm into a simple random search. In the case of the binary coding of the chromosome, mutation consists of inverting one or more bits of the chromosome.

Inverse reinforcement learning

In Chapter 9, *Robot Control System Using Deep Reinforcement Learning*, we addressed the amazing world of the reinforcement learning. Reinforcement learning aims to create algorithms that can learn and adapt to environmental changes. This programming technique is based on the concept of receiving external stimuli, the nature of which depends on the algorithm choices. A correct choice will involve a reward, while an incorrect choice will lead to a penalty. The goal of the system is to achieve the best possible rewards, of course. Often, the reward function can be difficult to define: it is not always easy to understand whether a certain action in a certain state is positive for the agent. The purpose of IRL is to identify it. In IRL, the reward function is derived from the observed behavior. As we have learned, in reinforcement learning, we use rewards to learn the behavior of a particular system. In IRL, this function is reversed; in fact, the agent observes the behavior of the system to understand what goal it is trying to achieve.

In IRL, we start from the following:

- Measurements of an agent's behavior over time
- Measurements of the sensory input to that agent
- A model of the physical environment

Based on this data, we determine the reward function that the agent is optimizing. An example of IRL being applied in simple domains such as Atari games was released from OpenAI and DeepMind in 2017. The DeepMind researchers have shown that these techniques may be economically scalable to modern systems.

Several algorithms have been proposed to solve the IRL problem:

- **Feature-expectation-based algorithms**: The algorithms in this family use a linear parameterization of the reward function, and consequently the value function. They aim to minimize a certain metric of dissimilarity, based on the difference between the feature expectation of the objective policy and that of the expert's policy.
- **Supervised or structured algorithms**: The algorithms of this family lead the IRL problem to a classification problem, then to either, a standard problem of supervised learning applied to raw data or to an appropriate reelaboration thereof. In these approaches, policies are used as classifiers to assign labels to inputs; the quality of the policy is measured on a score function based on the value function.
- **Likelihood-based algorithms**: These algorithms aim to estimate and subsequently optimize the likelihood of the expert's behavior. This is achieved by minimizing the distance between the behavior of the expert and the behavior of the target agent.
- **Algorithms based on probabilistic models**: The algorithms of this family aim to infer, through probabilistic models, the policy or the prize function of an expert starting from its trajectories. This probabilistic description allows to solve the problem of the intrinsic uncertainty of the IRL problem.

In IRL, we can use the calculated reward function to generate an agent that mimics the decision-maker's behavior. This is a useful approach to building an intelligent agent. Furthermore, the reward function is one of the most transferrable representations of agent behavior, because it represents the agent's goals and preferences in a compact way.

Summary

In this chapter, we have reviewed the deep neural network models that are most used in real-life applications. We started from deep feedforward network, which has a structure typical of a three-level neural network; the first layer receives the input signals, and the last returns the output signals. It is a good example of a network in which the signal flow proceeds in one direction.

Then we analyzed CNNs, which divide the input data into various overlapping fragments that are then analyzed to identify the particularities that characterize those fragments. This information is then passed on to the following layer in the form of a feature map containing the relations between neurons and particularities.

Then RNNs were addressed, which are a type of neural networks specializing in the processing of sequential data. This type of network is highly optimized for tasks related to speech and facial recognition. Finally, RBMs, DBNs, and GANs were reviewed.

In the second part of the chapter, we explored **Automated Machine Learning (AutoML)** applications, which are able to automate the end-to-end process of applying machine learning to real-world problems. Several solutions were looked at, such as Auto-Keras, Google Cloud ML Engine, Azure Machine Learning Studio, and Amazon Web Services.

Finally, some of the next challenges of the deep learning were introduced, such as DNCs, genetic programming and ES, and IRL.

Other Books You May Enjoy

If you enjoyed this book, you may be interested in these other books by Packt:

Keras Reinforcement Learning Projects

Giuseppe Ciaburro

ISBN: 9781789342093

- Practice the Markov decision process in prediction and betting evaluations
- Implement Monte Carlo methods to forecast environment behaviors
- Explore TD learning algorithms to manage warehouse operations
- Construct a Deep Q-Network using Python and Keras to control robot movements
- Apply reinforcement concepts to build a handwritten digit recognition model using an image dataset
- Address a game theory problem using Q-Learning and OpenAI Gym

Advanced Deep Learning with Keras
Rowel Atienza

ISBN: 9781788629416

- Cutting-edge techniques in human-like AI performance
- Implement advanced deep learning models using Keras
- The building blocks for advanced techniques - MLPs, CNNs, and RNNs
- Deep neural networks – ResNet and DenseNet
- Autoencoders and Variational AutoEncoders (VAEs)
- Generative Adversarial Networks (GANs) and creative AI techniques
- Disentangled Representation GANs, and Cross-Domain GANs
- Deep Reinforcement Learning (DRL) methods and implementation
- Produce industry-standard applications using OpenAI gym
- Deep Q-Learning and Policy Gradient Methods

Leave a review - let other readers know what you think

Please share your thoughts on this book with others by leaving a review on the site that you bought it from. If you purchased the book from Amazon, please leave us an honest review on this book's Amazon page. This is vital so that other potential readers can see and use your unbiased opinion to make purchasing decisions, we can understand what our customers think about our products, and our authors can see your feedback on the title that they have worked with Packt to create. It will only take a few minutes of your time, but is valuable to other potential customers, our authors, and Packt. Thank you!

Index